THE ANTHROPOLOGY OF GLOBAL PENTECOSTALISM AND EVANGELICALISM

The Anthropology of Global Pentecostalism and Evangelicalism

Edited by Simon Coleman and Rosalind I. J. Hackett

With an Afterword by Joel Robbins

NEW YORK UNIVERSITY PRESS

New York and London

NEW YORK UNIVERSITY PRESS
New York and London
www.nyupress.org

References to Internet websites (URLs) were accurate at the time of writing. Neither the author nor New York University Press is responsible for URLs that may have expired or changed since the manuscript was prepared.

Library of Congress Cataloging-in-Publication Data
The anthropology of global pentecostalism and evangelicalism / edited by Simon Coleman and Rosalind I. J. Hackett ; with an Afterword by Joel Robbins.
pages cm   Includes bibliographical references and index.
ISBN 978-0-8147-7259-1 (cl : alk. paper) — ISBN 978-0-8147-7260-7 (pb : alk. paper)
1. Pentecostalism. 2. Evangelicalism. 3. Anthropology of religion. I. Coleman, Simon, 1963–, editor.
BR1644.A58   2015
306.6'7083—dc23   2015013955

New York University Press books are printed on acid-free paper, and their binding materials are chosen for strength and durability. We strive to use environmentally responsible suppliers and materials to the greatest extent possible in publishing our books.

Manufactured in the United States of America

10 9 8 7 6 5 4 3 2 1

Also available as an ebook

CONTENTS

ACKNOWLEDGMENTS

This book has been a truly collaborative effort between the editors since our first discussions in a tea shop in Washington, DC. Innumerable cups of tea since, consumed on both sides of the Pond, we have worked with many others in the production of the volume and incurred some important debts of gratitude. Apart from thanking our authors for their patient responses to our numerous requests, we would like to convey our gratitude to people whose contribution to this text has been vital but much less visible. Jennifer Hammer of New York University Press has been the ideal editor, combining encouragement, advice, and the occasional nudge. Dr. Anna Stewart is an excellent and knowledgeable researcher on Pentecostalism in her own right, who came into the project at a vital moment and has steered communications among editors, authors, and press with considerable efficiency, as well as doing much checking of the text. We received constructive comments from reviewers both at the planning stage of the book and as the final manuscript was being prepared. Finally, Simon would like to thank his PhD supervisor, Dr. Malcolm Ruel (1927–2010), for being open to giving advice relating to a PhD on Swedish Pentecostalism, which seemed a much more eccentric topic in the 1980s than it does now, as well as Professor Jan-Åke-Alvarsson, director of the Institute for Pentecostal Studies in Uppsala, another scholar who combines interests in Pentecostalism and the drinking of tea in almost equal measure. Rosalind wishes to express her appreciation to the numerous Pentecostal and evangelical church leaders and members around the world, from Calabar to Manila to Atlanta, who have been willing to talk to an inquiring researcher, especially Rev. Dr. Mensa Otabil, the General Overseer of the International Central Gospel Church, in Accra, Ghana, with whom she has enjoyed meaningful conversations over many a year.

Introduction

A New Field?

SIMON COLEMAN AND ROSALIND I. J. HACKETT

The anthropological study of Pentecostalism and evangelicalism (P/e)[1] has undergone a striking transformation in recent years. In the 1980s, when the editors of this volume were beginning their careers, it was still seen as relatively unusual for an anthropologist to focus on *any* form of Christianity, let alone Protestantism. For much of the twentieth century, fieldworkers might have been very aware of the presence of missions where they carried out research, but they often saw these proselytizing Christians as background "noise"—sometimes deeply irritating noise—distorting their attempts to concentrate on what they saw as more authentic, local expressions of culture. Ethnographers visited the same regions where colonial officials and Western missionary churches had worked, but liked to think of themselves as engaged in a fundamentally different enterprise to either: listening rather than dictating to informants, and translating ways of life rather than attempting to transform them.

Nowadays, however, the anthropology of Christianity is a burgeoning subfield, reflecting a growth that has undoubtedly been led in its early stages by hugely increased interest in P/e. Many of the old ambivalences remain, but such Christians are beginning to be understood to represent far more than cultural noise, and to raise questions of key anthropological significance. The chapters of this book reflect such a shift in disciplinary focus. They are written by scholars whose careers trace the intellectual transformation we are describing: some contributors have been writing on Christianity over the past two to three decades, whereas others represent just a few of a newer generation of scholars whose intellectual development has emerged in and through the paradigm shift that we are sketching out. The authors come from different intellectual traditions within anthropology—British, Dutch, French, German, North American.[2] To some degree, then, we see this book as indicating a "coming of age" of anthropological studies of P/e, embodying a period when we can reflect back on what has been achieved so far, but also indicate what needs to be done.

Why, however, has such a paradigm shift begun to occur? The answers tell us about changes within both P/e and anthropology, and the combined histories of both. One set of reasons lies in developments within Christianity itself. Many social scientific scholars of the contemporary world—though not, in general, anthropologists—have spent much of the past century predicting the disappearance of religion in the West and possibly elsewhere; however, P/e (along with other expanding religious forces such as Islam) has proved capable of resisting secular forms of modernity and of thriving in environments characterized by global markets, cultural pluralism, industrialization and postindustrialization, mass migration, and the explosion of the mass media. Furthermore, an apparent shift in gravity in the weight and authority of Christianity has become increasingly evident. Lamin Sanneh (2013, xiv) tells us that in 1950, 80 percent of the world's Christians lived in Europe and North America; but by 2005 the vast majority of the world's two billion Christians lived in Asia, Africa, and Latin America. In line with such developments, the long-standing assumption that resources, prestige, and decision making would mostly emanate from liberal, Euro-American contexts has been replaced by recognition that powerful centers of religion have increasingly been "Southernized," rooted more and more in the Majority World, in regions such as Latin America or West Africa.[3] A notable example of such a shift came from a well-known secular source, the pages of *Newsweek*: in 2008 the magazine named Enoch Adeboye, Nigerian head of the Pentecostal Redeemed Christian Church of God, one of the fifty most powerful people in the world.[4]

Arguably, then, the cultural noise from P/e has become too loud for anthropologists to ignore, reinforced by these Christians' use of media technology and well-resourced missionary activities (Hackett 1998, 2012). But the shift in focus also indicates significant transformations within anthropology. The discipline retains its interest in the everyday details of life, but it has become difficult to sustain an older vision of anthropology as studying bounded cultures that can be analyzed without reference to much wider scales and spheres of reference (Coleman and von Hellermann 2010). Nor can one invoke the "ethnographic present" nowadays in naïve fashion without acknowledging the inherently shifting, historical, dynamic character of all cultural forms. These changes in the way that anthropology frames its research have been accompanied by the realization that sharp distinctions between "home" (where anthropologists live, teach, and write) and "the field" (where they gather data) are collapsing, as is the idea that anthropology is predominantly carried out by Western scholars in non-Western contexts. Thus Christianity in Euro-America is increasingly coming under scrutiny. There is also more awareness that anthropology must be seen as a discipline with a particular cultural as well as intellectual history, and one where a Christian heritage has had considerable influence in its understandings of culture, humanity, and religion.[5]

These observations about the changing shape and focus of anthropology are not new: they have been debated extensively since at least the 1980s. Our point is that they indicate some of the reasons why P/e has now become recognized by anthropologists as an exciting field of study. If anthropology in a world of accelerating globalization becomes interested in the links between different scales of analysis, in understanding how localities require work to be sustained rather than simply reproducing themselves, in seeing how informants develop their own theories of culture contact and culture change, then P/e comes into focus as a vital field of research.

Fascinating epistemological ambiguities, moral quandaries, and analytical challenges are created by such developments. Ethnographers have always worried about how to understand others' religion—this is typically called the "insider-outsider" problem—but such questions are often compounded in research on Christianity, given that it has been such a significant contributor to the history of Western thought despite the avowed secularity of many Euro-American ethnographers. Fenella Cannell (2006, 20), for instance, assesses the ways Protestant thought has been linked to ideas of the interior self as well as to ideas of the modern Western person. Furthermore, members of P/e often maintain their own, strongly held understandings of why an anthropologist has come to work amongst them: the fieldworker may explain that s/he has come to gather social scientific data, but informants may be equally convinced that God has sent *this* person to them and that it is their duty to convert someone who seems so keen to ask questions and participate in worship. Such encounters indicate the complex power dynamic involved in the study of P/e: older, paternalistic assumptions about giving oppressed peoples a voice gain little traction in encounters where informants have the confidence and motivation to redefine the ethnographic relationship on their own terms and through their own narratives. Such encounters also raise tricky methodological and ethical questions for secular fieldworkers: how far *should* they go in participating in as well as observing P/e worship practices? Is it all right to sing a hymn, but not appropriate to pray? Elaine Lawless (1992) has expressed parallel worries in her work on Pentecostal women preachers in Missouri: how should she reconcile her growing intimacy with a friend who also happens to be an informant, and one with ethical views so different from her own?

So far we have assumed that the anthropologist of P/e is likely to be secular. Again, this is too simple a preconception. Some members of the discipline either have been or still are practicing Christians (or are members of another tradition). In addition, the process of carrying out ethnography can take the fieldworker close to feeling that his/her identity has been taken over, however temporarily, by a P/e view of the world. In a famous piece, the anthropologist Susan Harding notes how her fieldwork interview with a Baptist pastor left her somewhat dazed, caught up in the language of her interlocutor, so that "I began to acquire the knowledge and vision and sensibilities, to share the experience, of a believer" (1987, 178; see also Harding 2000). Vincent Crapanzano also describes his unease at having an evangelist in Los Angeles questioning him astutely about his beliefs: "He caught me off guard and offered me no escape for more than four hours" (2000, 83).

Equally importantly, we might ask whether, from a social scientific point of view, it is reasonable to assume that there is a single, stable barrier that divides believer from nonbeliever. It is true that important research on P/e congregations has argued that believers learn specific ways to recognize signs of divine action in their lives (Luhrmann 2012). We add, however, that members of the same congregation may relate to common symbols and rituals in varied ways, and indeed differently at different times. There is also the tricky question of how culture in a broader sense relates to religion. As Brian Howell, an anthropologist at the evangelical Wheaton College, notes,

> My own experience, and I think our common sense, tells us that two people identifying as Christians, one from North America and one from, say, the northern Philippines, do not share as much "culturally" as would the North American Christian and his or her secular neighbor, regardless of how "orthodox" the beliefs of the Filipino and secularized the identity of the non-Christian North American. (2007, 374)

The dividing line between a person's past biography as religious believer and present status as academic nonbeliever can also be fascinatingly ambiguous. Michael Warner, currently professor of English literature and American studies at Yale University, recalls his youth growing up in a family that moved restlessly between congregations. He begins his piece by stating, "I was a teenage Pentecostalist" (2004, 215), but it might seem that Warner has traveled about as far as he can from his childhood—intellectually, culturally, spiritually, linguistically. He now characterizes himself as "a queer atheist intellectual" (215). However, he asks whether one's former self can go away quite so easily, even among "us who once were found and now are lost" (216). Thus, despite its use of the past tense, Warner's opening confession closely echoes Pentecostal testimony—a public declaration of personal religious conviction. The language of the pious youth seems to live on in the apparently secular adult. And perhaps the rupture between being secular and born-again, lost and saved—so much a part of the rhetoric of much radical Protestant culture—need not be quite as stark as we might have thought, even at levels beyond individual experience.

So we are beginning to learn about the uneasy but sometimes inevitable conjoining of academic, cultural, and P/e worlds. We also see how, in certain respects, anthropology has been subject to some of the same cultural and social forces as P/e in recent years. Our authors come from different religious backgrounds, and most would probably define themselves as agnostic or atheist in religious orientation. However, anthropological research always involves a fascinating kind of alchemy, a transformational blending of subject and object, discipline and case study. This book attempts to illustrate the power and the potential of such alchemy.

Defining Terms

In considering the difficulties of giving precise definitions of Pentecostalism and evangelicalism, we are tempted to quote the anthropologist Roy Wagner: "The things we can define best are the things least worth defining" (1981, 39; see Engelke and Tomlinson 2006, 8). Many of the people who are generally regarded by analysts as coming under the rubric of P/e would reject dry, academic terms as ways to describe their religious experience and sense of personal identification with God. Even among scholars, very different approaches are evident. It is common at academic conferences to hear the argument that the defining characteristic of a Pentecostalist must ultimately be the ability to speak in tongues. Such an apparently simple and clear approach has its initial attractions, and yet should also give us pause. How should we deal with believers who have spoken in tongues in the past, but have not done so for years? At what point would they cease to be classifiable as "genuinely" Pentecostalist? And what kind of tongues would qualify? Only that which involves syllables with no ready counterpart in any known language (*glossolalia*—described by St. Paul in I Corinthians 12–14)? What would we make of the (rarer) case of *xenoglossia*: the speaking of a recognized language, but one that is not consciously known by the speaker? And how should we classify somebody who is a fluent tongues speaker and yet is radically opposed to much of the theology of the congregation to which he or she belongs? Perhaps one-dimensional and rigid characterizations are not very helpful after all.

But we have to start somewhere. The word "Pentecostal" derives from a Greek term meaning "fiftieth" and points to the Christian festival of Pentecost (also called Whitsunday), which occurs fifty days after Easter Sunday. The festival corresponds with the Jewish celebration of Shavuot, a commemoration of the day that God gave the Torah to the Israelites on Mount Sinai; it also marks the event, described in the New Testament, of the descent of the Holy Spirit on the Apostles, when "they were all filled with the Holy Ghost, and began to speak with other tongues, as the Spirit gave them utterance" (Acts 2:6, KJV). As André Corten and

Ruth Marshall-Fratani put it (2001, 5), we see here a scriptural template for the contemporary Pentecostal desire to "reach a fusional relationship with God, in which the individual's praise and prayers may reach Him unmediated even by language."

"Classical" Pentecostalism is commonly associated with outbreaks of glossolalia in the United States in the early part of the twentieth century (as well as with earlier, Methodist roots [Martin 2002, 7–9]). In 1901 Agnes Ozman, a student of Charles Parham's Bethel Bible School in To-peka, Kansas, is reported to have spoken in tongues;[6] subsequently, an-other student of Parham called William Seymour, a black pastor and son of former slaves, led a congregation based in Azusa Street, Los Angeles, which in 1906 began to experience similar miraculous events. Seymour's congregation attracted considerable attention from the press and fel-low Christians, much of it deeply skeptical, but it was remarkable for its interracial character. It also seems to have acted as an international catalyst for the spread of the movement, which soon split up into dif-ferent groups. Allan Anderson (2013, 2) notes that Pentecostalism had reached perhaps fifty different nations within its first decade. In fact, the very idea, even the rhetoric, of global expansion has now become part of many Pentecostalists' self-image. It is possible that the number of ad-herents had climbed to over 600 million by 2010, constituting a quarter of the world's Christian population, though this estimate may well be inflated (Anderson 2013, 2).

The beginnings of Pentecostalism illustrate what was to become a characteristic desire to bypass the details of ecclesiastical history not only by establishing a direct relationship with the Early Church and with scripture, but also by placing a high value on the cultivation of powerful religious experience. Tongues and other spiritual gifts such as healing and prophecy were used to reenact the Acts of the Apostles.[7] Spiritual more than earthly authority was to be respected. After all, the first figures who "spoke" the movement into existence—a modest white woman and a black pastor—were certainly not representatives of any ecclesiastical elite.

At the same time, Pentecostalism is perhaps too slippery a movement to be confined in our interpretations to single origins in the United States. The venerable historian of Pentecostalism Walter Hollenweger (e.g., 1997) has emphasized the African roots of some of its worship styles. Another distinguished chronicler, Allan Anderson (2004, 35), argues that religious revivals occurring not only in different parts of Europe but also in Asia, Africa, and Latin America in the nineteenth century helped to lay the ground for the spread of Pentecostal practices.[8] Jean DeBernardi's chapter in this volume indicates very clearly the difficulties in attributing single places of origin to Spirit-filled religion. In any case, a movement or set of movements was being put in motion that could spread through shifting, expansive social networks and through a ritual "grammar" consisting of asserting the need to be born again, belief in the tangible results of prayer, focus on praise and worship, powerful sermons expecting direct responses from congregations, democratic exercise of gifts of the Spirit, frequent use of the "altar call" toward the end of the service (encouraging people to come up to the front to receive salvation or healing), the assumption that we are entering the "end -times" before the return of Jesus to the world,[9] and a valuing of ritual spontaneity over fixed liturgy or organizational hierarchy.

Of course, even a common grammar is eminently capable of producing quarrels over boundaries, especially given the chronic tendencies of Pentecostals to break off from established groupings to create new alliances and networks. Bitter disputes have been evident over such matters as the timing and character of God's grace and spiritual baptism, and over the extent to which maintaining piety and personal holiness is consonant with enjoying material luxury. Racial divisions have marked some parts of the movement for much of its history. Although historically American and European ministries have had considerable influence around the world, other groups in parts of Africa and countries such as Chile and Brazil have asserted their national independence.[10] While some congregations have remained autonomous, others have formed large denominations or allied themselves with fellowships of broadly like-minded Christians. As Anderson puts it,

"Pentecostalism" has been used to embrace large movements as widely diverse as the celibacy-practicing Pentecostal mission in India, the Saturday-Sabbath keeping . . . True Jesus Church in China, the uniform-wearing, highly ritualistic Zion Christian Church in Southern Africa, and Brazil's equally enormous, prosperity-oriented Universal Church of the Kingdom of God. (2013, 4)

Beyond classical Pentecostals, "neo-Pentecostal" churches have developed in recent decades, often taking on what is called "megachurch" status (by maintaining congregations of more than two thousand people) and frequently proving attractive to middle-class as well as working-class populations. The largest congregation in the world, Yoido Full Gospel Church, located in Seoul, South Korea, emerged in the late 1950s out of the Assemblies of God, and now claims over a million members while preaching a variant of the Prosperity Gospel—the idea, increasingly popular among some believers, that links the possession of faith with the ability to attract good health and material well-being (see, e.g., Bowler 2013; Coleman 2000; Hackett 1995; Marti 2008).

Meanwhile, "charismatic" is a term often used by scholars to refer to yet another variant in this religious landscape, namely, those Christians who practice spiritual gifts but retain their membership in older, established denominations. Elements of the grammar we described above have proved highly transferable to Catholic as well as Protestant congregations, as Thomas J. Csordas's chapter in this book illustrates. Some commentators claim that the emergence of classical Pentecostalism represents a "first wave" of revivalist history, while the "second wave" is constituted by the diffusion of Pentecostal and charismatic ideas to many Christians since the 1970s or so. According to this logic, the "third wave" of revival refers to the diffuse and dynamic growth of independent, broadly Holy Spirit–led churches that we see emerging in many parts of the contemporary world.[11] Such churches, we should note, often emerge in places where there has already been a long tradition of P/e mission, so that they may constitute something of a revival of a revival.

What, then, of evangelicalism? The word derives from Greek terms that, combined, mean "good news" ("gospel"). Mark Noll notes that at the time of the European Reformation in the sixteenth century it was broadly equivalent to Protestant (2004, 421), while the most common use of the term refers to revival movements of the eighteenth century onwards, initially based in Europe and North America and then spreading more globally. The word therefore encompasses movements such as Baptism, Lutheranism, Methodism, Presbyterianism, some streams within Anglicanism, and so on; occasionally—when used in its very broadest sense—it may also encompass Pentecostal and charismatic Christians.

Probably the most widely cited attempt to characterize evangelicalism has been produced by the British historian David Bebbington, who isolates four key and interlinked features (1989; Noll 2004, 422). We summarize these as follows:

1. Conversionism, implying the conviction that humans need to be turned away from sin and toward belief in God.
2. Biblicism, meaning that the Christian should see scripture as the ultimate guide in life, encouraging a close relationship to sacred text and potentially implying skepticism toward "merely" human traditions and institutions.
3. Activism, indicating the need to work at a number of levels, ranging from social reform to spreading the "Good News" and its associated salvation to others. In the United States and elsewhere, evangelicals have sometimes been deeply involved in politics, historically playing significant roles in Prohibition and the antislavery movement and more recently becoming involved in debates over the teaching of evolution in schools and legal frameworks surrounding abortion.
4. Crucicentrism, literally "cross-centered," expressing the notion that Christian existence is focused on Christ's death and subsequent resurrection; through his sacrifice, Christ is said to have paid the price for human sins, so that spiritual life is available to those who accept his atoning work.

As with Pentecostalism, these characteristics might be seen as constituting a "grammar" that takes varied expression in real-life communities. Evangelicals also clearly overlap with Pentecostal practices in their mistrust of fixed and hierarchical liturgies, emphasis on the need to proselytize, desire to develop a "personal relationship" with God and scripture, and distinctions between those who have and those who have not given themselves to Christ. While, as noted, evangelicalism is therefore sometimes used as a blanket term for activist, Reformed Protestants, it may also be distinguished from other revivalist orientations. Most evangelicals do not emphasize baptism in the Holy Spirit in the same way as Pentecostalists, for instance. Meanwhile, fundamentalism emerged in the United States at roughly the same time as Pentecostalism in opposition to what it saw as liberal tendencies within established American denominations, and thus reemphasized the need to "go back" to viewing the Bible as an infallible, literally true, and all-encompassing text.

The dividing line between fundamentalists and evangelicals can be a difficult one to draw, depending on ecclesiastical and cultural context. In Germany, for instance, *Evangelische* is a very broad term used to refer to a wide variety of Reformed churches, while in Hispanic contexts *evangélico* may refer to virtually any non-Catholic Christian.[12] Hunter (1987, 4), describing the American context, sees fundamentalism as "a faction *within* Evangelicalism and not a movement *distinct from* Evangelicalism." Famously, George Marsden (1980, 235) has defined a fundamentalist as "an evangelical who is mad about something." However, significant American figures such as Jerry Falwell (1933–2007) have been adamant in stating that they are fundamentalist *rather* than evangelical. We might ask, with David Goodhew (2013, 231–32), just how "angry" a believer has to be in order to be classified as fundamentalist. We might also worry with him that it has become a profoundly pejorative "f-word" in some circles, even as we understand that boundary formation has been a central, dynamic element in the identity of believers such as Falwell in their crusades against secular humanism and liberalism.

At least in the United States from the 1930s on, self-identified fundamentalists and many conservative evangelicals engaged in a relatively low-key consolidation of networks that provided parallel educational and communications institutions to those of mainstream society. They were therefore in a strong position to react when both the opportunity and the desire to reenter political and other public realms became ever more apparent from the 1960s in North America and elsewhere (Coleman 2000, 2011a). A world-renowned evangelist, Billy Graham, had already become the "preacher to the presidents" in America.[13] From the 1970s and 1980s, members of some of the more conservative evangelical and fundamentalist denominations and churches cooperated through such political lobbying groups as the Moral Majority, Religious Roundtable, and Christian Voice, in opposition to "secular humanism." Beyond the United States, analysts began to wonder whether the power of evangelicals could displace the hegemony of the Catholic Church in large parts of Latin America (Stoll 1991; see also, e.g., Martin 1990, 2002).

However, both evangelicalism and its study continue to evolve, and some of the most interesting current work examines believers whose relationship to more conservative political and worship stances is one of considerable ambivalence (Bielo 2011; Elisha 2011; compare also Miller 1999).

In this section we hope to have provided you with some background orientations, without drowning you in detail. We suggest that the most effective next step is for you to work inductively—as anthropologists tend to do—by seeing how these terms play out in practice in the case studies contained in this book. After all, life worlds have a habit of confounding definitions. One useful way to think about any example of P/e comes from the anthropologist Rodney Needham's description of "polythetic classification" (1975).[14] By this term, Needham essentially means that a polythetic class is defined by having a number of *possible* characteristics; while any given example of that class will contain a certain minimal number of those characteristics, it need not contain all of them. Different examples will therefore have certain similarities, certain family resemblances, but will not be identical. In this sense, the term "P/e" is itself useful because it not only points to these as sometimes separate religious orientations, but also indicates their frequent overlaps and parallels.

P/e, the Anthropology of P/e, and the Anthropology of Christianity

Important anthropological studies of Christianity have appeared before the current burst of research. For instance, Catholicism played a significant part of the context of work on "honor and shame" in the culture of the Mediterranean (Peristiany 1966). Accounts of churches in colonial and postcolonial contexts included J. D. Y. Peel's celebrated work *Aladura* (1968), an analysis of independent churches among the Yoruba of Nigeria, as well as Jean Comaroff and John Comaroff's (e.g., 1991, 1997, 2000; see also Comaroff 1985) well-known studies of the past and present impacts of relations among Christian mission, colonialism, and resistance in South Africa. Victor Turner and Edith Turner's *Image and Pilgrimage in Christian Culture* (1978) was both a pathbreaking study of pilgrimage and an attempt to characterize Christian (especially Catholic) culture across different sites.

However, it is only within the last fifteen years that the anthropological study of Christianity has become a marked subfield, with its own
specialists, commonly recurring themes, and growing literature. As we
have suggested already, the *recognition* of Christianity as a proper object of study had to overcome some opposition. In his important article
"What Is a Christian? Notes toward an Anthropology of Christianity,"
Joel Robbins argues (2003, 193), "Neither real others nor real comrades,
Christians wherever they are found make anthropologists recoil by un-
settling the fundamental schemes by which the discipline organizes the
world into the familiar and the foreign." A 1991 essay by Susan Harding had already described how scholars saw Christian fundamentalists
as "the repugnant cultural other," while in the introduction to her edited book *The Anthropology of Christianity*, Fenella Cannell (2006, 4)
referred to Christianity functioning as the "repressed" of anthropology
during the formation of the discipline, as part of its attempts to differentiate itself from theology.[15]

Adapting the work of another anthropologist of religion, Mary Douglas (1966), we might say that P/e functioned for years as a taboo object,
constituting cultural matter "out of place" for the discipline precisely because it inhabited borders between categories that had been kept apart:
self and other, local and "global," home and abroad, anthropology and
theology. As Douglas notes, such matter is both threatening and powerful precisely *because* it breaks down or challenges previously established boundaries. But we have seen how the study of P/e has followed
a fascinating trajectory, from being ignored or suppressed because of
its anomalous character to actually being highlighted for its powerful,
boundary-breaking orientations. In effect, it has become ethnographic
matter that is now much more "in place" because it now appeals to a discipline that is changing its own forms and boundaries. P/e has become
"good to think with."

Our argument is reinforced when we look at the direction that much
of the newer P/e literature has taken so far. Work has been carried out
on belief and conversion,[16] diasporas,[17] gender (sometimes linked with
ethnicity),[18] language,[19] materiality and media,[20] personhood,[21] and numerous intersections with economic and political practice;[22] but one of
the key theoretical tropes so far—and one that has in fact encompassed
many of the topics mentioned—has revolved around the question of

"rupture." What is meant by this term? In one sense, it has referred to the question of whether P/e has caused fundamental transformations in the societies and cultures that it has encountered. We have already mentioned the issue of whether Latin America is being "turned" away from Catholicism by evangelicals who are promoting a new, politically oriented Protestant ethic, but the notion of rupture has had still wider implications, suggesting that in various ways encounters with P/e have facilitated the shift of populations toward radically new forms of self-conception and practice involving engagement with "modernity" and rejection of past customs. Thus Peter van der Veer's (1996) important edited volume explores links between conversion and modern notions of personhood (see also Hann 2007, 391). Bialecki, Haynes, and Robbins (2008, 1149) note that discussions of Pentecostalism in Africa have emphasized its role in severing kinship ties and traditional economic obligations, thus freeing believers to participate more "freely" in market economies (Meyer 1999; van Dijk 1999). Such freedom takes on Weberian implications as conversion seemingly shifts the person's "obligation away from lateral [horizontal] social bonds among consociates towards dyadic [and more vertical] bonds between the individual and the divine" (Bialecki, Haynes, and Robbins 2008, 1147).

We can see why Robbins (2004b, 127; also 2004a, 2007) talks of Pentecostal and charismatic Christianity's "cult of discontinuity." Furthermore, such transformations can be seen as occurring at different scales, ranging from the individual's sense of becoming born again, to the conversion of particular ethnic or social groups, to society-wide shifts in attitudes in relation to tradition (Hefner 1993). Indeed, Robbins (2004b) argues that the emphasis on discontinuity plays an important role in the ways that such Christianity globalizes, as it pits itself against aspects of "local" culture while also accepting the reality of already existing spiritual forces. This use of locally meaningful idioms for talking about—and reclassifying—the past and thus continuing ritual engagement with local spirits not only distinguishes such Christianity from other forms, but also allows it to imply different things in different places: its ruptures may involve denial of kin relations, challenging the power of the elders, and so on (Robbins 2004b, 129).[23] Thus "even as it absorbs local content," it "maintains its globally recognizable shape as a struggle between the divine and the demonic" (129).

For our purposes, what is most striking is how the very imagery of rupture, of breaking from one state or category to another, speaks to how *anthropologists* as well as believers operate. Remember our use of Douglas's work to discuss how the analysis of P/e redraws cherished anthropological boundaries. In *temporal* terms, a perspective that draws on P/e to demonstrate cultural and religious discontinuity challenges ideas of the ethnographic present and assumptions anthropologists have had that, even under new circumstances, people tend to maintain the worldviews that they were first socialized into. In *cultural* terms, it asks how ethnographers of "local" culture are to deal with a heterogeneous and volatile religious orientation that takes on globally recognizable characteristics. In *spatial* terms, it forces the analyst to consider using "multi-sited" ethnography to capture the ways P/e often connects people from different parts of the world through use of mass media, religious imagination, and ritual events.[24] In *ethical* terms, it forces secular analysts to ask what they are to make of a cultural object that is powerful and may be pushing forms of change that they mistrust or find distasteful. Finally, in *epistemological* terms (i.e., those concerned with the nature and construction of knowledge), it upsets the traditional academic monopoly of anthropology itself, not only maintaining its own versions of truth but also sometimes using the very methods of anthropology to promote mission. One of us vividly remembers an ethnographic interview conducted in London with a member of the Redeemed Christian Church of God that concluded with the latter asking for advice on how to apply for master's courses in anthropology.

So there are good reasons why the notion of "rupture" (itself often associated with the idea of modernity) has cropped up so much in recent anthropological discussions of P/e. But the concept also has its limitations. To begin with, it should not tempt us into thinking that all converts somehow adopt similar visions of the modern world along with their adoption of Christianity. Equally problematically, it may encourage us to focus too much on one topic to the exclusion of others. As Cannell has pointed out (2006, 38), "It may be that the history of modernity is inextricably bound up with the history of Christianity, but this does not mean that the meaning of Christianity is sufficiently explained by the history of modernity." Furthermore, in arguing that P/e consistently causes transformations in many parts of the world, we are assuming that it has a coherence and influence that may be exaggerated. Ironically, despite the broad family resemblances that allow us to recognize P/e in different parts of the world, any strong assertion that P/e has an inherent and consistent cultural logic perhaps takes anthropologists closer to theology than they are likely to intend.[25] Very obviously, we need also to ask whether a focus on P/e has encouraged us to ignore the significance of Roman Catholicism and forms of Orthodoxy (Hann 2007, 403), with their own notions of temporality, salvation, materiality, and so on.

We end this section by suggesting that, just as three "waves" of P/e may be said to have emerged over the past century, so we might be able to discern three phases in its fate as an object of anthropological study.[26] The first phase refers to that period before a self-conscious anthropology of Christianity had been formed. Such work remained relatively rare and was not linked into a wider subfield or set of integrated conversations. The second phase has involved the recent formation of a subfield with its own dynamism, set of themes, and identity. This phase has allowed us to talk of the anthropology of Christianity as we might talk of the anthropology of Islam, in the knowledge that such subfields will have their own distinct conversations. The third phase, which may just be beginning, acknowledges the maturity and growth of the subfield, the sense that it is here to stay, but is beginning to branch out into new areas of research, including but also going beyond examinations of "rupture," and starting to link the study of P/e with other, wider themes in the anthropological literature. We see this book as itself on the borders between the second and third phases that we describe here, and we suggest just a few of these potential new directions for the study of P/e in the conclusions to this introduction.

Gathering the Book Together

If our volume can be located in the borderlands of the second and third phases of the anthropological study of P/e, then this position is reflected in the way it brings together pieces on both classic and newer areas of study of Pentecostalism and evangelicalism, at least for English-speaking academic contexts. It includes studies of the "epicenters" of these religious movements, such as the United States and Brazil, as well as research from scholars working in lesser-studied areas such as

Polynesia, Central, East, and Southeast Asia, and Lusophone Africa. These postcolonial and, in some cases, post-atheist contexts, at times fragile and insecure, reveal new conditions of possibility for Pentecostal and evangelical movements to take root and flourish. Even when more established P/e forms are the subject of some of the chapters in this book, the authors provide current data and fresh angles revealing a new interplay of "old" concepts, such as language and body, affect and power, prayer and politics.

A common concern of many of the chapters is to address the ambiguities, as well as the paradoxes, of this newer phase of P/e growth in their respective regions, often leading them to consider a reformulation of some of the assumptions about the parameters of these movements and their provenances. As might be expected in our study of this globalizing phenomenon, networks and networking feature prominently in the lives of P/e organizations and their members. Now empowered by modern media technologies, communities can become supercommunities; parachurch agencies and organizations can advertise and raise funds on a global scale; and individuals can communicate to their pastors, their headquarters, and fellow believers around the world.

Relatedly, another notable feature of this collection is the range of different scales and institutional forms for the expression of P/e—not just churches, but the whole spectrum from individual actors to cell groups to networks, popular culture, political and civic life, and so on. The concept of individualism, deriving from evangelical notions of salvation, looks very different when individuals are so transnationally interconnected via their P/e networks. In this regard, it is noteworthy that many of the contributors treat as central the idea of spatiality in their accounts of these movements, whether this is framed in terms of actual places or virtual spaces, centers or peripheries, emplacement or displacement, home territories or diasporic lands. Because nonchurch locations can be as important as churches themselves, we show P/e in dialogue with other areas of life—politics, economics, but also dieting, feminism, the city, music, and so forth. Again, many of the chapters demonstrate the blurring of public and private spheres in the activities of the newer generation of P/e movements, as much as the leaders (and perhaps some members too) seek to constitute discrete and distinctive organizations.

From the outset, we envisaged our primary audience as anthropological researchers and students whom we wanted to persuade that Pentecostalism and evangelicalism are productive and timely areas of inquiry—sometimes in ways that have not yet been fully explored. We remain intrigued by the way Pentecostalism and evangelicalism have indeed become much more popular topics of inquiry within anthropology, despite the ambivalent feelings, discussed above, that many anthropologists have had and in some cases still have toward these phenomena. This volume seeks to discuss and illustrate the specifically anthropological contribution to the topic, while also exploring some of the tensions and contradictions inherent in such contributions. For example, just one tension revolves around the ways such movements may present direct epistemological and moral challenges to the role and authority of the ethnographer as participant observer. We also seek to demonstrate to readers from other disciplines and/or nonanthropological analysts of these globalizing movements the merits of localized ethnographies (with an associated focus on language, embodiment, subjectivity, communities and networks, cultural practices, and so on). Several of our authors have long-term associations with the regions and movements that they study, allowing them to discern internal changes and multiple perspectives even after they have left the field.

To general readers, we recommend this work as an accessible resource on one of the most significant developments in contemporary Christianity. It provides an updated and diversified perspective on these increasingly influential religious movements. The chapters contain stories and vignettes from the authors' field experiences that bring alive the religious worlds of P/e but also serve as springboards for academic analysis. From these studies, readers will be exposed to a more multicentered and multilateral perspective on P/e as it has expanded from its early twentieth-century roots in the United States.

We have not set out to present a single theoretical framework to "explain" the spread of P/e movements. Rather, our aim is to provide studies of the landscape of those movements in particular regions. Each author operates with a particular conceptual or theoretical focus, such as language, gender, generation, or politics and power, which in turn shapes the methodological emphasis. In addition to their field research, some contributors use historical and archival materials, while others turn to mass and social media or popular culture. Just as the local movements are engaged by or in the translocal and transnational aspects of P/e, whether they are in the global north or global south, so too the researchers explore the dynamics of local and global interactions in their particular settings. Concomitantly, they reflect upon the possibilities and problems of comparison across movements, historical time periods, cultural settings, and geographical regions. For example, does the concept of the "individual" remain a viable comparative concept?

In several instances, in keeping with the methodological transparency of anthropology, our authors reflect critically on the challenges of conducting research on such a burgeoning field. Many of the P/e movements—driven by their conversionist impulses—are leaving their homelands to establish new diasporic communities, subsequently constituting new online networks to service their expanding virtual communities. These recent trends offer both logistical difficulties and opportunities for researchers. A new church website may be full of news and information, but will not reveal internal tensions in leadership or disagreements over public modes of representation. In sum, for present-day researchers on the globalizing phenomenon of P/e, skills of dexterity and multitasking are the order of the day.

We have therefore designed the book to provide both a geographical and an analytical map of Pentecostalism and evangelicalism. Moreover, it is intended to help readers navigate across a burgeoning field of study, as well as gain a sense of how it has been and is being constituted. Our four sections are designed to reflect key themes within the religious movements under study, but also to point us toward more generic issues in the anthropology of religion and the study of culture as a whole. Within sections, titles of chapters are meant to indicate some of the fundamental themes that readers might wish to reflect on in considering what makes up P/e, ranging from "Personhood" to "Prayer" to "Mediation," and so on.

Both Pentecostalism and evangelicalism are frequently depicted as providing "dualistic" ways of viewing the world, engaging in forms of "spiritual warfare" to combat evil in the self, in others, in particular objects and locations, and across territories and cultures. The first section, "Moralizing the World," asks how such general terms can be conceptualized and compared cross-culturally. How might they be refracted through local notions of agency, spatiality, temporality, and causality? How do notions of the Spirit as well as demonologies relate to processes of social, cultural, and economic change? In the first chapter, Omri Elisha draws on his fieldwork on evangelical megachurches in Knoxville, Tennessee. Focusing on the social interactions and spiritual aspirations of a men's fellowship group, Elisha argues that these groups should not be read in solely individualistic terms, as only "reinforcing Protestant ethics of self-discipline and self-actualization." As his ethnographic involvement in evangelicalism as a lived religion reveals, evangelicals are taught to become involved in the spiritual and emotional lives of others and to allow such involvement by others. This emphasis on what he terms the "immersive sociality" of these relational networks and communities of practice thus challenges—without completely displacing—the long-standing popular and academic assumption that the values of evangelical theology are primarily individuating in their emphasis and effects.

Jean DeBernardi writes about the emplacement of evangelical and Pentecostal Christianity in nineteenth- and early twentieth-century Singapore and Penang. Through archival and field research she is able to demonstrate the early indigenization of evangelism, through the agency of independent lay missionaries such as the Brethren and their Asian coworkers, and the creation of independent, locally led churches, whose revivalist impact was felt across Southeast Asia. She discusses how improved communication and travel facilitated this interconnected world for Christians, even in early modernity. She pays particular attention to the negotiations between local Christians and missionaries over the education and religious leadership of women, which led to the eventual transformation of gender roles in Asia.

Kristine Krause's chapter concerns how Pentecostal believers evaluate, sustain, and create moral geographies of their inner selves, their surroundings, and the wider world in their charismatic practices. She explores these practices based on fieldwork conducted with migrants from Ghana in London, but also on research in transnational Pentecostal networks of Ghanaian-founded churches based in Berlin and Hamburg. While her focus is on how moral subject positions are created in this "simultaneously universal and deeply personal" movement, she also emphasizes, as does Omri Elisha, that Pentecostal practices are inevitably relational. Importantly, she proposes that the question of rupture that dominated the anthropological literature for quite some time needs to be reformulated in light of the diversification of the Pentecostal scene; for young Ghanaian migrants born into born-again families, the challenge is how to preserve these moral boundaries.

Pentecostalism and evangelicalism focus on the holy word as an instrument of both instruction and power. However, as becomes clear in our second section, "Language and Embodiment," such a statement conceals the multiple ways words are articulated and understood by believers and embedded within nonverbal practices that question the divisions between scripture and orality, the written and the embodied. While the focus on language clearly overlaps with issues of transmission and mediation in the next section, the main emphasis in section 2 is on the links between bodily and linguistic practices in ritual and other contexts.

Drawing on his eight years of ethnographic engagement with the Vineyard, a hybrid evangelical/Pentecostal California-originated church planting movement (i.e., one that focuses on creating new local congregations), Jon Bialecki argues that by concentrating on affect, we can think about language and embodiment together without privileging either term. He defines affect as "the intensities and energies found in a particular moment or object that has consequences on others." He shows how affect serves to structure both linguistic and embodied performance and suggests that Pentecostal/charismatic Christianity has been particularly successful in using heightened levels of affect to "expand, reinvigorate, and reconfigure individual and collective identities." Tracing the "lines of affect," he proposes, would develop greater appreciation for the growth of Pentecostalism and evangelicalism in the twentieth and twenty-first centuries, as well as a greater theoretical understanding of broader religiosities.

Kelly H. Chong takes us to South Korea, renowned for the phenomenal success of its evangelical churches, to explore middle-class women's experiences and encounters with evangelicalism and patriarchy. Her focus on a female, small-group culture thus provides an interesting counterpart to Elisha's examination of a male fellowship group. She studies "the ways women become constituted as new feminine subjects through the development of a novel evangelical habitus, one that is constituted by new dispositions, both embodied and linguistic, and is

developed through ritualized rhetorical, bodily, and spiritual practices."
Through Chong's participation in cell groups, she could observe how
women sought healing for experiences of "intense domestic suffering,"
notably when "attempts at other solutions failed, such as psychotherapy
or shamanistic intervention." Yet in spite of the empowered sense of self
that many achieved through these therapeutic, charismatically oriented
communities, women were still resubjugated to the structures of social
and religious patriarchy.

Finally, in this section, Thomas J. Csordas explores the "global geography of the spirit" evident among Catholic charismatic communities, and he thus combines some of the spatial concerns evident in our
first section with the more language-based focus of the second. Csordas
takes geography to have both literal and metaphorical implications, and
thus to "refer to a figurative conceptual terrain as well as to the physical features on the face of the earth." Both of these meanings are at play
in Csordas's examination of the "cartographic self-representation" of
Catholic charismatics, who draw for instance on websites to exhibit a
powerful "sense of international presence and progress toward world
evangelization." He includes but goes beyond the examination of maps,
however, as he traces the workings of the geography of the spirit in the
everyday lives of members, their verbal and body languages, and their
(often gendered) experiences of space.

The high profile of evangelical and Pentecostal movements can be
attributed in part to their easy adaptation to numerous forms of (mass)
mediation and circulation, ranging from missionary tracts in the nineteenth century to Internet sites in the twenty-first. The chapters in section 3, "Transmission and Mediation," raise many questions about this
trend: How are we to understand the apparent resonances between these
religious movements and such (re)mediation, especially given the apparent valorization of immediacy and spontaneity expressed by many
believers? How are these trends related to discourses on fake/authentic
sources and practices of spiritual power? How are ritual practices being
adapted at the local level to accommodate the flows of global actors,
musics, texts, performances, images, and ideas?

Martin Lindhardt is interested in how Pentecostal and charismatic
beliefs and practices regarding spiritual warfare entail a specific stance
toward materiality. Most of the scholarship to date has centered on the

human body as the main material form in which spiritual powers are held to reside, but Lindhardt wants to explore the ways the battle against diabolic powers is fought through the handling of physical objects. Drawing on long-term fieldwork in south-central Tanzania, where P/e has experienced significant growth over the last three decades, he provides a range of ethnographic sketches of how people pray over money to cleanse it from evil powers. Using the lens of the "anthropology of things," he argues that coins and bills constitute a particularly significant object of mediation and a pointer to how adherents of P/e believe they can influence the spiritual world to generate wealth and prosperity in miraculous ways. He notes further that concerns about the moral and potentially dangerous aspects of exchange of money, and rumors about what he calls the "witchcraft of wealth," have been influenced by the increasing impact of the Gospel of Prosperity. In sum, he contends that spiritual warfare "provides a language for speaking about this-worldly concerns" and that money offers a material form for expression of these fears, demonstrating, in his view, the success of P/e in offering viable solutions to "problems of presence and mediation" in religion more generally.

Pentecostal media and music in Brazil have popular appeal, but particularly in the *favelas*, or slums, where conditions are tough. Martijn Oosterbaan's chapter begins with an account of a performance by the renowned gospel singer Elaine Martins at a crusade in a Rio de Janeiro *favela*. Drawing on her case, he seeks to show that Pentecostal musicians struggle with both the potential gain and loss of charisma owing to the current mergers between P/e and electronic media. Not only have media technologies transformed and expanded the "reproduction of charisma," but they have also generated controversies about the sincerity of the performers as converts and evangelists. To defend themselves in the face of the commercialization of the gospel music industry, singers integrate prayers and testimonies into their recordings and performances. Oosterbaan's analysis underscores the need to take seriously the spiritual aesthetic of popular music and its technological (re)mediation, as well as the structural life conditions and cultural backgrounds of the people involved, in understanding the localization and globalization (what some call the "glocalization") of P/e in settings such as Brazil.[27]

In his study of the Pentecostal advance in post-Soviet Central Asia, Mathijs Pelkmans opts to focus on the academically neglected area of miracles and their sustainability, not just because they characterize the effervescent qualities of Pentecostal conviction, but also because they illustrate its fragility. Using the many stories he collected during his research on Kyrgyzstan's largest Pentecostal church, the Church of Jesus Christ, he is able to identify the attractiveness of the Pentecostal message to those struggling with the vagaries of life in a former Soviet state. Miracles are central to this process, circulating through sermons and informal settings and allowing congregants to actively engage with questions of divine intervention and life transformation. However, they need to gain social and semiotic *recognition* as miracles first. Furthermore, the truth of miracles runs the risk of failure in those contexts where the miraculous is needed the most, but "in which it was most difficult to produce success in the form of jobs, regained health, and reliable husbands." The paradox of charismatic action involves its instability, as it is either repeated so often as to strain credibility, or is linked to institutions that destroy its effervescence. Doubt can lead to disaffection, and eventually a (re)turn to the rival tradition of Islam. Instability can both prompt and provide the death knell for faith in the miraculous.

As discussed in our final section, "The State and Beyond: New Relations, New Tensions," Pentecostal and evangelical Christians frequently display ambivalent relations to the state, sometimes seeking its patronage (and even supporting forms of sacralized nationalism), and sometimes self-consciously bypassing its jurisdiction, creating wider "publics" within and beyond state boundaries. The connections between missionary and development discourse are evident, often following old colonial pathways of influence. At the same time, the centers of gravity in Christianity are shifting, so that older sites and states of colonial and missionary power are themselves becoming the objects of proselytization.

Over the last twenty years or so, Angola's religious landscape has undergone considerable transformation. State-sponsored atheism has been replaced by a policy of strategic alliances with major religious institutions. Ruy Llera Blanes explores in his chapter how Pentecostal and evangelical movements are increasingly engaging in aspects of governance and partisan policy in the public sphere, and how they are negotiating these shifting developments and evolving state-sponsored religious policies. These developments raise the question for Blanes of how such movements translate "their transnational, universalizing ethos and narrative into specific, located engagements with national regimes." From the bottom-up perspective of anthropology, the "nationalization" of religion is anything but linear, as the complex field of P/e movements in this context reveals. Categories of foreignness and sovereignty, as well as economic value, intervene in the intersection of government and religious institutions in Angola. Blanes tries to find out from interviews and local media why some P/e churches receive differential treatment, ranging from public recognition to deregistration and persecution. He concludes that the growth and diversification of local and foreign P/e churches have resulted in greater competition and a peculiar system of "fracture and reconnection between government and religious institutions" in which the official narrative of nationalization and "partnership" is frequently overridden by "interpersonal logics."

A focus on the biographies of Pentecostal politicians does not yield the same insights as studies of the everyday experiences of believers who perform their politics through their Christian practices, especially prayer. So argues Kevin O'Neill in his analysis of formations of citizenship among Guatemalan Pentecostals, notably in relation to a particular cause, the decriminalization of drugs. He recounts how, in a visit to Washington, DC, in 2012, this cause was championed—somewhat counterintuitively—by Harold Caballeros, then foreign minister and one of Guatemala's leading Pentecostal politicians. This was an extension of the prayer campaigns he had led against drug trafficking in Guatemala. In this connection, churches such as the Guatemala City megachurch El Shaddai provide a body of literature that instructs members on how to win back the capital as well as the country from the Devil. Through his field research, O'Neill was able to observe how interceding in a spiritual war was primarily enacted as a private and personal activity, with prayer sheets kept at bedsides and workplaces and in individual Bibles, rather than used in public spaces. He stresses that even though such religious activity would not be classified as citizenship participation from the perspective of political science, for Guatemalan Pentecostals, it is a practice that works, and in fact *is* Pentecostal politics. It works primarily because it makes the individual, with his or her power of choice, the "very terrain upon which political action takes place." O'Neill's thematizing of the individual as location of action contrasts in interesting ways with Elisha's emphasis on the relationality of evangelicals in Knoxville. Rather than seeing a simple contradiction in such an apparent disjunction, however, we might be better advised to explore how different dimensions of P/e personhood can be foregrounded according to temporal and social, as well as cultural, context.

Yannick Fer opens his chapter by showing how the histories of Polynesian island nations are very much bound up with Christianity. As nineteenth-century Protestant missionaries translated the Bible into vernacular languages, they became enmeshed in social life and local cultural traditions, serving to shape a common Pacific Christian culture. In contrast, the early classical Pentecostal churches arriving later in the region from North America were more ambivalent about local culture as they sought ethical respectability. Yet the growth of charismatic movements in Polynesia, against a backdrop of rapid social change and transnational circulations between the island states and strong diasporic communities in New Zealand, Australia, and the United States, has resulted in a type of "nonconformist liberation." Polynesian youth are drawn to what Fer terms the more "individuated understanding of moral consciousness," as well as the new possibilities for bodily movements and cultural expression such as dance. Thus, local culture might in fact have a positive moral valency for contemporary Christians, and we see how contemporary forms of Pentecostalism may have very different emphases than more classical forms. As with DeBernardi's chapter, Fer shows us the value of locating current manifestations of P/e in relation to much longer histories of local Protestantism.

Moving into the Future

When we talk of the anthropology of P/e, we might want not only to explore links and complementarities between cases, as just described in our summaries of the chapters of this book, but also to contrast it with other ways of studying P/e: historical, sociological, theological, geographical, and so on. Admittedly, divisions between disciplines are not always so simple. We have indicated how the development of a more historical sensibility has helped anthropologists assess whether P/e has or has not made fundamental changes in a given society or group.[28] Overlaps with more qualitative forms of sociology are obvious (e.g., Ammerman 1987), though anthropologists have generally been less concerned with framing the (re-)emergence of P/e as a reversal of secularization. This latter theme has played a less prominent role in the discipline partly because of a general mistrust of theories suggesting linear trajectories in human history, and partly because many non-Western fields showed few signs of becoming secular. The discipline's relationship with theology has at times been troubled, but in recent years the study of Christianity has encouraged some dialogue between scholars and themes. Interestingly, a focus on rupture has suggested the possibility of interdisciplinary reflections on Pauline notions of conversion (see Robbins and Engelke 2010). Anthropology's links with geography in studying P/e have been least discussed and yet have great potential, given how believers focus so much on territorial spirits and mapping of the world (literally and metaphorically), and are so oriented toward a global view of mission. Both geographers and anthropologists are likely to perceive any vision of the "global" not as a set of ideas to be taken for granted, but as a particular cultural framework whose specific motivations and assumptions need to be examined, as Kristine Krause and Thomas Csordas demonstrate in this volume.

The anthropology of P/e has gained some of its distinctiveness through the kind of fieldwork and case-study approach that you will find in the chapters of this book. It has also taken on a particular character through the kinds of themes and conversations that have developed in the past fifteen years. But, in conclusion, how might the conversation be opened up in ways that complement but also go beyond "rupture"? Very briefly, we suggest a few areas that might help us move into a "third phase" of studying P/e. We divide these areas into three: "reflexivity," "recalibration," and "reframing."

Our first area relates to a common feature of P/e, but one that contradicts somewhat stereotypical views of believers as being somehow seduced into unthinking forms of religious engagement: the extent to which P/e encourages certain forms of *reflexivity* and *flexibility* in relation to questions of truth and culture. By this we do not mean the kind of reflexivity involved in more extreme versions of rupture, whereby tradition may be objectified and morally condemned, but more complex and ambiguous forms of accommodation and negotiation between moral, epistemological, and/or cultural alternatives. Pelkmans's chapter provides one example of what we mean here, as his focus on miracles shows how people can become "actively engaged with the epistemological and social dimensions of different bodies of knowledge." In Oosterbaan's piece, Pentecostal testimony and popular culture come together in the fragile construction of charisma, which can work on both secular and spiritual registers. Fer's tracing of the way the Island Breeze movement deploys a perhaps surprising strategy of taking up Polynesian cultural forms such as dancing as a means of negotiating a relationship not only with secularization, but also with more classical Pentecostal attitudes, is another case in point. More generally, we note that members of P/e congregations often have to live alongside members of other religious communities for much of their lives (Daswani 2013), and may even themselves move back and forth between different religious frameworks in a given period of time. Engagement with P/e practices and ideologies is likely to involve many more situational stances than even ethnography has sometimes revealed (Walton 2012, 109), and we need more work on how P/e practices may become backgrounded as well as foregrounded in people's ethical lives. Related to this point, although less covered in our book, is the fact that anthropologists and others have tended in their studies of P/e to focus on more triumphalist narratives and examples of P/e—in other words, cases where believers are demonstrably successful in attracting numbers and commitment. But the global diffusion of P/e will also entail many cases of failure or halfhearted engagement, and such cases of more stuttering, diffuse forms of P/e may well reveal little-known dimensions of religious practice (compare Premawardhana 2013, in press).

Second, we are interested in the ways P/e can *recalibrate* boundaries commonly used by scholars, including many anthropologists, in their analyses of religion and society at large. Many ethnographers have the tendency to assume that they can "explain" religious conversion and engagement by identifying the function that it plays in addressing some gap in a person's life, whether it be lack of personal or political direction, poverty, desire for healing, or psychological trauma. There is no doubt that P/e can play such a role in people's lives, as for instance Pelkmans's chapter demonstrates. However, a particular challenge for secular anthropologists is the need to study engagement in P/e without assuming that religious commitment is "really" about something that scholars often see as more fundamental and measurable, such as economic or political benefit. Consider then the implications of O'Neill's argument that the text he studies "repositions the meaning of Pentecostal politics to include prayer itself. To perform this Pentecostal prayer, this chapter argues, is to participate politically." One of the things that O'Neill is asking us to do here is not only to rethink what prayer is, but also to reconsider how we are to understand political action when viewed from a different way of viewing the world. Bialecki may be doing something similar in his analysis of a notion of affect that allows us to see a thread that runs through the secular *and* the religious. As Lindhardt does in his piece on money, these scholars are prompting us to reimagine categories of secular analysis, including politics, the secular/sacred divide, and the economy, by showing how conventional distinctions do not capture the complexities of the practices being analyzed. While anthropologists have long delighted in showing how non-Western populations blend spheres of life that Western "modernity" has separated (such as religion, politics, and the economy), we need to bear in mind that many P/e advocates are aware of the assumptions of Western modernity, but are—whether consciously or not, with greater or lesser degrees of agency—attempting to remake them.

Finally, by "reframing," we mean that the opportunity exists to go back to one advantage that studies of Christian contexts had before the self-conscious anthropology of Christianity emerged as a subfield. In other words, we ask, How do we frame our work on P/e by comparing it with and to a much wider set of anthropological questions and literatures than those concerned with Christianity per se? Are there significant ways we might see P/e as comparable to certain manifestations of Islam in its use of mass media, for instance? How might we see P/e through the lens of such theoretical frameworks as the anthropology of elites or, say, the anthropology of organizations? The list of potential comparisons is never-ending. There is clearly much still to do.

NOTES

We would like to thank our editor, Jennifer Hammer, and an anonymous reviewer for their very helpful comments on a draft of this introduction.

1. When these two terms occur together in this introduction, we will refer to them as P/e.

2. Given size constraints for this text, our coverage of traditions cannot be comprehensive. An obvious and important gap in our coverage is the lack of scholars who

have held posts for a significant period in university settings outside Europe and North America, although many of the scholars here have experience of such contexts. The Nigerian scholar Ogbu Kalu (2007; see also Kalu 2008) has traced the history of scholarship on African Christianity, using works by African scholars themselves. Mariz and Campos (2011) discuss Brazil as a cultural context not only for Pentecostalism, but also for the study of Pentecostalism. Anderson and Tang (2005) examine the study of Asian Pentecostalism.

3. See, for example, Freston 2008.

4. *Newsweek*, December 22, 2008, http://www.newsweek.com/newsweek-50-e-adeboye-83039 (accessed June 8, 2013).

5. See, e.g., Asad 1993. Hann (2007, 383) notes that Christianity was the dominant religion of the countries in which sociocultural anthropology was originally established.

6. Her fellow students said that she appeared to be speaking Chinese, and thus a form of xenoglossia.

7. See also Saint Paul's instruction in 1 Corinthians 12 and 14.

8. Anderson is editor of the journal *PentecoStudies*, a very useful source for up-to-date analyses of Pentecostalism and charismatic developments in particular.

9. However, disagreements exist as to the exact timing and nature of the end-times, and thus whether a tribulation will occur before the reign of Jesus on earth (premillennialism), or whether a glorious period of peace will be followed by war against, and ultimately vanquishing of, the Antichrist (postmillennialism).

10. For an overview of Scandinavian Pentecostalism, see Alvarsson 2011.

11. For a more extended discussion of Pentecostal history, see, e.g., Anderson 2004.

12. We are grateful to our anonymous reviewer for reminding us of this last point.

13. From midcentury on, Graham and other evangelicals such as Carl Henry had been important in encouraging more engagement with the world than fundamentalists (we are grateful to our anonymous reviewer for reminding us of this point). Starting in 1956, Henry worked as founding editor of the important evangelical magazine *Christianity Today*.

14. For an alternative to this approach in considering Christianity as a whole, see Bialecki 2012.

15. See Sahlins's (1996) discussion of links between Christianity, social sciences, and modernity. We should also remember the work of historians of religion such as Ninian Smart and Peter McKenzie, who also made the case from the 1970s for studying Christianity historically and comparatively.

16. See, e.g., apart from texts already mentioned, Anderson et al. 2010; Barker 2012; van de Kamp 2011; Gooren 2010.

17. See, e.g., Coleman and Maier 2013; Hunt 2002; Knibbe 2009; Krause 2008; Ukah 2009; van Dijk 2002.

18. See, e.g., Austin-Broos 1997; Brusco 2010; Frederick 2003; Stewart and Coleman in press.

19. See, e.g., Bialecki 2011; Bielo 2009; Csordas 1997; Lindhardt 2011; Luhrmann 2012; Schieffelin 1996; Shoaps 2002; Stromberg 1993; Tomlinson 2012.

20. See, e.g., de Witte 2008; Engelke 2007; Keane 2006, 2007; Meyer 2012; Oosterbaan 2011.

21. See, e.g., Bielo 2007; Mosko 2010; Coleman 2011b; Daswani 2011; Klaits 2011; Werbner 2011.

22. See, e.g., Coleman 2011c; Comaroff and Comaroff 2000; Gifford 2004; Hackett 1995; Haynes 2013; Marshall 2009; O'Neill 2010.

23. Bialecki, Haynes, and Robbins (2008, 1151) note that forms of Christianity that look fiercely anti-modern in the context of the "developed" West appear to be strong upholders of modernity when placed in other contexts. See also Strathern and Stewart (2009, 31) on ways that the implications of apparent Christian "rupture" can vary considerably cross-culturally.

24. See Hackett 1996.

25. This is not to say that P/e is any more or less coherent in its relationship between theology and practice than any other religious expression.

26. One model we had in mind here was the Kuhnian notion of paradigm shifts and the distinction between normal and revolutionary science. This theme is discussed in Robbins's afterword to this volume, and in Coleman (in press).

27. In fact, despite its importance, Pentecostal music remains a remarkably understudied area.

28. See also, e.g., Maxwell 2006; Peel 2000.

REFERENCES

Alvarsson, Jan-Åke. 2011. "Scandinavian Pentecostalism." In European Pentecostalism, edited by William K. Kay and Anne E. Dye, 19–39. Leiden: Brill.

Ammerman, Nancy. 1987. Bible Believers: Fundamentalists in the Modern World. New Brunswick: Rutgers University Press.

Anderson, Allan. 2004. An Introduction to Pentecostalism: Global Charismatic Christianity. Cambridge: Cambridge University Press.

———. 2013. To the Ends of the Earth: Pentecostalism and the Transformation of World Christianity. Oxford: Oxford University Press.

Anderson, Allan, Michael Bergunder, André Droogers, and Cornelis van der Laan. 2010. Studying Global Pentecostalism: Theories and Methods. Berkeley: University of California Press.

Anderson, Allan, and Edmond Tang, eds. 2005. Asian and Pentecostal: The Charismatic Face of Asian Christianity. Oxford: Regnum.

Asad, Talal. 1993. Genealogies of Religion: Discipline and Reasons of Power in Christianity and Islam. Baltimore: Johns Hopkins University Press.

Austin-Broos, Diane. 1997. Jamaica Genesis: Religion and the Politics of Moral Order. Chicago: University of Chicago Press.

Barker, John. 2012. "Secondary Conversion and the Anthropology of Christianity in Melanesia." Archives des Science Sociales des Religion 157:67–86.

Bebbington, David. 1989. *Evangelicalism in Modern Britain: A History from the 1730s to the 1980s*. London: Unwin Hyman.

Bialecki, Jon. 2011. "No Caller ID for the Soul: Demonization, Charisms, and the Unstable Subject of Protestant Language Ideology." *Anthropological Quarterly* 84:679–703.

———. 2012. "Virtual Christianity in an Age of Nominalist Anthropology." *Anthropological Theory* 12 (3): 295–319.

Bialecki, Jon, Naomi Haynes, and Joel Robbins. 2008. "The Anthropology of Christianity." *Religion Compass* 2:1139–58.

Bielo, James. 2007. "'The Mind of Christ': Financial Success, Born-Again Personhood, and the Anthropology of Christianity." *Ethnos* 72:316–38.

———. 2009. *Words upon the Word: An Ethnography of Evangelical Group Bible Study*. New York: New York University Press.

———. 2011. *Emerging Evangelicals: Faith, Modernity, and the Desire for Authenticity*. New York: New York University Press.

Bowler, Kate. 2013. *Blessed: A History of the American Prosperity Gospel*. Oxford: Oxford University Press.

Brusco, Elizabeth. 2010. *The Reformation of Machismo: Evangelical Conversion and Gender in Colombia*. Austin: University of Texas Press.

Cannell, Fenella, ed. 2006. *The Anthropology of Christianity*. Durham: Duke University Press.

Coleman, Simon. 2000. *The Globalisation of Charismatic Christianity: Spreading the Gospel of Prosperity*. Cambridge: Cambridge University Press.

———. 2011a. "Actors of History? Religion, Politics and 'Reality' within the Protestant Right in America." In *Religion, Politics and Globalization: Anthropological Approaches*, edited by Galina Lindquist and Don Handelman, 171–88. Oxford: Berghahn.

———. 2011b. "Introduction: Negotiating Personhood in African Christianities." *Journal of Religion in Africa* 41 (3): 243–55.

———. 2011c. "Prosperity Unbound? Debating the 'Sacrificial Economy.'" *Research in Economic Anthropology* 31:23–45.

———. In press. "Christianity: An (In-)Constant Companion?" In Research Companion to Anthropology, edited by Pamela J. Stewart and Andrew Strathern. Farnham: Ashgate.

Coleman, Simon, and Katrin Maier. 2013. "Redeeming the City: Creating and Traversing 'London-Lagos.'" *Religion* 43 (3): 353–64.

Coleman, Simon, and Pauline von Hellermann, eds. 2010. *Multi-sited Ethnography: Problems and Possibilities in the Translocation of Research Methods*. New York: Routledge.

Comaroff, Jean. 1985. *Body of Power, Spirit of Resistance: The Culture and History of a South African People*. Chicago: University of Chicago Press.

Comaroff, Jean, and John Comaroff. 1991. *Of Revelation and Revolution*. Vol. 1, *Christianity, Colonialism, and Consciousness in South Africa*. Chicago: University of Chicago Press.

———. 1997. *Of Revelation and Revolution*. Vol. 2, *The Dialectics of Modernity on a South African Frontier*. Chicago: University of Chicago Press.

———. 2000. "Millennial Capitalism: First Thoughts on a Second Coming." *Public Culture* 12 (2): 291–343.

Corten, André, and Ruth Marshall-Fratani. 2001. *Between Babel and Pentecost: Transnational Pentecostalism in Africa and Latin America*. Bloomington: Indiana University Press.

Crapanzano, Vincent. 2000. *Serving the Word: Literalism in America from the Pulpit to the Bench*. New York: New Press.

Csordas, Thomas. 1997. *Language, Charisma and Creativity: The Ritual Life of a Religious Movement*. Berkeley: University of California Press.

Daswani, Girish. 2011. "(In-) Dividual Pentecostals in Ghana." *Journal of Religion in Africa* 41:256–79.

———. 2013. "On Christianity and Ethics: Rupture as Ethical Practice in Ghanaian Pentecostalism." *American Ethnologist* 40 (3): 467–79.

De Witte, Marleen. 2008. "Spirit Media: Charismatics, Traditionalists, and Mediation Practices in Ghana." PhD diss., University of Amsterdam.

Douglas, Mary. 1966. *Purity and Danger: An Analysis of Concepts of Pollution and Taboo*. London: Routledge.

Elisha, Omri. 2011. *Moral Ambition: Mobilization and Social Outreach in Evangelical Megachurches*. Berkeley: University of California Press.

Engelke, Matthew. 2007. *A Problem of Presence: Beyond Scripture in an African Church*. Berkeley: University of California Press.

Engelke, Matthew, and Matt Tomlinson, eds. 2006. *The Limits of Meaning: Case Studies in the Anthropology of Christianity*. Oxford: Berghahn.

Frederick, Marla. 2003. *Between Sundays: Black Women's Everyday Struggles of Faith*. Berkeley: University of California Press.

Freston, Paul. 2008. "The Changing Face of Christian Proselytizing: New Actors from the Global South." In *Proselytization Revisited: Rights Talk, Free Markets and Culture Wars*, edited by Rosalind I. J. Hackett, 108–38. London: Acumen.

Gifford, Paul. 2004. *Ghana's New Christianity: Pentecostalism in a Globalising African Economy*. London: Hurst.

Goodhew, David. 2013. "Evangelical, but Not 'Fundamentalist': A Case Study of the New Churches in York." In *Evangelicalism and Fundamentalism in the United Kingdom during the Twentieth Century*, edited by David W. Bebbington and David Ceri Jones, 230–50. Oxford: Oxford University Press.

Gooren, Henri. 2010. *Religious Conversion and Disaffiliation: Tracing Patterns of Change in Faith Practices*. New York: Palgrave Macmillan.

Hackett, Rosalind I. J. 1995. "The Gospel of Prosperity in West Africa." In *Religion and the Transformations of Capitalism*, edited by Richard Roberts, 199–214. London: Routledge.

———. 1996. "New Directions and Connections for African and Asian Charismatics." *Pneuma* 18, no. 1 (Spring): 69–77.

————. 1998. "Charismatic/Pentecostal Appropriations of Media Technologies in Nigeria and Ghana." *Journal of Religion in Africa* 28 (3): 258–77.

————. 2012. "Devil Bustin' Satellites: How Media Liberalization in Africa Generates Religious Intolerance and Conflict." In Displacing the State: Religion and Conflict in Neoliberal Africa, edited by James H. Smith and Rosalind I. J. Hackett, 153–208. South Bend: University of Notre Dame Press.

Hann, Chris. 2007. "The Anthropology of Christianity per Se." *Archives of European Sociology* 48 (3): 383–410.

Harding, Susan. 1987. "Convicted by the Holy Spirit: The Rhetoric of Fundamental Baptist Conversion." *American Ethnologist* 14:167–81.

————. 1991. "Representing Fundamentalism: The Problem of the Repugnant Cultural Other." *Social Research* 58:373–93.

————. 2000. *The Book of Jerry Falwell: Fundamentalist Language and Politics.* Princeton: Princeton University Press.

Haynes, Naomi. 2013. "On the Potential and Problems of Pentecostal Exchange." *American Anthropologist* 115 (1): 85–95.

Hefner, Robert, ed. 1993. *Conversion to Christianity: Historical and Anthropological Perspectives on a Great Transformation.* Berkeley: University of California Press.

Hollenweger, Walter. 1997. *Pentecostalism: Origins and Developments Worldwide.* Peabody, MA: Hendrickson Publishers Marketing.

Howell, Brian M. 2007. "The Repugnant Cultural Other Speaks Back: Christianity as Ethnographic Standpoint." *Anthropological Theory* 7:371–91.

Hunt, Stephen. 2002. "'Neither Here nor There': The Construction of Identities and Boundary Maintenance of West African Pentecostals." *Sociology* 36 (1): 147–69.

Hunter, James D. 2010. *To Change the World: The Irony, Tragedy, and Possibility of Christianity in the Late Modern World.* Oxford: Oxford University Press.

Kalu, Ogbu, ed. 2007. *African Christianity: An African Story.* Trenton: Africa World Press.

————. 2008. *African Pentecostalism: An Introduction.* New York: Oxford University Press.

Keane, Webb. 2006. "Anxious Transcendence." In *The Anthropology of Christianity,* edited by Fenella Cannell, 308–23. Durham: Duke University Press.

————. 2007. *Christian Moderns: Freedom and Fetish in the Mission Encounter.* Berkeley: University of California Press.

Klaits, Frederick. 2011. "Introduction: Self, Other and God in African Christianities." *Journal of Religion in Africa* 41:143–53.

Knibbe, Kim. 2009. "'We Did Not Come Here as Tenants, but as Landlords': Nigerian Pentecostals and the Power of Maps." *African Diaspora* 2 (2): 133–58.

Krause, Kristine. 2008. "Spiritual Spaces in Post-industrial Places: Transnational Churches in North East London." In *Transnational Ties: Cities, Identities, and Migrations,* edited by Michael Peter Smith and John Eade, 109–30. London: Transaction.

Lawless, Elaine. 1992. "'I Was Afraid Someone Like You . . . an Outsider, Would Misunderstand': Negotiating Interpretive Differences between Ethnographers and Subjects." *Journal of American Folklore* 105 (417): 302–14.

Lindhardt, Martin, ed. 2011. *Practicing the Faith: The Ritual Life of Pentecostal-Charismatic Christians.* Oxford: Berghahn.

Luhrmann, Tanya. 2012. *When God Talks Back: Understanding the American Evangelical Relationship with God.* New York: Knopf.

Mariz, Cecilia, and Roberta Campos. 2011. "Pentecostalism and 'National Culture': A Dialogue between Brazilian Social Sciences and the Anthropology of Christianity." *Religion and Society: Advances in Research* 2:106–21.

Marsden, George. 1980. *Fundamentalism and American Culture.* Oxford: Oxford University Press.

Marshall, Ruth. 2009. *Political Spiritualities: The Pentecostal Revolution in Nigeria.* Chicago: University of Chicago Press.

Marti, Gerardo. 2008. *Hollywood Faith: Holiness, Prosperity, and Ambition in a Los Angeles Church.* Berkeley: University of California Press.

Martin, David. 1990. *Tongues of Fire: The Explosion of Protestantism in Latin America.* Oxford: Blackwell.

———. 2002. *Pentecostalism: The World Their Parish.* Oxford: Wiley.

Maxwell, David. 2006. *African Gifts of the Spirit: Pentecostalism and the Rise of a Zimbabwean Transnational Religious Movement.* Oxford: James Currey.

Meyer, Birgit. 1999. *Translating the Devil: Religion and Modernity among the Ewe in Ghana.* Edinburgh: Edinburgh University Press.

———. 2012. "Religious Sensations: Media, Aesthetics, and the Study of Contemporary Religion." In *Religion, Media and Culture: A Reader,* edited by Gordon Lynch and Jolyon Mitchell, with Anna Strhan, 159–70. New York: Routledge.

Miller, Donald. 1999. *Reinventing American Protestantism: Christianity in the New Millennium.* Berkeley: University of California Press.

Mosko, Mark. 2010. "Partible Penitents: Dividual Personhood and Christian Practice in Melanesia and the West." *Journal of the Royal Anthropological Institute* 16:215–40.

Needham, Rodney. 1975. "Polythetic Classification: Convergence and Consequences." *Man* 10 (3): 349–69.

Noll, Mark. 2004. "The Future of Protestantism: Evangelicalism." In *The Blackwell Companion to Protestantism,* edited by Alister McGrath and Darren Marks, 421–38. Oxford: Blackwell.

O'Neill, Kevin. 2010. *City of God: Christian Citizenship in Postwar Guatemala.* Berkeley: University of California Press.

Oosterbaan, Martijn. 2011. "Virtually Global: Online Evangelical Cartography." *Social Anthropology* 19 (1): 56–73.

Peel, J. D. Y. 1968. *Aladura: A Religious Movement among the Yoruba.* London: Oxford University Press.

———. 2000. *Religious Encounter and the Making of the Yoruba*. Bloomington: Indiana University Press.

Peristiany, Jean, ed. 1966. *Honour and Shame: The Values of Mediterranean Society*. Chicago: University of Chicago Press.

Premawardhana, Devaka. 2013. "Between River and Road: Circular Migrations and Reversible Conversions in Northern Mozambique." Working paper, Colorado College, Harvard University, Cambridge, MA, April 19, 2013. http://ssrn.com/abstract=2253759.

———. In press. "Continuities of Change: Conversion and Convertibility in Northern Mozambique." In What Is Existential Anthropology?, edited by Michael Jackson and Albert Piette. Oxford: Berghahn.

Robbins, Joel. 2003. "What Is a Christian? Notes toward an Anthropology of Christianity." *Religion* 33 (3): 191–99.

———. 2004a. *Becoming Sinners: Christianity and Moral Torment in a Papua New Guinea Society*. Berkeley: University of California Press.

———. 2004b. "The Globalization of Pentecostal and Charismatic Christianity." *Annual Review of Anthropology* 33:117–43.

———. 2007. "Continuity Thinking and the Problem of Christian Culture: Belief, Time and the Anthropology of Christianity." *Current Anthropology* 48:5–38.

Robbins, Joel, and Matthew Engelke. 2010. Introduction to "Global Christianity, Global Critique." Special issue, *South Atlantic Quarterly* 109 (4): 623–31.

Sahlins, Marshall. 1996. "The Sadness of Sweetness: The Native Anthropology of Western Cosmology." *Current Anthropology* 37:395–415.

Sanneh, Lamin. 2013. "Introducing the Oxford Series." In *To the Ends of the Earth: Pentecostalism and the Transformation of World Christianity*, edited by Allan Anderson, xiii-xvi. Oxford: Oxford University Press.

Schieffelin, Bambi. 1996. "Creating Evidence: Making Sense of the Written Word in Bosavi." In *Interaction and Grammar*, edited by Elinor Ochs, Emanuel Schegloff, and Sandra Thompson, 45–60. Cambridge: Cambridge University Press.

Shoaps, Robin. 2002. "'Pray Earnestly': The Textual Construction of Personal Involvement in Pentecostal Prayer and Song." *Journal of Linguistic Anthropology* 12 (1): 34–71.

Stewart, Anna, and Simon Coleman. In press. "Contributions from Anthropology." In *The Oxford Handbook of Sexuality and Gender*, edited by Adrian Thatcher. Oxford: Oxford University Press.

Stoll, David. 1991. *Is Latin America Turning Protestant? The Politics of Evangelical Growth*. Berkeley: University of California Press.

Strathern, Andrew J., and Pamela J. Stewart. 2009. "Introduction: A Complexity of Contexts, a Multiplicity of Changes." In *Religious and Ritual Change: Cosmologies and Histories*, edited by Pamela J. Stewart and Andrew J. Strathern, 3–68. Durham: Carolina Academic Press.

Stromberg, Peter. 1993. *Language and Self-Transformation: A Study of the Christian Conversion Narrative*. Cambridge: Cambridge University Press.

Tomlinson, Matthew. 2012. "God Speaking to God: Translation and Unintelligibility at a Fijian Pentecostal Crusade." *Australian Journal of Anthropology* 23 (3): 274–89.

Turner, Victor, and Edith Turner. 1978. *Image and Pilgrimage in Christian Culture*. New York: Columbia University Press.

Ukah, Asonzeh. 2009. "Reverse Mission or Asylum Christianity: A Nigerian Church in Europe." In *Africans and the Politics of Popular Cultures*, edited by Toyin Falola and Augustine Agwuele, 104–32. Rochester, NY: University of Rochester Press.

Van de Kamp, Linda. 2011. "Converting the Spirit Spouse: The Violent Transformation of the Pentecostal Female Body in Maputo, Mozambique." *Ethnos* 76 (4): 510–33.

Van der Veer, Peter, ed. 1996. *Conversion to Modernities: The Globalization of Christianity*. London: Routledge.

Van Dijk, Rijk. 1999. "The Pentecostal Gift: Ghanaian Charismatic Churches and the Moral Innocence of the Global Economy." In *Modernity on a Shoestring: Dimensions of Globalization, Consumption and Development in Africa and Beyond*, edited by Richard Fardon, Wim van Binsbergen, and Rijk van Dijk, 71–89. Leiden: EIDOS.

———. 2002. "The Soul Is a Stranger: Ghanaian Pentecostalism and the Diasporic Contestation of 'Flow' and 'Individuality.'" *Culture and Religion* 3:49–66.

Wagner, Roy. 1981. *The Invention of Culture*. Chicago: University of Chicago Press.

Walton, Jonathan. 2012. "Stop Worrying and Start Sowing! A Phenomenological Account of the Ethics of 'Divine Investment.'" In *Pentecostalism and Prosperity: The Socio-Economics of the Global Charismatic Movement*, edited by Katherine Attanasi and Amos Yong, 107–29. New York: Palgrave Macmillan.

Warner, Michael. 2004. "Tongues Untied: Memoirs of a Pentecostal Boyhood." In *Curiouser: On the Queerness of Children*, edited by Steven Bruhm and Natasha Hurley, 215–24. Minneapolis: University of Minnesota Press.

Werbner, Richard. 2011. *Holy Hustlers, Schism, and Prophecy: Apostolic Reformation in Botswana*. Berkeley: University of California Press.

SECTION 1

Moralizing the World

1

Personhood

Sin, Sociality, and the Unbuffered Self in US Evangelicalism

OMRI ELISHA

Trevor paused, held his fist to his mouth, and cleared his throat. Standing in front of a dozen men, including some of his closest friends, he struggled to regain a masculine composure but made no effort to conceal his emotion or downplay the poignancy of the moment. "In the week since my diagnosis, I've learned a lot about this disease, this diabetes, and how to live with it." His eyes grew more determined. "I'm also realizing that this disease is my repentance," he said, "repentance for years of gluttony. When I became a Christian years ago, I gave up most of my sinful ways, but I never gave up overeating, even though I knew that God wanted me to make that sacrifice too."

The men, all members of an evangelical men's group, listened quietly as Trevor spoke. His humbling indictment seemed all the more damning with empty pizza boxes and grease-soaked paper plates scattered around the table where we all sat. As he raised a Bible in his hand, the other men instinctively reached for theirs, patiently awaiting chapter and verse.

"Now that I'm repenting," Trevor continued, "I really appreciate it because, as we learn in Romans 2, repentance is a gift." His tone shifted, as the emphasis of his discourse changed. Words of confession now assumed the force of instruction. "And if you pray for me, I don't want you to pray that I'll be healed from this disease, but pray that I'll be healed from the sinful lifestyle that made me sick. Pray that I'll be obedient to God and begin to live a more healthy life, and pray that my wife will support me." Heads nodded in agreement. "I need you guys to keep me accountable," Trevor concluded. "*I will fail if I go through this alone.*"

Trevor's testimony—introspective and confessional—was clearly about more than a middle-aged family man telling his friends he had type 2 diabetes. By presenting himself as a contrite sinner and beneficiary of God's grace, Trevor framed a narrative that was at once deeply personal and standard fare in a milieu where themes of repentance, redemption, and regeneration are routinely invoked. At Eternal Vine Church (pseudonym), a megachurch in the suburbs of Knoxville, Tennessee, "fellowship groups" like this one (also known as "small groups") are valued precisely as zones of intimacy where soul-searching evangelicals come together to nourish and reform their inward selves through Bible study, prayer, and discussion. Intrinsically, such groups attend to the needs, fears, and desires of individual believers, reinforcing Protestant ethics of self-discipline and self-actualization.

Yet the interactions among members of this fellowship group should not be read in purely individualistic terms, as if it were merely the sanctification of atomized selves at stake. Exchanges triggered by moments like the one described are morally and theologically significant in ways beyond privileging the individual as the locus of ethical cultivation. Seen in context, Trevor's words and the responses that followed were fueled by a relational imperative, a model of sociality (that is, how social connections are formed and maintained) that stresses the virtues of radical interdependence among people of faith. This imperative is crucial when it comes to how evangelicals inhabit the world as Christians, and how they guard themselves from sin and other forces that might cause spiritual harm or impede the mission of the church.

Drawing on field research, including the above anecdote to which I will return, this essay argues two main points. First, being part of a Christian community, for many US evangelicals, means entering into voluntary social networks where one is expected to become closely implicated in the lives of others. It is a relational dynamic that must be nurtured and upheld with commitment and vigilance. Prayer, fasting, and biblical immersion are common methods for bolstering faith, resisting temptation, and overcoming demonic influences, but they are not the only means at evangelicals' disposal. Relationships built on transparency, and the monitoring of self and other, are enacted as vehicles of spiritual discipline, mediating biblical truth and the power of the Holy Spirit. To borrow the idiom of spiritual warfare—a language more closely tied to Pentecostalism, but increasingly ubiquitous in evangelical circles as well—social relationships help constitute the armor and arsenal of the Christian warrior.

Second, I argue that the corresponding model of sociality challenges the independence and impermeability of what Charles Taylor (2007) calls the "buffered self," thus destabilizing individualism even while accommodating it in other respects. For evangelicals, sociality is ideally meant to facilitate intersubjectivity, a form of communion among coexisting selves, an alternative reality that nearly approximates the divine. As I will demonstrate, this meaningful nuance suggests that even as evangelical theology reproduces Western hegemonic values and individuating norms, the manner in which such values and norms are expressed in actually existing Christianities is rarely straightforward or unself-conscious.

Like many Americans, US evangelicals champion the virtues of self-reliance and personal responsibility, not least because they reflect the moral fortitude expected of those who have been "saved." At the same time, evangelicals aspire toward "redemptive relationships," in which the boundaries of individual moral autonomy are partially broken down. Marked by terms such as "fellowship" and "discipleship," evangelical sociality is a religious end unto itself, in which familiar conditions of personhood are revised to promote new configurations of self and other. Spiritual and emotional lives are meant to intersect, unhindered, in the confines of religious affinity.

There are limits, of course. Such principles do not nearly amount to a relational social ontology like that found, for example, among the Urapmin of Papua New Guinea, where identities are determined by patterns of social differentiation and "no one ever appears as an individual outside of relationships" (Robbins 2004, 302). Western evangelicals retain their status as self-determined, impartible individuals, no matter how much personal sovereignty they relinquish to friends and spiritual kin. Yet evangelical indoctrination is a process that features prescribed forms of immersive sociality, seen as correctives against the atomizing pressures of secular society. As James Bielo has shown, while US evangelicals "remain individual adherents of faith," a growing number are "fed up with their own individualist heritage." In turn, they "ground their visions of authentic faith in relationality," in efforts to achieve "a desired moral community in which mutual dependence is lived in the everyday" (2012, 259). This model of mutual dependence, which reinforces the believer's utter dependence on God, is instrumental in the formation of evangelical subjects. And despite the potential obligations, risks, and entanglements involved, it is important for their sense of how divine as well as satanic forces become manifest in their lives.

That They All May Be One

The liberation of the individual from social, political, and economic constraints is a core paradigm of Western modernity, with deep resonances in American life. In a devotedly democratic and capitalist society that privileges the possessive rights and responsibilities of individuals, evangelicals—especially white conservative evangelicals—embrace these values with noted consistency and zeal. They are, so to speak, individualists par excellence, and are routinely characterized as such by scholars and critics alike. Undeniably, the conservative social attitudes of most American evangelicals are strongly influenced by ethics of modern individualism as well (Smith 1998).

This long-standing ideological affinity stems from the very heart of Reformed theology, in which salvation is linked to notions of individual agency purified of material and social entanglements (Keane 2007). The evangelical concept of being "born again" is itself strongly individuating, as is the expressive culture of evangelical worship and prayer, typically performed in first-person singular terms. Ministries of charity and social outreach tend to rely on personalistic "one-on-one" strategies as well, reinforcing the primacy of the individual as the site of radical transformation.

But what are the limits of this dominant worldview? How do evangelicals imagine or create new interpersonal boundaries when their Christian idealism compels them to relate to others with uncommon devotion? Is there room for extension and nuance in standard evangelical conceptions of the bounded autonomous self, standing alone before God?

Charles Taylor considers "the replacement of the porous self by the buffered self" (2007, 539) to be one of the defining features of "the secular age" and its disenchantments. However, one need not look far to see that there is more to the story. As powerful as the force of individualism may be, it is "perpetually and irremediably haunted by its opposite" (Dumont 1986, 17). Evangelical practice aims to reduce the strain of this binary opposition, summoning alternatives that reflect perennial modernist concerns regarding both the privileges and pitfalls of individuality. In this regard it is worth noting that norms of religious sociality, though typically invoking the authority of sacred texts and doctrines, are inevitably shaped by specific social, historical, and institutional conditions (see Chipumuro 2014; Limbert 2010; Zigon 2011).

Since the 1960s, widespread innovations in Protestant revivalism have led to a proliferation of evangelical churches and ministries fostering "spirituality" and personal fulfillment as standards of authentic faith (Miller 1997). Contemporary megachurches, para-church organizations, and Christian media industries exemplify a style of evangelical populism that assigns great value to the virtues of therapeutic individualism and choice, even while advancing a conservative theology. At the same time, as Donald Miller observes, evangelical churches put structures in place to ensure that members become morally accountable to one another, thereby subsuming part of their individuality in the collective Body of Christ: "Typically this accountability occurs in small group Bible study settings where mentored friendships are valued. As a Christian, one does not live for oneself. . . . While considerable emphasis is placed on individual choice and personal interpretation, the committed Christian is held to a purpose beyond self-actualization" (Miller 1997, 21–22).

Such elucidations are useful correctives against the tendency to overgeneralize when describing the social habits of evangelicals. Critics, including evangelicals themselves, are inclined to accuse modern churches and media enterprises of promoting spiritual narcissism and self-help capitalism under the guise of a watered-down gospel, which they suggest has the effect of debasing sacred traditions of piety and selfless altruism (e.g., Hunter 2010). This critique, whatever its merits, overlooks an essential aspect of evangelicalism as a lived religion: it is often oriented toward communities of practice and relational networks that bring individuals into sustained contact with authoritative disciplines, informal social controls, and moral norms that destabilize and reconstitute the modern self.

As churchgoers are frequently reminded in sermons, books, and study groups, the straight and narrow path of salvation is a personal journey, but it is a journey that one best not undertake alone. This is about more than the sentimental value of togetherness, or the church as a moral community. There is, one could say, an almost sacramental quality in how evangelicals idealize relationships founded on Christian virtues, as though social bonding through mutual dependence, selflessness, instruction, sympathy, and affection should not only evoke key aspects of one's relation to Jesus, but will in effect instantiate and enhance them.

Virtual surrender of one's moral autonomy and self-reliance to pastors, spouses, and friends, whose very presence in one's life reflects the will of God, reaffirms complete surrender to God. Seen in this light, the fusion of spirituality and self-help evident in contemporary evangelicalism does not necessarily preclude deep piety and altruism, but is in fact aligned with theological claims that valorize "human relationships as part and parcel of supernatural grace" (Bialecki 2009, 118).

Of course, evangelical relationships are not all the same, depending on the relative status and social positions of those involved. Relations between pastors and congregants, and husbands and wives, or even between seasoned Christians and new converts, are defined less by egalitarian sensibilities than by structures of uneven or "vertical" authority. Individuals are expected to recognize and abide by traditional power dynamics (e.g., wives submitting to their husbands), and to show deference to those whom God has chosen to exercise authority in their lives (see Kelly H. Chong's chapter in this volume). And yet evangelicals do retain the overall sense, in principle if not practice, that everyone is a sinner and that all godly relationships are basically symbiotic.

So while my discussion of evangelical relationalism and its application in terms of sociality is based here on a discussion of one fairly homogeneous group (all male, all white, but not without their own internal power dynamics), it is fair to say that the imperative with which I am concerned—the emphasis on exemplary relationships and networks, and their potential to make the boundaries of the self more permeable—is relevant in the lives and commitments of evangelicals more broadly. And although the decision to embrace an *unbuffered* (if not entirely porous) selfhood is largely voluntary, and applies to some social contexts more than others, it remains a critical component of evangelical indoctrination and sanctification, and represents a preferred path for keeping oneself and one's friends out of the Devil's hands.

The Fellowship of the Salad

As illustration, specifically with regard to the concept of fellowship (I address discipleship in the next section), let us return to the scene that opened this essay. The reader will recall that Trevor ended his diabetes speech with an emphatic appeal: "*I will fail if I go through this alone.*" More than just a sentimental plea, his statement was a normative command with the full weight of scripture behind it. By reminding his born-again brethren that they had to keep him "accountable" not only to his own resolution but more importantly to God, Trevor indicated that the bonds they shared were of no small consequence, and he implied that the way forward would likely require interventions involving more than prayer alone.

In the discussion that ensued, the men assured Trevor that they too were sinners, equally vulnerable to weaknesses of the flesh such as over-eating and poor diet, and that they were obliged to confront the issue together as a group. I noted during this discussion that it made little difference whether or not the men were all actually in the same boat with regard to health and diet. What mattered was the underlying effort to mark a collective shift in their discourse from a confessional mode to a redemptive one. Their ability to make this shift was meaningful as reaffirmation that their very existence as a group was itself the fruit of divine intervention. While much of the conversation was not unlike that found in secular support groups and AA meetings, the implications for self-reliance and individual autonomy are distinctive here in that they are linked to a Christian metaphysics of communion, or in evangelical parlance, fellowship.

The concept of fellowship in evangelical circles has theological connotations beyond everyday ideas of camaraderie and companionship. Translated from the Greek *koinonia*, "fellowship" refers to the spiritual unity of God's people and the qualities associated with it. Evangelicals value fellowship as a blessing from God and a covenant with God. They stress the benefits of fellowship for safeguarding faith and moral fortitude, and avoiding relapses into sin. In his mega-bestseller, *The Purpose Driven Life*, an entire section of which is devoted to fellowship, Pastor Rick Warren writes, "None of us are immune to temptation. Given the right situation, you and I are capable of any sin. God knows this, so he has assigned us as individuals the responsibility of keeping each other on track. . . . We are called and commanded to be involved in each other's lives" (2002, 135).

Fellowship groups at churches like Eternal Vine usually meet in the homes of members, and often include men and women together. The goal is to experience fellowship with a small group of friends and confidantes, in weekly sessions that are meant to provide levels of intimacy that are harder to achieve in large worship services. At Eternal Vine, men's group meetings typically start with dinner—usually pizza, sometimes cold-cut sandwiches, accompanied by chips and soda—followed by an hour of Bible study and discussion (devotional texts may be read as well), which is normally led by volunteers who prepare their lessons in advance. Evenings conclude with prayer requests, followed by a period of group prayer. At the time of my fieldwork, a retired preacher named Chuck served as the group's informal leader, but as with most small groups, lay members determined much of the tone and content of each weekly gathering.

The men's efforts to explicate biblical texts were instructive for me as an ethnographer, allowing me to access a lay theology drawn from authoritative sources (the Bible, sermons, handbooks, etc.) and shaped by individual experiences and idiosyncrasies (Elisha 2008). The men were so eager to deepen their knowledge and appreciation of the "Word of God" that they would spend months at a time working through a single book of the Bible. But mulling over the details of biblical exegesis was not the only reason why they took so long. Much of their time together was spent sharing the details of their personal lives, from family and career concerns to struggles with doubt and temptation. They discussed these topics at great length, drawing connections and applications from scripture. It was by listening to these discussions, not to mention general banter, and hearing the confessions and prayer requests of men like Trevor, that I came to understand the religious value of the group, and how it functioned as a social unit.

Although the composition of the group fluctuates, most of the members during my fieldwork were middle-aged white men from the greater Knoxville area. While a number of them were married with children, several core members were unmarried or divorced. Most were employed as skilled laborers or midlevel managers, and a few were unemployed.

The weekly meetings offered the men a much-needed refuge, a place to nurse the emotional wounds of stressful jobs, troubled marriages, and corporate downsizing. It was also a time to relax, refocus, and enjoy the company of like-minded peers. Above all, the group represented an opportunity for Christian men to practice fellowship, an ideal rarely afforded by the circumstances of daily life.

Prayer requests at the end of each meeting were essential in this regard. Individual requests were varied but tended to focus on personal challenges (e.g., anger, addiction, unemployment), crises (e.g., a sick friend or loved one, a family conflict), and opportunities (e.g., job interviews, trips abroad, new relationships). The men, in response, prayed aloud and promised to be vigilant intercessors on each other's behalf. Chuck, the group leader, was a strong advocate for intercessory prayer, which he described as "a Christian's best protection against the Enemy."

The men also responded to prayer requests with encouragement, advice, and promises to "watch over" one another. The solidarity expressed in these exchanges was often quite moving to observe, but its impact was more than sentimental. Group prayer and other rites of fellowship clarified and validated the idea that the men's spiritual concerns and aspirations were immediately served by their ongoing sociality. As a defense against life's pitfalls and dangers, both self-inflicted and diabolic, fellowship is embodied as a religious calling, whereby quotidian relationships become the stuff of divine providence.

Turning back to the case of Trevor, we see an example of how this plays out. At one point during the discussion that took place that night, someone suggested that they all needed to make an effort to change their eating habits, especially when they were together as a group (see 1 Cor. 8:13). This meant forgoing the usual pizzas and cold cuts for healthier fare. Doug, a recent divorcee with a particularly sympathetic demeanor, went so far as to suggest that they put together a "men's night cookbook," with ideas for low-fat, heart-healthy alternatives, but this idea was met with little enthusiasm.

In the end it was decided that they would start making salads every week. A couple of the men would buy ingredients—lettuce mixes, tomatoes, chicken or ham strips, grated cheese, and dressing—and everyone would make their own salad as they pleased. Potato chips and soda were kept on the menu, and some white bread was kept in the vicinity for those who preferred a sandwich. The culinary experiment lasted several weeks, which surprised me, since the men had notoriously large appetites. The topic of food normally brought out a certain male bravado that I figured wouldn't go very well with salad. But in a sense, this was exactly the point. Their collective effort to eat better was a self-consciously counterintuitive gesture, an abstention verging on sacrifice for the sake of a greater good. As members arrived early to sort the ingredients and slice the tomatoes, they took pleasure in the idea of God's grace working through them, enriching their bonds and bridging their gaps as individuals, much as prayer and worship are meant to bring them closer to God.

Within a few months, however, the salad experiment came to an end without remark. Someone's brother-in-law got a job running the concessions stand at a local motor speedway, so the men were now privy to free leftovers of fast food, which restored their taste for greasy comfort carbs. Coincidentally, Trevor no longer attended meetings regularly, though he was still considered a member (he enrolled in a training course for Christian counselors that met on the same night). The end of the group's literal salad days should not, however, be interpreted as a failure or shortcoming, but rather as part of ongoing social interactions and relational dynamics that are meant to enhance fellowship and, as I discuss below, make disciples out of friends.

"The Devil Was Really after Ronnie"

The figure of the disciple is of course crucial in Christian thought and practice. In Matthew 28:19, Jesus instructs his followers to "go and make disciples of all nations," inspiring centuries of Christian missions and evangelization. In modern churches, discipleship usually refers to the condition of following Christ, but it is also closely associated with a relational condition among believers in which recent converts and those who stumble in their faith are mentored by church elders and peers (Barna 2000). Whether in the context of a dyadic relationship or wider group dynamics, discipleship is another category through which we can examine how evangelicals reimagine the boundaries and buffers of individual autonomy.

Ronnie, a blond and blue-eyed corporate manager in his late thirties, was a member of the Eternal Vine men's group for just over a year when I started attending meetings. I knew this because members repeatedly pointed out that his first "anniversary" was approaching, referring to his born-again conversion that occurred shortly after he became a part of the group. Though raised in a churchgoing family, Ronnie was "never fully committed" to Christ. Now, a year after his decision to accept Jesus as his savior, the men were excited to celebrate his status as a changed man and his entry into their lives. One night, at a meeting where Ronnie was absent for family reasons, Chuck announced that it would be a good idea to formally recognize the occasion by throwing Ronnie a surprise "re-birthday party."

By most accounts, including his own, Ronnie's personal transformation was a long time coming and not a moment too soon. It was also clear that he had still some ways to go. Before he converted and got involved in the men's group, Ronnie was a frustrated and violent man. His family was falling apart: his wife distrusted him, and his two adolescent sons feared and resented him. It was a classic "wretch like me" scenario: a lost and unrepentant sinner, overcome by sins of passion and rage, eventually broken and ultimately "saved."

The story was a familiar one, but it took on an added dimension for the men of the group, since they contributed to the process that led to Ronnie's "rebirth." His successful integration into their social circle was extolled as a case of discipleship in action. The fact that he still had some difficulty being humble, transparent, and accountable did little to diminish their assurance. It actually reinforced it. Ronnie's susceptibility to occasional lapses in judgment—at one meeting he confessed to losing his temper and knocking his son down "with one punch"—exposed the insecurities many of them felt when it came to walking the precarious line between sin and self-control. While glowing reports of Ronnie's transformation were cause for celebration, the group's awareness of his persistent struggles with anger and impatience was likely part of what motivated the idea for his "re-birthday party."

Ronnie symbolized the work in process that the other men recognized in themselves; his vulnerability was their own. Moreover, since he was the newest addition to their fellowship, his willingness to receive their encouragement and submit to their watchful guidance directly reflected his obedience to God and, to some extent, the spiritual viability of the group as a whole. This would be reinforced further by the authority that others were willing to grant him in return.

Indeed, Ronnie was already taking advantage of opportunities to assume the kind of role that others served for him. One night during prayer requests, another member named Cole spoke at length about the hard time he was having coming to terms with his divorce, and the strain it was causing him with his children. Chuck admonished Cole for always trying too hard to control his life rather than placing trust in God, and then asked for a volunteer to pray over him. Ronnie promptly stepped to the plate. Afterwards, when Chuck suggested that two men offer to "check up" on Cole periodically, guiding him and keeping him from dwelling on his anger, Ronnie likewise volunteered.

The surprise party for Ronnie took place one evening at the same time as the group's weekly meeting, and was attended by the active group members, their wives, and other friends, all of whom arrived early. The element of surprise was successfully achieved, and Ronnie was clearly moved. He beamed as his friends spoke in turn, showering him with praise for his "incredible" transformation. Almost every testimony emphasized how troubled he was before; how, as one friend put it, "the Devil was really after Ronnie."

Chuck described how dire Ronnie's family situation was only a year before, and how they counseled and prayed for him continuously. Trevor, who allowed himself to indulge in a slice of "re-birthday cake," pointed out how impressed he was that Ronnie found the humility to repent at a relatively young age, adding that "it takes a special man" to repent at a time in life when family and career pressures are especially high. Ronnie's wife spoke as well, echoing similar themes with an even more personal touch, as did his sons, who prepared a video message just for the occasion.

What struck me the most about the evening was how the men around Ronnie implicated themselves in the unfolding story of his conversion. They *expanded* it, so to speak, stretching its narrative contours to include them as well, not merely as individuals who have undergone conversions of their own but as figures in a shared teleology, interwoven selves in a tale of relational redemption. As they showered Ronnie with praise for his accomplishment, they upheld the standards and expectations on which their cohesion as a group ostensibly relied. Furthermore, their testimonies were implicit warnings and cautionary reminders that sins and transgressions have the power to resurface at any moment, thus requiring the aid of external and even critical supervision, as much as self-control. The goal of subjecting oneself to the authority of reliable others (reserving total submission only for God) is thus conceptually grafted onto the more individuating aims of salvation and sanctification, acquiring some measure of their urgency and theological heft.

Conclusion

Evangelicals take their views on sin very seriously, believing, as a matter of doctrine, that every one of us is born in sin, to a sinful world, and vulnerable to all manner of depravity and suffering. We are possessed of rebellious spirits and corrupted hearts, and surrounded by evil forces that thrive on our inability to escape our fallen nature by means of our own efforts. In this orthodox view of the human condition, nothing but the blood of Jesus saves us from ourselves; and, as evangelicals confidently affirm, nothing but a personal relationship with Jesus stands between the individual sinner and eternal damnation.

And yet, despite the explicit personalism of these fundamental tenets of Protestant theology, such doctrines are invariably expressed and worked out in collective contexts, in congregations and relational networks where the bonds of salvation and sociality intersect. The "obvious" fact that evangelicals convene in groups may not seem worth emphasizing, unless one considers that some of the most celebrated virtues and disciplines of evangelical religiosity are enacted in relationships and settings where the presence of others is not merely conducive or convenient but essential. This has been demonstrated in a variety of ethnographic contexts, including evangelical Bible study groups (Bielo 2009), outreach ministries (Elisha 2011), fitness and diet ministries (Griffith 2004; Gerber 2011), and "reparative therapy" programs where, for example, Christian "ex-gays" suppress their homosexual urges through strict, mutually enforced regimens of confession, surveillance, and homosocial bonding (Erzen 2006). In these and other instances, intersubjectivity among otherwise differentiated selves becomes something to strive for, both for its perceived personal benefits and for the supremacy of God's kingdom.

The hegemony of Western individualism in the modern world is rarely absolute, and never without its oppositional tensions. This is especially true of course in non-Western, post-conversion societies, where normative demands imported by Western missionaries disrupt but often fail to completely uproot native ontologies and models of partible personhood (Robbins 2004; Keane 2007; Bialecki, Haynes, and Robbins 2008). While missionization and revivalism recast local traditions and identities in powerful ways, a great deal of cultural ambiguity remains, as social actors negotiate between competing moral systems and categories of social being (Van Vleet 2011). Across the global spectrum of evangelicalism and Pentecostalism, modern Christians inhabit "a living tension between states of individuality and dividuality" (Daswani 2011, 257).

The foregoing discussion has been an attempt to show that this "living tension" is not entirely alien to evangelicals in the West, though they may experience it less intensely and for very different reasons. For a vast majority of churchgoing evangelicals in the United States, self-determination and personal responsibility are cherished ideals, consistent with the will of God. Individual regeneration involves the transformation of an embodied yet interior self, whose boundaries must remain impermeable to material and social forces that otherwise infringe upon or threaten one's inviolable autonomy. At the same time, though deeply invested in the ideological staying power of individualism, many evangelicals are drawn to ritualized relational practices that allow them to experience, however transiently, what I call an *unbuffered* sense of self. Biblical ideals of fellowship and discipleship offer what evangelicals see as a radical alternative to lives of quiet desperation and uncertainty. They also indicate, and anticipate, the future "Kingdom come," which represents the final union of earth and heaven, the ultimate communion of self and Other.

As with most high ideals, these are hard to maintain in practice. In the men's fellowship group at Eternal Vine, where members were encouraged to open their souls and become morally accountable to others, even to the point of giving up aspects of their privacy and self-reliance, there were clear cases of resistance on occasion. In times of tension, as when group members chastised another for actions or life decisions they found disagreeable, it was not uncommon for the individuals in question to leave the group, temporarily or even permanently, in order to avoid having to answer for themselves, or perhaps to seek fellowship somewhere else.

The dynamics of evangelical sociality, then, are not without challenges, especially as they affect people in moments of their lives when they feel particularly disinclined to concede to the moral demands of others. Nonetheless, the socialization of unbuffered selves is ingrained in the institutional culture of US evangelicalism, defining a cultural style and countercultural consciousness that believers seek to master. Evangelicals turn to relational principles and disciplines, and the structures of religious authority on which they rely, as they struggle to manage the adversities and opportunities of life, and as they learn to recognize the disadvantages of going it alone.

REFERENCES

Barna, George. 2000. *Growing True Disciples*. Ventura, CA: Issachar Resources.

Bialecki, Jon. 2009. "Disjuncture, Continental Philosophy's New 'Political Paul,' and the Question of Progressive Christianity in a Southern California Third Wave Church." *American Ethnologist* 36 (1): 110–23.

Bialecki, Jon, Naomi Haynes, and Joel Robbins. 2008. "The Anthropology of Christianity." *Religion Compass* 2 (6): 1139–58.

Bielo, James S. 2009. *Words upon the Word: An Ethnography of Evangelical Bible Study*. New York: New York University Press.

———. 2012. "Belief, Deconversion, and Authenticity among U.S. Emerging Evangelicals." *Ethos* 40 (3): 258–76.

Chipumuro, Todne Thomas. 2014. "Pastor, Mentor, or Father? The Contested Intimacies of the Eddie Long Sex Abuse Scandal." *Journal of Africana Religions* 2 (1): 1–30.

Daswani, Girish. 2011. "(In-)Dividual Pentecostals in Ghana." *Journal of Religion in Africa* 41:256–79.

Dumont, Louis. 1986. *Essays on Individualism: Modern Ideology in Anthropological Perspective*. Chicago: University of Chicago Press.

Elisha, Omri. 2008. "Faith beyond Belief: Evangelical Protestant Conceptions of Faith and the Resonance of Anti-Humanism." *Social Analysis* 52 (1): 56–78.

———. 2011. *Moral Ambition: Mobilization and Social Outreach in Evangelical Megachurches*. Berkeley: University of California Press.

Erzen, Tanya. 2006. *Straight to Jesus: Sexual and Christian Conversion in the Ex-Gay Movement*. Berkeley: University of California Press.

Gerber, Lynne. 2011. *Seeking the Straight and Narrow: Weight Loss and Sexual Reorientation in Evangelical America*. Chicago: University of Chicago Press.

Griffith, R. Marie. 2004. *Born Again Bodies: Flesh and Spirit in American Christianity*. Berkeley: University of California Press.

Hunter, James D. 2010. *To Change the World: The Irony, Tragedy, and Possibility of Christianity in the Late Modern World*. Oxford: Oxford University Press.

Keane, Webb. 2007. *Christian Moderns: Freedom and Fetish in the Mission Encounter*. Berkeley: University of California Press.

Limbert, Mandana E. 2010. *In the Time of Oil: Piety, Memory, and Social Life in an Omani Town*. Stanford: Stanford University Press.

Miller, Donald E. 1997. *Reinventing American Protestantism: Christianity in the New Millennium*. Berkeley: University of California Press.

Robbins, Joel. 2004. *Becoming Sinners: Christianity and Moral Torment in a Papua New Guinea Society*. Berkeley: University of California Press.

Smith, Christian. 1998. *American Evangelicalism: Embattled and Thriving*. Chicago: University of Chicago Press.

Taylor, Charles. 2007. *A Secular Age*. Cambridge: Harvard University Press.

Van Vleet, Krista E. 2011. "On Devils and the Dissolution of Sociality: Andean Catholics Voicing Ambivalence in Neoliberal Bolivia." *Anthropological Quarterly* 84 (4): 835–64.

Warren, Rick. 2002. *The Purpose Driven Life*. Grand Rapids, MI: Zondervan.

Zigon, Jarrett. 2011. *"HIV Is God's Blessing": Rehabilitating Morality in Neoliberal Russia*. Berkeley: University of California Press.

2

Circulations

Evangelical and Pentecostal Christianity in Nineteenth-Century Singapore and Penang

JEAN DEBERNARDI

Introduction

In 1963 Kong Duen Yee (1923–1966), a famous Hong Kong movie star turned Christian evangelist, toured Malaysia and Singapore with support from a Pentecostal denomination, the Assemblies of God (AOG). In revival meetings, she exhorted Chinese Christians to speak in tongues, and claimed to have the gifts of healing and prophecy. Throughout the Malay Peninsula, Christians left missionary-led churches to start new charismatic churches linked not to the AOG but to the independent New Testament Church that Kong had founded.

In Singapore the dissident Chinese Christians formed a house church that became the Church of Singapore, the first of many large independent charismatic churches. In Penang the converts to Pentecostalism met in the seaside bungalow of the Chinese businessman and former Brethren elder Teh Phai Lian.[1] More than thirty years after Kong's revival campaign, members finally received permission from the Malaysian government to build a new church. They modeled the Charismatic Church of Penang (CCOP) and its sound system on Grace Chinese Alliance church in Richmond, British Columbia, and elder Teh's daughter and son-in-law returned from Canada as the CCOP's new ministers.[2]

Just down the street from the Charismatic Church of Penang is the old Chinese temple known as the Snake Temple, a popular tourist destination.[3] At the height of the spiritual warfare movement that the American evangelist Peter Wagner promoted worldwide, the new CCOP minister led prayers against the temple's patron deity daily at 6:00 a.m.[4] When attendance dwindled, he berated them at Sunday service, comparing them unfavorably to the enthusiastic Christians whom he regularly visited at a house church in Mainland China. Soon thereafter, he and his wife resigned from the CCOP, and a small group of members followed them to form a new church, returning only to claim the high-end sound system.

This vignette, which is based on interviews and observations conducted in the 1990s, seems to point to the newness of Pentecostal and charismatic practices in Singapore and Malaysia. But through these interviews I also learned that the founders of the new charismatic churches had "come out" of the Brethren movement, a nondenominational lay evangelical movement whose members had supported missionaries in Singapore and Penang since the 1860s. I decided to conduct further research in British archives, seeking to learn more about the long dialogue between Christianity and Chinese culture that had unfolded in these two cities. I began my research in Brethren archives, and continued it in the archives of the London Missionary Society, the Chinese Evangelisation Society, the Bible Society, and the Female Education Society.

This chapter focuses on three aspects of the circulation of Christian values and practices in Asia: the promotion of female education, the spread of indigenous independent churches, and the impact of waves of Pentecostal revival. I draw on an extensive archive of letters published in missionary agency magazines, annual reports, and memoirs that were distributed worldwide. These include letters from lay nondenominational missionaries associated with the Brethren movement.

In the nineteenth century, evangelical Christians not only circulated their ideas and practices through publications, they also traveled extensively. The Brethren founder John Nelson Darby (1800–1882) made five trips to Canada and the United States between 1862 and 1877 to promote his theological views, which influenced the growth of fundamentalism and end-times theology in North America. The Scriptural Knowledge Institution founder George Müller, who raised funds to support Brethren missionaries, traveled extensively between 1875 and 1892. In 1887 Müller preached almost every day for two weeks in Singapore. The written word informed Asian Christians of events elsewhere, and travelers brought new doctrines and practices to Asia.

Many assume that the indigenization of Christianity did not occur until after World War II, when the end of colonial empires closed doors to foreign missionaries. Many also date the "explosive starburst" growth of Pentecostal Christianity to the early twentieth century, and pinpoint its origin in the Los Angeles Azusa Street Revival.[5] But the longer history of the emplacement of evangelical and Pentecostal Christianity in Southeast Asia demonstrates that the indigenization of Christianity was already well advanced in that part of the world by the mid-nineteenth century, and that the roots of global Pentecostalism are deeper than the conventional narrative suggests.

Let me now turn to a more detailed consideration of education, indigenization, and revival.

The London Missionary Society, 1814–1843

When the Charter Act of 1813 granted missionaries access to territories that the British East India Company controlled, the London Missionary Society (LMS) established the Ultra-Ganges mission in a network of cities in Southeast Asia.[6] Because these European-controlled cities had attracted Chinese immigrants, the LMS missionaries could study Chinese languages and seek Chinese converts as they waited for China to open its doors to foreign missionaries (see Harrison 1979).

When they began work in Penang in 1819, the LMS missionaries established Malay and Chinese boys' schools with support from the government. By 1823 they had built a mission house and laid the foundations of a new mission chapel. Although they required their Asian student boarders to attend services, Asian converts were few. But the mission chapel also served European Christians associated with so-called dissenting Christian denominations, who in 1826 formally declared themselves to be an independent nondenominational church.

In the Penang boys' schools, the LMS missionaries followed a "new system of education" that included teaching in the vernacular, an emphasis on exegesis and comprehension rather than rote learning, and some training in mathematics and geography. But the missionaries had to compromise with local expectations about the curriculum. Muslims would not send their sons to the missionary schools unless they studied the Koran, and Chinese expected their sons to learn to read the Confucian classics. Confucian philosophy teaches that human nature is fundamentally good, a tenet that contradicted the missionaries' perspective that humans were sinners until they were saved by religion. Frustrated by the situation, the LMS missionary Samuel Dyer and his wife, who arrived in Penang in 1827, moved the schools into town, where they could supervise them more closely.

Dyer's wife, Maria Tarn Dyer, was the daughter of Joseph Tarn, director of the LMS. She started Penang's first Christian girls' school with the support of a private network of British Christian women who collected donations on her behalf, including handmade goods that they shipped to Penang to be sold. As I discuss in more detail below, British Christians had concluded that female education was essential to their success, and in 1834 formed the Society for the Promotion of Female Education in the East.

After the 1842 Treaty of Nanking forced China to open five treaty ports to European residents, the LMS moved its mission from Southeast Asia to China. But on her husband's death in 1843, her friends in England urged Maria Dyer to return to Penang to run the girls' school she had founded. There, she married George Bausum (1812–1855), an independent missionary who had taken responsibility for the Penang mission and schools.

Female Education

The founding of the Charismatic Church of Penang and its sister church, the Church of Singapore, marked a radical turn toward Pentecostal practices like divine healing and speaking in tongues. But individuals involved in the schism observed in interviews that wives had urged their husbands to separate from the Brethren movement. The Brethren taught—and still teach—that a woman cannot teach or have authority over a man. In 1963 conservative Brethren elders objected not only to Kong Duan Yee's teachings, but also protested against her taking on the role of public evangelist. By leaving the Brethren assemblies to form independent churches, female Christians had claimed the possibility to lead and teach.

Even today, conservative Brethren assemblies do not allow women to be elders. But in the longer view, evangelical Christians (including the Brethren) contributed to the transformation of gender roles in Asia. In their work partnerships with their missionary husbands, wives like Maria Tarn Dyer modeled the Christian ideal of marriage as a working partnership. The missionaries also promoted and supported girls' education in Asia. Their efforts were also connected to the moral agenda of the antislavery movement: the missionaries adopted and educated Asian orphans and young girls who had been sold as slaves or prostitutes (which they viewed as a form of slavery).[7]

In Penang and Singapore, girls' schools were supported by the fundraising efforts of British evangelical Christian women, first through a private network of women who supported the Penang Girls' Schools (est. 1822), then through a new Female Education Society (est. 1834). The society was formed on the urging of David Abeel, who in 1830 had gone to Asia on behalf of the American Seaman's Friend Society to work as a chaplain to foreign sailors in Hong Kong. Abeel had traveled throughout Southeast Asia on behalf of the American Board, and spent five months in Java. He visited England in 1834, and wrote a book entitled *Appeal to Christian Ladies on Behalf of Female Education in China.*

In July 1834, a network of elite British women formed the new Society for the Promotion of Female Education in the East, known simply as the Female Education Society (FES), to raise funds for girls' education in Asia, and to recruit and train female missionaries to work in this field. The founders were aware that the Baptist Missionary Society had undertaken similar work in India in 1820, and knew that girls' schools existed at Ultra-Ganges mission stations in Penang, Malacca, and Singapore, including the one that Maria Tarn Dyer had founded.

The FES founders observed that when the established missionary societies emphasized training boys and neglected the education of girls, they put at risk the transmission of Christianity to a new generation. Their leaders proposed that a Ladies' Society raise funds to train, equip, and support single women to go to Asia as teachers. Ironically perhaps, Asian and European gender segregation created an exclusive sphere of work for Christian women (FES 1847; see also Doran 1996).

After Maria Tarn Dyer's death in 1846, George Bausum married an FES missionary, Jemima Poppy, who ran the Penang missionary girls' school until Bausum's death in 1855. After Bausum's death his widow followed her stepdaughters to China, and the Chinese Evangelisation Society and FES sought new workers for Penang.

The missionary wife who took over running the Penang Girls' Boarding School wrote a letter to the FES directors in 1857 describing the schools as "a medley of nations, like the population of the island. The girls comprise eighteen Chinese, ten Burmese, four Malays, three Armenians, one Siamese, one Kling [Tamil], and one European." All of her students learned to read both Malay and English (typically Chinese education was reserved for boys).[8] In addition to learning scripture and hymns, students studied history, geography, arithmetic, and writing (in both Arabic and Roman script). They also spent the afternoon studying needlework of all kinds. The missionaries reported that when a female student reached puberty, her parents might remove her from school and confine her at home until her marriage.

A girls' school that Maria Tarn Dyer established in Singapore in 1842 still exists, and is now called Saint Margaret's School. When Dyer returned to Penang in 1843, the FES sent Miss Grant to Singapore to replace her as this school's new principal.[9] Miss Grant openly sought converts among her students, and described her rhetorical strategies in letters to the FES directors. Much as male missionaries did in street-corner orations, she sought to convince them of the powerlessness of Chinese gods.

As Miss Grant explained her approach, verses 4–7 of the 115th Psalm "formed the groundwork" of "instruction to the young heathen" when a student was first placed in her care (Walker 1899, 18). The missionaries and Chinese both recognized parallels between Old Testament descriptions of idols and the lifelike statues that Chinese devotees placed on temple and family altars:

4 Their idols *are* silver and gold, the work of men's hands.

5 They have mouths, but they speak not: eyes they have, but they see not.

6 They have ears, but they hear not: noses have they, but they smell not.

7 They have hands, but they handle not: feet have they, but they walk not: neither speak they through their throat. (Ps. 115: 4–7, King James Version)

After reading them this passage, Miss Grant asked her students to smell a flower, then asked whether their experience would have been different if she had given them a durian to smell. The durian fruit has a penetrating smell that some compare to that of rotting onions or smelly gym socks. Smiling, the children agreed.

She then took a pin and threatened to prick them. They resisted, and when asked why, the students responded that it would hurt them or make them bleed. "Having pointed out to them the power of sensation in this very simple but practical way, I used to ask them when they went home to put the same test to their idols, and on their return to school to tell me whether they evinced the same sensation of which the children had proved themselves possessed" (Walker 1899, 18).

Most of her students never acted on this suggestion, but the younger brother of one student jumped on the family altar, took a three-pronged fork, and plunged it into the god image's cheek. When he saw no blood flowing and heard no "voice of pain" from the paper god, he decided that he no longer believed in "idols." On seeing what he had done, his sister called their aunt, who cautioned him to remain quiet and not tell his grandmother. As the aunt anticipated, when the grandmother saw the damaged paper god, she feared that some evil would befall the family. But then she calmed herself with the notion that a cat must have scratched it (Walker 1899, 19–20).

Although some adults were curious about Christianity, traditional Chinese parents feared that if their children converted, they would not perform rituals to look after their spirits after their death and that their neglected spirits would become hungry ghosts. According to Miss Grant, in one case a mother allowed her three eldest children to convert, but wanted her youngest daughter and favorite child to remain traditional. After her death the daughter honored her mother's wishes for a while, but finally sought baptism (Walker 1899, 25).

Some of the female students who converted worked as teachers in Christian schools. As they moved within the growing network of girls' schools in Southeast and East Asia, the young teachers kept in touch with their classmates through letters, some of which the missionaries published. In other instances the missionaries lamented that despite their influence, favorite students were forced by their parents to marry traditional men rather than Christians, and to participate in so-called idol worship.

Evangelical Practice and the Brethren Movement

The vignette that I offer at the beginning of this chapter may suggest to the reader that Penang Chinese Christians had to secede from their missionary-led Brethren gospel hall in order to fully indigenize their leadership. But by 1963—the year of the schism—Brethren missionaries had worked in Penang for over a century. Despite the long history of Christianity in Southeast Asia, European missionaries did not leave Malaysia until changing immigration policies made it difficult for them to stay long-term. Although the missionaries may have remained, the process of indigenization began in the nineteenth century in both China and Southeast Asia.

One early influence on British evangelical Christians, including the Brethren, was Karl Friedrich August Gützlaff (1803–1851), an ordained German missionary and Chinese translator who became an independent missionary. Gützlaff and seven Chinese formed an organization called the Chinese Union in 1844 in order to indigenize Christian proselytism in China. To that end, the Chinese Union raised funds to train Chinese to distribute tracts and New Testaments in the interior of China, where Europeans were not permitted to travel. The Chinese workers had reported spectacular successes, but some of these reports turned out to be fraudulent, and the Chinese Union did not survive long after Gützlaff's death in 1851.[10]

Gützlaff had returned to Europe in 1849 to promote his method of indigenizing proselytism, and in 1850 British evangelical Christians formed the Chinese Society for Furthering the Promulgation of the Gospel in China, and Adjacent Countries, by Means of Native Evangelists, which they renamed the Chinese Evangelisation Society (CES). Although they soon broke their connection with the Chinese Union, among their first projects was printing ten thousand copies of a corrected edition of Gützlaff's Chinese translation of the New Testament.[11]

After the LMS missionaries left Southeast Asia, the CES became an important source of funding for independent missionaries in Penang and Singapore. George Bausum, who had taken responsibility for the LMS schools and mission in Penang in 1843 (and who married Maria Tarn Dyer in 1845, and the FES missionary Jemima Poppy in 1848), was among the first successful applicants to the CES. He asked for funding to train three Chinese boys who were students in his Penang school and a Malay.[12] In 1854 the CES directors noted that the "native youths" went out in Penang and did street-corner evangelism. But they hoped that they would return to China, where they believed that the Taiping Rebellion (1851–1864) might result in the overthrow of a dynasty and the establishment of a new government by a rebel leader who claimed to worship the same God as the Christians.[13]

After Bausum's sudden death in 1855 and the departure of his widow, Jemima Poppy Bausum, the CES found new independent lay missionaries for the Penang mission and schools. But by 1859, no European missionary remained, and the CES once again sought missionaries for Penang.

In 1859 John Chapman and his wife embarked for Penang with support from the CES and Müller's Scriptural Knowledge Institution. The CES directors noted that Chapman was independent of any missionary society, but had a connection with Bethesda Chapel in Bristol.[14] With his arrival in Penang, the Brethren movement had claimed the old LMS mission for their growing network of lay missionaries.[15]

As members of the Brethren movement, Chapman and his wife associated themselves with a network of nondenominational Christians who sought to restore the simplicity of the first-century New Testament Church. The Brethren practiced adult immersion baptism and, like Quakers, had no ordained ministers. Their first lay missionary, Anthony Norris Groves (1795–1853), had pioneered the practice called "living by faith," proposing that Christians look to God and providence alone for support.

Like other evangelical Christians, the Brethren viewed donating to support charitable projects as a means to realize their moral values and make them visible to others (see DeBernardi 2011). Independent lay missionaries who engaged in a variety of projects wrote letters describing their work to the editors of Brethren publications. In an early form of social media, the editors made digests of missionary letters from all parts of the world and distributed them to a global diaspora of evangelical Christians. The editors then collected and transmitted funds to the missionaries.

The missionaries' letters described the details of their outreach, including their collaboration with and dependence on local evangelists, whose work they also publicized. These letters reveal that revival movements traveled through global Christian networks much earlier than the Azusa Street Revival.

The most well-known of these was a revival in India led by John Christian Arulappan (1810–1867), an Indian evangelist who became independent of the Church Missionary Society and lived by faith after working with the Brethren movement's first missionary, Anthony Norris Groves. From reading the Brethren magazine the *Missionary Reporter*, Arulappan learned about the 1859 Great Awakening in Britain and North America. He urged his followers to confess their sins, and launched a local revival at which participants had visions of heaven and hell and saw signs; some offered prophecies and others spoke in "unknown tongues with their interpretations" (Dann 2004, 358–59; see also Anderson 2013, 18–25).

Teh Phai Lian, the Penang leader of the 1963 schism that I describe above, had been an elder in the Burmah Road Gospel Hall before his turn toward charismatic Christianity. The Burmah Road Gospel Hall is a Brethren assembly, and dates its foundation to 1860, the same year that John Christian Arulappan launched a revival in India. In 1860 evangelical Christianity was already a diffuse, borderless, multicentered network, just as it is today.

Indigenization: A Brethren Vignette

Especially after the missions in China began to gain converts in the mid-nineteenth century, Chinese Christians who migrated to areas of Southeast Asia where there was no mission sometimes formed small Christian gatherings. Chinese Christians often helped one another: when Chinese Christians in Singapore built a new gospel hall, for example, Chinese Christians in Batavia (Java) sent them a donation.

The Brethren missionaries and their Chinese partners often took long tours to visit isolated Christians and to seek possible sites for new missions. In 1884 an English-educated Asian Christian living in Phuket wrote a letter to the Brethren missionary in Penang to report that a few Chinese met with him in his house for "prayer and edification," and to ask for their help. The missionary and a Chinese evangelist took the twenty-four-hour boat trip and visited the small gathering. Excited by what they found, they frequently exchanged letters with the Christians in Phuket and often traveled there to meet with them, sometimes presiding over baptisms.

In 1886 they proudly reported that a Chinese cake seller had built a Gospel Hall in the upstairs room of his bakery. Through missionary letters and lectures praising the devout Chinese cake seller, this indigenous Chinese Gospel Hall became renowned in Brethren circles. In 1890 one of the Brethren missionaries, W. D. Ashdown, decided to work there and initially stayed with the cake maker. For a time the two had meetings every night and did street evangelism together, reporting conversions.[16]

As the Brethren missionaries described it, the Phuket mission brought together diverse activities and projects, some locally led, others led by the missionaries. In 1892 a medical missionary opened a clinic in Phuket and worked there until 1917, treating opium addicts and injured tin miners, and offering medical assistance during frequent epidemics of cholera and plague. In that period, the Chinese cake seller held Tuesday and Friday night prayer meetings in his house, and on Sunday afternoons and evenings, the missionaries held meetings in the preaching hall of the dispensary.

This vignette illustrates that the Brethren practice of forming local churches led by the adult men of the assembly (the so-called priesthood of all believers) favored indigenization. Individuals like the Chinese cake seller who had energy and financial means could create new Christian gatherings in the absence of missionaries or external financial support. The Brethren missionaries celebrated his efforts, holding him up to their readers as an icon of the devoted indigenous Christian, but also as evidence of the success of their approach to emplacing Christianity.

Pentecostalism and Conversion

The history of Christianity in Singapore and Penang suggests the importance of influential individuals and personal networks in the emplacement of the religion. Although more difficult to document than the growth of brick-and-board churches and schools, nonetheless these relationships and connections are often described in missionary letters.

From the perspective of evangelical networks, one of the most influential early evangelists in China was the Scots Presbyterian missionary William Chalmers Burns. Burns was a renowned evangelist who at age twenty-four had sparked the Kilsyth Revival of 1839 in Scotland. He preached with intense passion, and people cried and fell to the ground at revival events that his brother compared to the day of Pentecost "both in its immediate features and in its after results, and in everything except the miraculous gift of tongues" (Burns [1870] 1975, 98).

Burns arrived in China in 1847, and soon traveled with Chinese evangelists who had worked with Gützlaff. He adopted many of Gützlaff's methods, including learning to speak regional Chinese languages, and traveling widely with Chinese partners to distribute tracts and do street-corner oration. Initially discouraged by the lack of response, he soon proved to be an effective orator who sparked intense devotion among his Chinese converts.

Murray Rubinstein explains the success of twentieth-century charismatic and Pentecostal Christianity in Taiwan in light of cultural congruency between these forms of Christianity and Taiwanese popular religion, including the practice of spirit mediumship (Rubinstein 1996). In Fujian, which shares religious traditions with Taiwan, Burns not only won an audience with his passionate street-corner orations, but also through Pentecostal revival meetings that in one famous case resulted in mass conversion. Another missionary described the penitent revival known as the Pechuia Awakening as the first "outpouring of the Holy Spirit" in China (Burns [1870] 1975, 489, 510).

Because Burns left the work of building churches to others, historians like Stephen Neill (1986, 242) do not regard Burns as a significant figure in the history of Christian missions in China. But Burns influenced both his Chinese converts, some of whom became full-time evangelists, and his coworkers, including the founder of the China Inland Mission, John Hudson Taylor.

The Presbyterian Mission in China sent one of Burns's coworkers, Alexander Grant, and an early Chinese convert, Tan See Boo, to work with Chinese immigrants in Singapore. Both decided to join the Brethren movement and to "live by faith." In 1867 Grant became the first missionary at Singapore's Bethesda Hall, and Tan their first Chinese evangelist.

In Southeast Asia, Grant and his Chinese coworkers used the same strategies for evangelical outreach that they had used in China. Like Burns, Alexander Grant had learned to speak Southern Min fluently and worked closely with his Chinese partners. He and Tan made widespread itineration part of their regular practice, and through the exchange of letters and visits supported autonomous indigenous churches. Grant did not describe Pentecostal revivals in Singapore or Penang, but he did witness the introduction of Pentecostal practices in Java.

In his travels, Grant and his Chinese partners frequently visited independent gatherings of Asian Christians in Java. He reported in one letter that in Batavia (Java), a small group of thirty or so Chinese Christians met both in a private home and at a Gospel Hall (*Hok-Im-Koan, Fuyin Guan*) in Pinang-town. In 1871 or 1872, members of this small Gospel Hall requested help from Grant in "having the Word ministered to them." Grant went to visit them with Mr. Jeffrey, a Scotsman who sometimes preached at Singapore's Gospel Hall, and together they visited Batavia, Semarang, and Depok, preaching to Chinese Christians and to Malay-speaking Javanese.

Grant and Jeffrey went to Depok because they had heard that there was a community of Christians there, formed when a well-to-do Dutchman had left his estate to his former servants on condition that they become Christian. They discovered over a hundred people gathered to study *Pilgrim's Progress* and the sermons of the British Particular Baptist preacher Charles Haddon Spurgeon (1834–1892).[17] When Grant visited Depok again in 1902, he found two Australian Salvation Army workers there, noting that "the fruit of those days has remained."[18]

Grant reported in an 1883 letter to the editors of the *Echoes of Service* that the Catholic Apostolic Movement had reached Java. Members of an independent Gospel Hall (including a Chinese Christian woman who had studied in the Singapore girls' school that Maria Dyer had founded) were doubtful about these new teachings and sought advice from Grant. He traveled to Java, where he discovered that a retired Dutch judge who had assisted the Batavian Chinese Christians financially was now a so-called apostle of a denomination that he had joined while visiting Europe. The judge and his wife, who had the "gift of prophecy," sought to spread their new faith.

As Grant described their meetings,

The way Mr. A——has proceeded is this. His wife stands up, and in an excited manner, in language resembling that of the prophets of Israel, delivers a few sentences in Dutch, which are then written down and translated.

On such occasions she names someone for a special office. Mr. A——then lays his hands on that person, and he is said to receive the Holy Ghost. In this way a Javanese has been appointed apostle; and a Java-born Chinese, the son of a Christian recently departed, to be a priest.[19]

The judge and his wife almost certainly belonged to the German branch of the Catholic Apostolic Movement, which formed in 1862 as an offshoot of an Irvingite group, a precursor to twentieth-century Pentecostal movements. Like the Irvingites, the Catholic Apostolic Movement emphasized gifts of prophecy and the appointment of prophets as a means of hastening the end-times. As the editor of *Echoes of Service* noted in his comment on Grant's letter, "It is instructive to observe how far winds of doctrine reach."[20]

In the early twentieth century, the waves of revival that gave birth to Pentecostalism also reached the Brethren in Southeast Asia and China. Many Christians refer back to the Azusa Street Revival in Los Angeles as a crucial starting point for Pentecostalism, but the Welsh revival of 1904 also convinced Christians that the end-times were near, and led to the foundation of Pentecostal-style churches. Although the leader of the Welsh revival, Evan Roberts, was Methodist, the form of worship practiced at the revival meetings resembled that of the Brethren. As participants described it, he was "led by the Holy Spirit" in his teachings, and they spontaneously prayed and offered hymns.

Brethren in the Malay States and Singapore heard news of the Welsh revivals, and in 1905 one missionary reported that "we had all been strongly impressed for some time that we should expect greater things from the Lord, and many were getting stirred up in heart." Consequently, his assembly organized a week of prayer in Kuala Lumpur. He reported to the editors of *Echoes of Service* that their meeting room was overflowing with persons who offered spontaneous testimonies, prayer, and praise, and he claimed a number of conversions among students and adults.[21]

His coworker also reported that "quite a revival" had broken out among them, and that many new converts "were full of joy and zeal for the spread of the gospel," including one multilingual Chinese who was "wrought upon by the Holy Spirit."[22] While many authors assume there to be a strict division between Pentecostal groups and fundamentalist evangelical groups like the Brethren, the latter were receptive to the teachings of Holiness movement authors, and also claimed to enjoy gifts of the Holy Spirit (albeit stressing the gifts of powerful teaching and conversion).

The next reported waves of revival originated not in Europe or America, but in Asia. In the 1930s the Chinese evangelists Watchman Nee and John Sung led revivals that demonstrated the increasing indigenization of Christianity. Both toured Southeast Asia, where they sparked the establishment of new churches in Singapore and Malaysia that were independent of Western control long before Kong Duen Yee sparked the 1963 schism.

Conclusion

In this chapter I have explored the circulation of Christian values and practices in Southeast Asia. After 1860, the nondenominational lay missionary movement known as the Brethren movement widely promoted Christianity in the region. Their inclusive leadership practices (at least for men) led to the early creation of autonomous, locally led Christian groups in Southeast Asia. But because all male elders are trained to lead, the Brethren are prone to schism. When former members form new churches and para-church groups, they remove themselves from Brethren networks and may soon forget their Brethren roots. I opened this chapter with one such example when I described the 1963 creation of the Church of Singapore and the Charismatic Church of Penang.

As this chapter demonstrates, in the nineteenth century evangelical Christians circulated their values and practices to Singapore and Penang as part of a global social movement. Although some describe fundamentalists like the Brethren as anti-modern, in nineteenth-century Asia evangelical Christians were active in the antislavery movement, in building modern schools and clinics for the poor, and in promoting girls' education and improving the status of women. If globalization defines the modern era, then the Brethren have been modern since the 1830s, when transportation, empire, and mass print media opened a door for them to expand their influence to the entire world.

NOTES

This chapter is based on an unpublished manuscript on the Brethren movement in Singapore and Penang, Malaysia. The Social Science Research Council of Canada and the Wenner-Gren Foundation for Anthropological Research provided funding for this program of research from 1997 to 2000. Grants from the University of Alberta Humanities, Fine Arts, and Social Sciences Research Committee funded additional periods of archival research in England in 2005 and 2006. For their assistance I thank Dr. Ernest Chew, Ch'ng Oon Hooi, Goh Ewe Kheng, and members of Brethren Gospel Halls in Singapore and Penang. I base the chapter on research done in British evangelical Christian archives, including those of the London Missionary Society (est. 1795), the Society for Promoting Female Education in the East (FES) (est. 1834), and the Chinese Evangelisation Society (CES) (est. 1850), which supported independent missionaries and also provided funds to train indigenous evangelists. I also thank the staffs at Echoes of Service in Bath and Müller House in Bristol for access to Brethren archives; Graham Johnson, archivist at the John Rylands Christian Brethren archive at University of Manchester, which now houses the Echoes of Service archives; the staffs at the library of the School of Oriental and African Studies, which holds LMS and CES archives, the University of Birmingham Special Collections Department, which holds records of the FES, and the Bible Society's Library at Cambridge University.

1. Teh's nephew Goh Ewe Kheng was one of the founders of the Church of Singapore.

2. Richmond is a city near Vancouver known for having the highest proportion of Asian residents in North America.

3. This temple is dedicated to a popular healing deity, the Clear Water Patriarch (Qingshui Zushi). Because pit vipers used to enter the temple from the jungle, the temple's patron deity came to be known as the Snake God. In Chinese culture, the snake is an auspicious symbol, but evangelical Christians view snakes as demonic. For details on this temple, see DeBernardi 2006.

4. For an analysis of the impact of the spiritual warfare movement on Christians in Singapore, see DeBernardi 1999.

5. David Martin observes that Pentecostalism is "an extension of Methodism and of the Evangelical Revivals (or Awakenings) accompanying Anglo-American moderniza-tion," recognizing Methodism as "a global movement prior to globalization" (Martin 2002, 7). He describes the 1906 Azusa Street Revival as an "explosive starbust" that sent people in all directions with a fusion of the faiths of culturally despised poor blacks and poor whites (Martin 2002, 5). He does note that the nineteenth- and early twentieth-century history of revivals in India "would even support the claim that the movement was as much generated there as among North American poor whites and poor blacks," but does not pursue this insight further (Martin 2002, 154). Allan Anderson recognizes that nondenominational faith missions, including the China Inland Mission, from 1865 promoted a form of revivalism, but still dates the introduc-tion of Pentecostalism to China to 1906 (Anderson 2009, 119–21).

6. The LMS established missions in Java and Amboyna (1814), Penang (1819), and Singapore (1819), and the Anglo-Chinese College in Malacca in 1818.

7. Some of these children became Christian and took European names, which makes them difficult to trace through written records.

8. Mrs. Pruen, "Native Girls' School at Penang," *Female Missionary Intelligencer*, n.s., 1 (March 1, 1858): 35.

9. Miss Sophie Cooke (1814–1895) replaced her in 1853 and led the school for the next forty-two years (Walker 1899).

10. For background on Gützlaff and his approach to the indigenization of Christianity in China, see Lutz 1985 (67), and Lutz and Lutz 1998.

11. Chinese Evangelisation Society, 1853 annual report, 2.

12. Ibid., 5.

13. CES, 1854 annual report, 10. The Taiping Rebellion encouraged British Christians, but also resulted in increased government restrictions on their activities, including an 1854 campaign to print and distribute one million New Testaments in China (DeBernardi 2011).

14. CES, *Chinese Missionary Gleaner*, n.s., 4, no. 44 (October 1, 1859): 103.

15. Jemima Poppy Bausum accompanied the Chapmans to Penang, introducing them to old friends before continuing to Ningpo, China, where her stepdaughters were teaching in a girls' school that an FES-sponsored female missionary had established in 1843.

16. Ashdown, "Lower Siam," *Echoes of Service*, July 1890, 205–7.

17. Lucy A. Grant, "Our Departed Brother Alexander Grant," *Echoes of Service*, March 1914, 106.

18. Alexander Grant, "Between Java and Singapore," *Echoes of Service*, November 1902, 411.

19. Alexander Grant, "Semarang, 26 June 1883," *Missionary Echo*, September 1883, 123–24.

20. Editorial preface to letter from Alexander Grant, "Semarang, 26 June 1883," *Missionary Echo*, September 1883, 122.

21. Alfred E. Green, "Special Prayer Followed by Rich Blessing," *Echoes of Service*, June 1905, 210.

22. T. R. Angus, "Reviving and Conversions," *Echoes of Service*, June 1905, 210–11.

REFERENCES

Anderson, Allan. 2009. "Pentecostalism in India and China in the Early Twentieth Century and Inter-Religious Relations." In *Global Pentecostalism: Encounters with Other Religious Traditions*, edited by David Westerlund, 117–35. New York: Taurus.
———. 2013. To the Ends of the Earth: Pentecostalism and the Transformation of World Christianity. Oxford: Oxford University Press.
Assembly Record Book. N.d. Ang Mo Kio, Singapore: Bethesda Gospel Hall.
Burns, Islay. (1870) 1975. Memoir of the Rev. Wm. [William] C. [Chalmers] Burns: Missionary to China from the English Presbyterian Church. New York: Robert Cater and Brothers. Reprint, San Francisco: Chinese Materials Center.

Chinese Evangelisation Society. 1851–1859. *Report of the Chinese Evangelisation Society*. London: Nisbet.

Dann, Robert Bernard. 2004. *Father of Faith Missions: The Life and Times of Anthony Norris Groves*. Waynesboro, GA: Paternoster/Authentic Media.

DeBernardi, Jean. 1999. "Spiritual Warfare and Territorial Spirits: The Globalization and Localization of a 'Practical Theology.'" *Religious Studies and Theology* 18 (2): 66–96.

———. 2006. *The Way That Lives in the Heart: Chinese Popular Religion and Spirit Mediums in Penang, Malaysia*. Stanford: Stanford University Press.

———. 2011. "Moses' Rod: The Bible as a Commodity in Southeast Asia and China." In *Chinese Circulations: Capital, Commodities and Networks in Southeast Asia*, edited by Eric Tagliacozzo and Wen-chin Chang, 380–404. Durham: Duke University Press.

Doran, Christine. 1996. "'A Fine Sphere for Female Usefulness': Missionary Women in the Straits Settlements, 1815–45." *Journal of the Malaysian Branch of the Royal Asiatic Society* 69 (1): 100–111.

Echoes of Service. 1885–present. Bath, UK: Echoes of Service.

FES (Society for Promoting Female Education in China, India, and the East [London]). 1847. *History of the Society for Promoting Female Education in the East: Established in the Year 1834*. London: E. Suter.

Harrison, Brian. 1979. *Waiting for China: The Anglo-Chinese College at Malacca, 1818–1843, and Early Nineteenth-Century Missions*. Hong Kong: Hong Kong University Press.

Lutz, Jessie. 1985. "Karl F. A. Gützlaff: Missionary Entrepreneur." In *Christianity in China: Early Protestant Missionary Writings*, edited by Suzanne Wilson Barnett and John King Fairbank, 61–87. Cambridge: Harvard University Press.

Lutz, Jessie G., and Rolland Ray Lutz. 1998. *Hakka Chinese Confront Protestant Christianity, 1850–1900; With the Autobiographies of Eight Hakka Christians and Commentary*. Armonk, NY: M. E. Sharpe.

Martin, David. 2002. *Pentecostalism: The World Their Parish*. Oxford: Blackwell.

The Missionary Echo. 1872–1884. Bath, UK: Echoes of Service.

The Missionary Reporter. 1853–1858. James Van Sommer, editor. London: n.p.

Neill, Stephen, and Owen Chadwick. (1964) 1986. *A History of Christian Missions*. 2nd ed. London: Penguin.

Rubinstein, Murray. 1996. "Holy Spirit Taiwan: Pentecostal and Charismatic Christianity in the Republic of China." In *Christianity in China from the Eighteenth Century to the Present*, edited by Daniel H. Bays, 353–66. Stanford: Stanford University Press.

Walker, E. A. 1899. *Sophia Cooke; or, Forty-Two Years' Work in Singapore*. London: Elliot Stock.

3

Orientations

Moral Geographies in Transnational Ghanaian Pentecostal Networks

KRISTINE KRAUSE

Can't remember if I told you but:
I have moved out from Beggars Alley, located at 2 Poverty Lane at the corner of Down and Out Circle. As of today, I have a brand new home.
My new address is Living Well on 231 Abundance Terrace, located at the corner of Blessings Drive and Prosperity Peak. It's in the God Can neighborhood.
No longer will I allow myself to travel to the other side of town on Begging Peter to Pay Paul Route, located at a dead end intersection called I Don't Have, which connects with Borrowers Junction! I no longer hang out at Failure's Place, near Excuses Avenue, next to Procrastination Point.
I now belong to an upscale community club called Higher Heights with unlimited potential and opportunities for me to succeed.
I can do ALL things through CHRIST who strengthens me! Life is good because God is good! Care to change your address? There are lots of empty flats around me.

This motivational text, which I received through a Christian e-mail list, draws on the well-known truth that a neighborhood in a city is more than just a spot on a map, but is also a position in socioeconomic terms. Here this insight is combined with the prototypical idea of evangelical and Pentecostal teaching that the ability to rise to a higher socioeconomic status means to reach a morally higher ground as well. In order to achieve this end, the believer needs to be proactive and disciplined. He or she does not move to "Abundance Terrace" and "Prosperity Peak" just like that, but has to leave the intersection "I Don't Have" and "Excuses Avenue" by his or her own willpower.[1]

The moral layout of the economic stratification of the city evoked in this e-mail resonates on a deeper level with the concern of born-again Christians that the world is a "site of war between God and the devil" (Meyer 2010, 115), in which every Christian has to take part. Even if there are "lots of empty flats," there are evil forces that will work against the efforts of people to move up from "Procrastination Point."

Taking these ideas as a starting point, in this chapter I will look at how Pentecostal believers evaluate, sustain, and create moral geographies of their inner selves, their surroundings, and the wider world in their charismatic practices—that is, practices relying on the power of the Holy Spirit. I will explore these practices based on fieldwork conducted with migrants from Ghana in London, but also on research in transnational Pentecostal networks of Ghanaian-founded churches based in Berlin and Hamburg. Thus, the argument I want to bring forward has to be seen as being based in a very specific empirical context: at the intersection between transnational migration from West Africa to Europe and the establishment of transnational Pentecostal churches from West Africa in Europe.

Clarification of Terms

"Moralizing the world"—the title of the section in which this chapter is placed—refers to the ways Pentecostal knowledge equips the believer with the ability to evaluate what is good and what is evil. I conceive thereby of morality as an activity and not as a "Pentecostal" or "Ghanaian" totality.[2] Moral geographies then bring in dimensions of hierarchy and power, pointing to the ways moral superiority and inferiority are constructed in relation to upward and downward mobilities and projected onto imaginative landscapes. This means that the term "geography" is used here in various ways: I am referring to the geographer Doreen Massey's concept of global power geometries (1996)[3] when talking about how migrants from West Africa are positioned globally, but at the same time use the term more metaphorically when talking about imagined geographies,[4] which contain a moral evaluation: the higher the better, as in the example of moving from "Down and Out Circle" to "Prosperity Peak." Moral geographies are constructed through knowledge about the concrete city space and its buildings, but also when talking about the places that an individual inhabits. The social position of a person is thereby moralized: the higher somebody is placed within socioeconomic topographies, the more elevated the person also becomes in spiritual terms, as expressed in the opening example of the e-mail.

The terms "subject position" and "subjectivities" are used to talk about how Pentecostal practice is related to questions of authority and power. We gain a position from which to speak and be heard by subjecting ourselves to specific ways of behaving and using our bodies.[5] When we do so, others recognize us and respond to us. Understood in this way, Pentecostal practices are inevitably relational: what born-again subjects say and do is directed toward an audience and is part of crafting the ways of being a person and belonging somewhere.

The moral geographies I am going to explore in this chapter are related to questions of subjectivities, as they provide the locations from which the born-again subject speaks and assesses the world she finds herself in. It is thereby crucial to how we understand the idea of becoming born again. The question of rupture, as expressed in the Pentecostal discourse on making a "complete break with the past" (Meyer 1998) that dominated the anthropological literature for quite some time, needs to be reformulated in light of the diversification of the Pentecostal scene. The young people, for instance, who have traveled from Ghana to Europe since the beginning of the 2000s were born into families in Ghana who had already been practicing born-again Christianity for two decades. In many cases, the crucial point is therefore no longer *how* somebody becomes born again, but how she stays it. Thus the ethnographic question at hand is, How do people remain born again and re-create moral boundaries in their daily lives?

In the following I will first summarize a few points about the migration of Pentecostalism from West Africa to Europe before moving on to the example of how moral subject positions are created, physical space is evaluated, and the inner self of the born-again subject is built up and maintained in Pentecostal belief and practice.

New Mission Churches in Europe

Churches founded by West Africans in Europe emerged from the complex history of Christianity in Africa.[6] We can distinguish two main strands that branched out to Europe, namely, *Aladura* or *sunsum asore*,[7] founded mainly in the 1960s and 1970s by worker students (Harris 2006, 19–40), and neo-Pentecostal churches[8] brought along by students and labor migrants and linked to the Christian renewal movements that spread throughout West Africa from the 1980s onwards (Asamoah-Gyadu 2008; Marshall 2009; Van Dijk 1997). A third strand can be seen in "ethnic missions" that were established by mainline churches such as the Catholic, Anglican, Methodist, and Presbyterian churches, often catering in African languages to their constituencies (Fumanti 2010).

The term "church" hardly captures the variety of organizational forms that make up the phenomenon being discussed: next to megachurches such as the Kingsway International Christian Centre (KICC) in London, which gather their flocks in huge stadiums and converted warehouse buildings, we also find smaller formations, often consisting of only a few people who meet regularly in someone's living room. Some groups have their headquarters in West Africa and have built branches elsewhere at the request of members living abroad, or have sent apostles to implant the church in Europe. Others were founded in Europe and inaugurate networks of churches across the globe, including branches in the home country. Another important feature is the density of activities that take place outside organized church contexts: individuals who have received a calling for healing or preaching might set up their "ministries" through their personal contacts and word of mouth, building up their networks of followers, who are often members of different churches and denominations.

Despite this variation, there are some common elements, such as the emphasis on a personal relationship with God, a conduct of life according to strict ethical rules, and a belief in the gifts of the Holy Spirit, which include speaking in tongues, the driving out of evil spirits, the achievement of success and wealth, and miraculous healing. Worship is practiced in idioms of popular performance, and the churches are staffed with the latest sound equipment and video technologies to bring their message to their congregations and into public forums more generally

(Hackett 1998). Over the last few decades, charismatic Pentecostalism has in this way created its own public sphere in Ghana (Meyer 2004b; de Witte 2011), which expands into transnational Ghanaian households located in Europe and North America via satellite TV and circulating DVDs.

The literature on Pentecostal churches in Ghana and West Africa as well as on the transnational offshoots of these churches is too vast to review here.[9] Regarding the question of how moral geographies are created, a few points are nevertheless important. In the case of Ghana, scholars have shown how the ritual practices and teachings of Pentecostal churches are marked by the entangled history of the appropriation of missionary discourses, modernization, postcolonialism, and transnational encounters (Meyer 1999; Van Dijk 2004; Lauterbach 2009; Daswani 2013). Thus, charismatic-Pentecostal churches have to be regarded as stemming from a particular history, which was "transnational and translocal from the onset" (Maxwell 2006, 14), yet neither influenced solely by preachers from the United States (Gifford 2004), nor based only on African traditions (Kalu 2008), as two extreme poles of the literature suggest. It is the intersection of all these different influences and the fact that the new mission churches challenge traditional versions of European Christianity and situate themselves as morally superior that make them an important subject of study. Although the term "reverse mission movement" cannot capture the multidirectional movements of missionizing today,[10] it points to the inversion of power relations that provide the ground for the alternative subject position for people from the global south who experience marginalization and downward mobility as migrants in the global north.

The tendency among Pentecostal churches to demonize any element that can be associated with ritual forms of African traditional religions has led scholars to view Pentecostalism as a machine of conversion to modernity and as an antipode to spirit possession cults. But this interpretation entails two flaws: the conflation of spirit possession with tradition and of Christianity with modernity. Historians such as Tom McCaskie (2008) have instead shown that many forms of spirit possession are of even more recent origin than Christianity in Ghana. In general it can be said that it is the intrinsic relation between the Holy Spirit and the many other spirits that brings about the specific Pentecostal practice. As Birgit Meyer writes, the "occult" spirits that Pentecostalism disavows remain firmly linked to it as its ever-present Other (Meyer 1999, 171ff.; 2004a, 455).

The embodiment of spirits in the manner of spirit possession cults, which is prevalent and quite elaborated in particular in the central ritual of deliverance, has been replaced in some strands of transnational Ghanaian Pentecostalism by an embodied experience of God's presence.[11] The argument is that time and energy should not be wasted on evil spirits but on building up a connection with God and the Holy Spirit. Thus, instead of engaging in demonology, prayer warriors and ministers should work on "self-deliverance," meaning the driving out of any evil by carrying the spirit in the inner space of the person.

The maintenance work that needs to be done in order to sustain these subjectivities is strongly gendered and links the personal with the public by focusing simultaneously on personal growth and the city space, as the following example shows.

Being in Tune and Free to Serve

Jennifer Wallace[12] is one of the female ministers whom I met during my research in London, who work attached to, but independently from, organized churches. She offers training courses and spiritual capacity building for Christian women and men. Her teaching is characterized by lucidity and warmth, based not only on her university education in sociology, but also on her own life experience as a woman, wife, and mother. Her base is in London, but she travels regularly throughout Africa (Ghana, Nigeria, Cameroon, Kenya, and Uganda) to launch her books and to expand the networks of the ministry. Her work reflects well how the building up of an intimacy with God can be linked with the specific positioning of a transnational female migrant in London, who struggles to find a position adequate for her education, and is engaged in a universal battle against evil forces in multiple geographical contexts.

The starting point in her ministry, "Women in Tune: Restoring, Raising, Releasing Women to take the Kingdom," is the question of identity as a Christian woman. As she explains, the problem of women is that they are always defined by somebody else, first by their fathers, then by their husbands, and later by their children. Instead of calling for rebellion, however, Wallace advises finding the source of belonging in God. In one of the invitations to her workshops, she writes, "Our identity in Christ is not based on gender. It is based on the finished work of the Cross. Therefore, both men and women have equal identity in Christ (Gal. 3:26–29)." During a conversation we had in a café in a shopping mall in North East London, she explained this further to me: "In regard to feminism, I always had the problem that it asks for equality, which implies that somebody has this equality for me and can give it to me. But on the contrary, equality is something God has given to me. It is nothing which can be given by an institution or a man" (cf. Wallace 2006, 196).

Instead, she says, women have to live up to their full potential by recognizing that they have been "designed for purpose," as one of her books is called (Wallace 2008). Women have been created by God to be "free to serve" (Wallace 2006), as the title of another goes. In her workshops the aspect of submission is therefore central. This point is reminiscent of what Saba Mahmood has written in regard to how young Egyptian women learn to be pious and gain a new subject position from it: "agency [is] not simply . . . a synonym for resistance to relations of domination, but . . . a capacity for action that specific relations of *subordination* create and enable" (Mahmood 2001a, 210).[13] Similar to the Muslim women Mahmood worked with, the Christian women in the training sessions with Wallace learn techniques on how to "'spontaneously' [express] the right attitude" (Mahmood 2001b, 833), to be "free to serve." The subject position as "woman in tune" is thereby not dismissive and passive, but characterized by the unique purpose God has created for women:

> Since purpose determines design, God created the woman with a unique reproductive system and an ability to incubate, nurture and birth life. Therefore, a woman can take the tiny seed of man, incubate and multiply it in her womb, with her whole being aligning itself to the sole purpose of creating life! (Wallace 2008, 56)

By drawing on the biological capacities of the female body, Jennifer Wallace places her message in line with strong voices of difference-based feminism and distances herself from claims that the rank of male leaders should be equaled by women.[14] Instead, the task of the woman "free to serve" is to take the ideas of the male leadership, to nurture them and bring them into fruition in the social body of the church as well as in the family. This peculiar subject position for women requires a matching partner on the male side, who accepts being the responsible leader in the congregation and the church.

At first glance this line of teaching seems to assign women to the traditional realms of the family. However, boundaries between family and church life become blurred when daily life in the city is placed at the center of moral practices. This is particularly evident in Wallace's "prayer school," in which women learn to build themselves up as "quivers": containers of God's arrows, to be used to fight against evil. Women are trained to build groups of five, and to deliver their environment from evil influences under the motto "Take ownership of your street."[15] Similar to the e-mail quoted in the beginning, we find here again the interlinkage between concrete city spaces and individual capacities. Since upward mobility for most migrant women is hard to achieve, it is suggested to take their destiny in their own hands by claiming the location on the city map and to clean it from spiritual blockages.

Jennifer Wallace's own story is an example of how to do this and how to carve out a particular position to speak from, not only by drawing on quasi-essentialist notions of womanhood but also by placing herself within a particular moral geography.

Moral Geographies of the City

Knowledge about the city space is gathered by born-again Christians while they move around in their daily lives, "walking with God" (Luhrmann 2004, 521), but also through attention to media representations and historical information, often linked with information lifted from the Bible. I met John, a middle-aged Ghanaian accountant who worked as a cleaner, at a week of intercessory prayers organized by one of the interdenominational prayer networks in Berlin in 2006. He told me how he perceived Europe when he arrived ten years earlier. Not only did the houses in Berlin appear surprisingly old and ugly, but also the manner people employed in the public space disgusted him. In particular, the fact that people drink, caress, and kiss in public was particularly strange for him, only topped by his discovery of the naked bodies, exposed the minute the first rare sunshine touches the ground, in Berlin's biggest public park, the Tiergarten. While he has learned about the prestige attached to the generosity of high ceilings in apartments located in old buildings, he has confirmed his impression that there is something wrong with the Tiergarten Park. For him the park has accumulated evil spirits through the immoral ways people use the green space: parts of the park are well-established meeting points for gay men, and the street that runs through the park has been the central route for festivals such as the Love Parade[16] and the Christopher Street Parade.[17] Both are events where people enjoy dancing on the street, exposing their barely dressed and erotically decorated bodies.

In his view, which was confirmed by the teaching and preaching we listened to, the immoral behavior of people strengthens the capacity of places to accumulate evil forces. The idea that spirits live in places is closely linked to teaching about territorial spirits. They are thought to reign over places, buildings, regions, and whole nations, and can cause poverty and be an obstacle to development (Asamoah-Gyadu 2005, 180ff.). Territorial spirits are powerful principalities because they can prevent other spirits from operating within their territory. Thus, if someone sends an evil spell or harming spirit to somebody, the permission of the territorial spirit is first needed before the harming action can be performed.

Whereas the spirit possession priests I talked to in research conducted in Ghana in 2008 insisted that these territorial spirits are neither evil nor good, and that it is the deeds and wishes of humans who bring in the moral quality, Christians in Ghana and Europe in contrast explained to me that any spirit other than the Holy Spirit is potentially evil and needs to be controlled. Evil deeds conducted on the territory of a spirit contribute to its powers. This happens even when people are not aware of it. John tried to explain the point more clearly in an interview by using the metaphor of a control desk, which displays the distribution of electrical energy, here equivalent to spiritual forces:

> Imagine a map with a control desk in which you can see the spiritual powers: you will see that the Tiergarten is highly charged with evil spiritual energy, but when we go and pray, this energy vanishes and is replaced by the power of the Holy Spirit. You will also see that where we meet for

our prayer meeting [*points to place on map*], there is a lot of power. It is like a cloud of power. God has shown me in prayer that this city needs our prayer; Berlin needs us in order to solve its problems. (Interview with John, August 1, 2006)

The view that how people use city space impacts the spiritual battle going on was also expressed by a guest preacher from Nigeria, who lectured at a prayer revival I attended the same summer. He mentioned the street festival Carnival of the Cultures,[18] which was taking place that same weekend, and warned his audience about the spiritual effect of the parade. Several of the groups who take part in the carnival refer positively to "African" cultures in drumming and dance performances on the street. One very popular drumming formation is the group La Forêt Sacrée. Comprising mainly white Germans, the group offers performances inspired by Guinean culture and art, with masks and drums on the street. The performance of cultural dances and drumming was condemned by the guest preacher, and he warned his audience, comprising mainly brethren who self-identified as African in origin, to watch out for what the carnival is doing spiritually in Berlin.

The spiritual charging of the city space evolves also from historical events, sedimented in buildings, monuments, and museums. One example of this is the well-known Pergamon Museum, on the Museumsinsel in the center of Berlin, named after one of the treasures of the museum, the Pergamon altar.[19] As I learned at a prayer meeting, this altar is viewed by some Christians as the throne of Satan, referring to a verse in Revelation (Rev. 2:12–14). The problems of the city, including unemployment, the high level of debts, violent conflicts among youths, the presence of neo-Nazis, and the fact that the mayor of that period, a well-known politician, is openly gay, are attributed to the presence of this throne in the midst of the city. Some Christians, including members of churches founded by Ghanaian pastors, but also white Germans, pray in front of the museum for removal of the altar.

The propensity among Pentecostals to appropriate big warehouses in European cities and to convert them for worship purposes resonates with the belief that certain practices such as drumming can invoke evil spiritual forces. Although the conversion of industrial buildings happens mainly for pragmatic reasons (affordable rent and an absence of neighbors who would be disturbed by late and loud worship), warehouse churches have become a pattern. At the risk of overinterpreting, I want to suggest that former warehouses and industrial buildings, besides their practicality, are attractive locales because they are spiritually and socially empty (Marshall 2009, 138, 140). As I have argued elsewhere (Krause 2014), they can therefore be filled with a new spirituality following Pentecostal principles.

The task of charging places with the power of the Holy Spirit and discharging others of evil forces requires those involved to be strong in prayer and to be able to identify the moral geography of the city space. Both talents are cultivated in prayer schools and complemented by a finely tuned routine of self-inspection.

Building Up a Moral Inner Self

The concept of building up skills to become a weapon against evil in the hands of God, as in Jennifer Wallace's ideas of the "quiver," is at the center of the activities of prayer warriors, who are often found among younger members of churches, and here particularly among young men. A fervent prayer warrior can pray for hours, "at any point in time, for every person who needs it and for any problem which needs to be solved, and any evil which needs to be fought back," as Matthew, one of the prayer warriors at Destiny Changing Church,[20] in which I did fieldwork in North East London, explained to me. The warriors train themselves to pray forcefully on the spot, but also over a longer stretch of time. Ruth, another prayer warrior of the same church, compared this with bodybuilding and sports for fitness: prayer warriors practice so that they can pray for long duration, and they also build up specific skills in praying, as one does in bodybuilding when training specific muscles.[21]

The ability to pray rests on the cultivation of introspection, an inner space in which the Pentecostal practitioner can interact with God. Ruth explained to me how every morning when she wakes up, she takes some quiet time to read the Bible or just to contemplate in order to create the space to "hear" God's voice. The hearing of God's voice is thereby to be understood as a translation of different moods or vibes that sweep to the surface of the mind into messages from God. Emerging sentiments are watched carefully in order to evaluate whether these were caused by the Holy Spirit in order to send a message. An often-heard example for this technique is the story of somebody who in the morning felt very reluctant to get up and go to work and later heard that there was a terrible road accident in which several people died. The reluctance of the person to get up and go, which otherwise could be interpreted as sheer laziness, is understood here as a way God communicated with the person and protected her from becoming involved in an accident.

The way the banal and idiosyncratic condition of an individual is translated into a specific intervention by divine forces furthermore shows how carefully people have to cater for this inner space, in order to be able to "discern" the right from the wrong. They have to be able to monitor their own moods, to ascertain whether the moods could be linked to God's attempt to create points of contact or whether they were sent by the Devil to destroy their plans.

Whereas in the preceding example, the person is being spared from an accident by God's interference into the emotional state of a person, other forms of intervention can take more drastic forms. Unforeseen negative events, for instance, from which the individual has not been spared, are seen as tests sent by God and as chances to grow spiritually. The story of Charles, a student who came to London on a holiday working visa during term break, serves as an example of divine intervention as a test. He did not return to finish his degree in Ghana, but overstayed his visa and worked instead on construction sites in London. He decided consciously to live as an undocumented person, attempting to exploit the "status paradox" of transnational migration (Nieswand 2011), hoping for a higher status in the home context by accepting temporarily a lower status in the migration context.

During a random police patrol, following the London bombing in 2006, Charles was detected as having no valid visa and was first kept in a detention center for several months and then deported with only one suitcase containing the clothes he used in the prison. After the experience in the detention center, he had to endure the humiliation of coming back with empty hands, and not living up to the expectations of his relatives and his peers, who had moved on in their lives, some in good jobs, with a family, a car, and a house. This opened his eyes to a harsh reality: instead of making it to Abundance Terrace (to invoke the motivational text cited at the beginning of this chapter), Charles was stuck at the "dead end intersection called I Don't Have." He had to live from the support of his cousins before eventually procuring another visa and returning to London.

During the time in the detention center, he framed what happened in terms of a test God was submitting him to. In his view, deceiving the visa regime of the United Kingdom was not a sin, but a way of trusting God, that He would lead him through to what he wanted from life. The example of Charles shows that everything that happens can become integrated into the moral world the born-again subject inhabits. It points to a kind of freedom from conventional understanding of good and evil resulting from the moral subject position of being born again.

Conclusion: Pentecostal Moral Geographies

The specific imaginative geography on which the moral world of Pentecostal migrants from Ghana in Europe is built, is based on the evaluation of linkages. There is first the link between the African continent and Europe. By appropriating and inverting the traditional missionary discourse, migrants project the image of the former "dark continent" onto Europe, a place where homosexual couples can marry and the majority of heterosexual couples raise children without being married. In the view of the born-again believers, the places where most of these things happen, such as Berlin, London, or Amsterdam, are in need of deliverance. On another level, the European cities are used as a base from which to engage in missionary work in West Africa. Here, many churches buy into development discourses, which again position them in a positive light, as organizations that have something to contribute to the world.

Another aspect of Pentecostal geography is the concrete level of a city in which a person lives. The history of a place and the activities of the people inhabiting the city contribute to the accumulation of evil or good spiritual powers. In order to discern good from bad, the Pentecostal practitioner needs to build up an inner space in which he or she can receive guidance from God. The main translator between all these different spaces and levels is the Holy Spirit. Compared to all the other spirits that inhabit this geography, the Holy Spirit seems to be strangely dislocated. It is everywhere and nowhere; it remains unmarked, or can perhaps be best understood as a spiritual equivalent of the "global" within Pentecostalism.[22]

Through the Holy Spirit, the daily life of the Pentecostal subject is placed in a global frame of reference, namely, Pentecostalism. Being part of a project that is simultaneously universal and deeply personal is one of the defining and most attractive features of Pentecostalism and charismatic Christianity. It describes in a nutshell how the world and the born-again subject become moralized in Pentecostalism. In Pentecostal geographies, city spaces shaped by particular historical heritages become linked to individual trajectories and are seen as embedded in the wider project of good against evil. The spatial manifestation of failure ("Beggars Alley" and "Poverty Lane" in the e-mail posting) is spiritually backed by territorial spirits, while socioeconomic success goes hand in hand with the moral higher ground that results from living a righteous Pentecostal life.

NOTES

Acknowledgment: To Jennifer Wallace and all the people who made time to speak to me, I owe deep thanks. I acknowledge the inspiring input of Gertrud Hüwelmeier and Rijk van Dijk on several aspects discussed in this chapter and comments by the editors and reviewers. Research in Germany and Ghana was funded by the German Research Foundation (HU 1019/1–2 and HU 1019/1–3, grant holder Gertrud Hüwelmeier); research in London by an ESRC Centre linked scholarship (PTA—042–2003–00032 with COMPAS, University of Oxford).

1. A superficial Internet search reveals that this text can be found on several Christian webpages dedicated to motivational Christian texts. The author is unknown.

2. I draw here on conceptualizations of morality as "unique local assemblages" (Zigon 2010, 5) that can be mobilized to construct "acceptable ways of living in the world" (5).

3. Massey suggested this notion to express that globalization does not mean the same thing for people all over the world: depending on the country or region people live in and their class position, they have different access to global flows.

4. Edward Said coined the term "imaginative geography" in his seminal book *Orientalism* (1978), in which he deconstructed the way Europeans imagined other places in the world as different and exotic, thereby constructing them as inferior. Since then, the term has been taken up by geographers to analyze how specific worldviews are used to legitimate power relations.

5. This is a very crude summary of what philosophers like Michel Foucault and Judith Butler have said. See Mahmood's study on pious women for an application to the study of religious subjectivities (Mahmood 2001a).

6. Following Claudia Währisch-Oblau (2009), I refer to the charismatic-Pentecostal churches founded by migrants in Europe as "new mission churches" rather than as "migrant," "African Initiated" or "African Independent churches," since the former term more adequately captures the vision of these groups to engage in missionary work worldwide.

7. *Aladura* (Yoruba for "praying people") and *sunsum asore* (Twi for "spirit churches") are the terms used in Nigeria and Ghana to refer to churches that were founded by black Africans as early as the end of the nineteenth century in reaction to the neglect of healing and spiritual protection in missionary churches and the exclusion of black Africans from offices in the church hierarchy (Oymenyo 2006). These churches soon became very successful and spread over all West Africa (Peel 1968).

8. In the Ghanaian context, the term "neo-Pentecostal" or "charismatic-Pentecostal" is used to differentiate these churches from an earlier generation of classical Pentecostal churches, such as Assemblies of God or the Church of Pentecost.

9. See Meyer (2004b) and Peel (1968) on African Christianities. On new mission churches in Europe, see the special issue edited by Knibbe and Van der Meulen (2009) and the volume edited by Adogame and Spickard (2010) for examples.

10. Movements that hardly fit any conventional model include proselytization from Brazil to Southern Africa (Van de Kamp and Van Dijk 2010) as well as from Nigeria to Ukraine (Wanner 2007).

11. See Bialecki (2011) and Brahinsky (2012), who write about the Vineyard Church and an Assemblies of God missionary training institute in North America, respectively, and the role sensation plays in building up specific subjectivities.

12. Since she is recognizable in her teachings, which I describe further down, this is her real name.

13. In this quotation, Mahmood draws on Judith Butler's conceptualization of the subject (Butler 1997).

14. In her books Wallace develops the idea of "sonship," which men and women both can inhabit when they live a life surrendered to Christ, although her argument about the different purposes of men and women is based on bodily difference. It is beyond the scope of this chapter and my competency to explore the question of whether these ideas derive from mainstream Christian or Pentecostal thinking, or respond to the broader African constituency Wallace is serving. I think, however, that Wallace's theology reflects her critical engagement with mainstream European feminism and her own specific positioning as a female minister in Europe who identifies as having her roots in Africa.

15. Women in Tune, "Welcome to our Homepage" and "Quiver—Women Praying in Groups of Five for Revival in the United Kingdom," http://www.womenintune.org (accessed February 9, 2014).

16. The Love Parade is a street parade consisting of sound systems carried on trucks that drive slowly through the streets, followed by people who dance for hours to techno, house, and drum 'n' bass music. The parade was founded in 1989 by a group of people involved in the specific club culture of Berlin after the reunification of Germany,

characterized by the utilization of spaces such as unused underground stations, base-ments, and industrial halls for experimental clubs. It started in the west of the city and was later relocated to the Tiergarten. It became a mega-event attracting several million people.

17. Named after the uprising that followed assaults by the police in New York's Christopher Street in 1969.

18. The festival Karneval der Kulturen was inaugurated in 1996 based on the Notting Hill Carnival in London, in order to celebrate the cultural diversity of Berlin.

19. The altar was brought to Berlin at the beginning of the twentieth century; German Christian groups began protesting against it soon after its arrival.

20. Fictional name of church.

21. This resonates with what Luhrmann, Nusbaum, and Thisted describe in regard to "skilled learning" in evangelical Christianity (2010, 66). See also Brahinsky, who talks about the "sensorium" of Pentecostalism (2012, 216), "a given arrangement of sensory modalities" (218) that enables the transfer of Pentecostal practices over time and cultural boundaries.

22. See Simon Coleman (2010) on the "globe as the sublime" in charismatic Christianity.

REFERENCES

Adogame, Afe, and James V. Spickard, eds. 2010. *Religion Crossing Boundaries: Trans-national Religious Dynamics in Africa and the New African Diaspora*. Leiden: Brill.

Asamoah-Gyadu, Kwabena J. 2005. *African Charismatics: Current Developments within Independent Indigenous Pentecostalism in Ghana*. Leiden: Brill.

———. 2008. "'I Will Put My Breath in You, and You Will Come to Life': Charismatic Renewal in Ghanaian Mainline Churches and Its Implications for African 'Diaspo-ran' Christianity." In *Christianity in Africa and the African Diaspora: The Appropria-tion of a Scattered Heritage*, edited by Afe Adogame, Roswith Gerloff, and Klaus Hock, 193–207. London: Continuum.

Bialecki, Jon. 2011. "Quiet Deliverances." In *Practicing the Faith: The Ritual Life of Pentecostal-Charismatic Christians*, edited by Martin Lindhardt, 249–76. Oxford: Berghahn.

Brahinsky, Josh. 2012. "Pentecostal Body Logics: Cultivating a Modern Sensorium." *Cultural Anthropology* 27 (2): 215–38.

Butler, Judith. 1997. *The Psychic Life of Power: Theories of Subjection*. Stanford: Stanford University Press.

Coleman, Simon. 2010. "Constructing the Globe: A Charismatic Sublime?" In *Travel-ing Spirits: Migrants, Markets and Mobilities*, edited by Gertrud Hüwelmeier and Kristine Krause, 186–202. London: Routledge.

Daswani, Girish. 2013. "On Christianity and Ethics: Rupture as Ethical Practice in Ghanaian Pentecostalism." *American Ethnologist* 40 (3): 467–79.

De Witte, Marleen. 2011. "Business of the Spirit: Ghanaian Broadcast Media and the Commercial Exploitation of Pentecostalism." *Journal of African Media Studies* 3 (2): 189–205.

Fumanti, Mattia. 2010. "'Virtuous Citizenship': Ethnicity and Encapsulation among Akan-Speaking Ghanaian Methodists in London." *African Diaspora* 3 (1): 12–41.

Gifford, Paul. 2004. *Ghana's New Christianity: Pentecostalism in a Globalising African Economy.* London: Hurst.

Hackett, Rosalind. 1998. "Charismatic/Pentecostal Appropriation of Media Technologies in Nigeria and Ghana." *Journal of Religion in Africa* 28 (3): 258–77.

Harris, Hermione. 2006. *Yoruba in Diaspora: An African Church in London.* New York: Palgrave Macmillan.

Kalu, Ogbu Uke. 2008. *African Pentecostalism: An Introduction.* Oxford: Oxford University Press.

Knibbe, Kim, and Marten Van der Meulen. 2009. "The Role of Spatial Practices and Locality in the Constituting of the Christian African Diaspora." *African Diaspora* 2 (2): 125–30.

Krause, Kristine. 2014. "Space in Pentecostal Healing Practices among Ghanaian Migrants in London." *Medical Anthropology* 33 (1): 37–51.

Lauterbach, Karen. 2009. "Wealth and Worth: Pastorship and Neo-Pentecostalism in Kumasi." *Ghana Studies* 9:91–121.

Luhrmann, Tanya M. 2004. "Metakinesis: How God Becomes Intimate in Contemporary US Christianity." *American Anthropologist* 106 (3): 518–28.

Luhrmann, Tanya, Howard Nusbaum, and Ronald Thisted. 2010. "The Absorption Hypothesis: Learning to Hear God in Evangelical Christianity." *American Anthropologist* 112 (1): 66–78.

Mahmood, Saba. 2001a. "Feminist Theory, Embodiment, and the Docile Agent: Some Reflections on the Egyptian Islamic Revival." *Cultural Anthropology* 6 (2): 202–36.

———. 2001b. "Rehearsed Spontaneity and the Conventionality of Ritual: Disciplines of Salat." *American Ethnologist* 28 (4): 827–53.

Marshall, Ruth. 2009. *Political Spiritualities: The Pentecostal Revolution in Nigeria.* Chicago: University of Chicago Press.

Massey, Doreen. 1996. "Power-Geometry and a Progressive Sense of Place." In *Mapping the Futures: Local Cultures, Global Change*, edited by John Bird, Barry Curtis, Tim Putnam, George Robertson, and Lisa Tickner, 59–69. London: Routledge.

Maxwell, David. 2006. *African Gifts of the Spirit: Pentecostalism and the Rise of a Zimbabwean Transnational Religious Movement.* Oxford: James Currey.

McCaskie, Tom C. 2008. "Akwantemfi—in Mid-Journey: An Asante Shrine Today and Its Clients." *Journal of Religion in Africa* 38 (1): 57–80.

Meyer, Birgit. 1998. "'Make a Complete Break with the Past': Memory and Post-colonial Modernity in Ghanaian Pentecostalist Discourse." *Journal of Religion in Africa* 28 (3): 316–49.

———. 1999. *Translating the Devil: Religion and Modernity among the Ewe in Ghana.* Edinburgh: Edinburgh University Press; Trenton, NJ: Africa World Press.

———. 2004a. "Christianity in Africa: From African Independent to Pentecostal-Charismatic Churches." *Annual Review of Anthropology* 33:447–74.

———. 2004b. "'Praise the Lord. . . .': Popular Cinema and Pentecostalite Style in Ghana's New Public Sphere." *American Ethnologist* 31 (1): 92–110.

———. 2008. "Mami Wata as a Christian Demon: The Eroticism of Forbidden Pleasures in Southern Ghana." In *Sacred Waters: Arts for Mami Wata and Other Divinities in Africa and the Diaspora*, edited by Henry J. Drewal, 383–98. Bloomington: Indiana University Press.

———. 2010. "Pentecostalism and Globalization." In *Studying Global Pentecostalism: Theories and Methods*, edited by Allan Anderson, Michael Bergunder, André Droogers, and Cornelis van der Laan, 113–30. Berkeley: University of California Press.

Nieswand, Boris. 2011. *Theorising Transnational Migration: The Status Paradox of Migration*. New York: Routledge.

Omenyo, Cephas N. 2006. *Pentecost outside Pentecostalism: A Study of the Development of Charismatic Renewal in the Mainline Churches in Ghana*. Zoetemeer, Netherlands: Boekencentrum.

Peel, John D. Y. 1968. *Aladura: A Religious Movement among the Yoruba*. London: Oxford University Press.

Said, Edward. 1978. *Orientalism*. London: Routledge and Kegan Paul.

Van de Kamp, Linda, and Rijk Van Dijk. 2010. "Pentecostals Moving South-South: Brazilian and Ghanaian Transnationalism in Southern Africa." In *Religion Crossing Boundaries: Transnational Religious Dynamics in Africa and the New African Diaspora*, edited by Afe Adogame and James V. Spickard, 123–42. Leiden: Brill.

Van Dijk, Rijk. 1997. "From Camp to Encompassment: Discourse of Transsubjectivity in the Ghanaian Pentecostal Diaspora." *Journal of Religion in Africa* 17 (2): 135–59.

———. 2004. "'Beyond the Rivers of Ethiopia': Pentecostal Pan-Africanism and Ghanaian Identities in the Transnational Domain." In *Situating Globality: African Agency in the Appropriation of Global Culture*, edited by Wim M. J. van Binsbergen, Rijk van Dijk, and Jan-Bart Gewald, 163–89. Leiden: Brill.

Währisch-Oblau, Claudia. 2009. *The Missionary Self-Perception of Pentecostal/Charismatic Church Leaders from the Global South in Europe: Bringing Back the Gospel*. Leiden: Brill.

Wallace, Jennifer. 2006. *Free to Serve: God's Liberated Woman*. Maitland, FL: Xulon.

———. 2008. *Designed for Purpose: Woman, Fearfully and Wonderfully Made*. London: NOBRICH.

Wanner, Catherine. 2007. *Communities of the Converted: Ukrainians and Global Evangelism*. Ithaca: Cornell University Press.

Zigon, Jarett. 2010. "Moral and Ethical Assemblages: A Response to Fassin and Stoczkowski." *Anthropological Theory* 10 (3): 3–15.

SECTION 2

Language and Embodiment

4

Affect

Intensities and Energies in the Charismatic Language,
Embodiment, and Genre of a North American Movement

JON BIALECKI

This is an essay about a talk presented at a conference that was very
rigorous, scholastic, and engaging but also offered, according to the program, "a time of worship, prayer, and prophetic ministry" after the first
plenary speaker. It was an academic conference that was sponsored by
the Vineyard, a fast-growing, neo-charismatic denomination that has
been influential not just in North American charismatic Christianity,
but globally as well. I want to discuss this not because the idea of charismatic scholarship is so odd that it necessitates being documented as
an anthropological curio; it is not. I mention this rather because the
juxtaposition between papers and passion implicit in this meeting tells
us something *interesting* about the twin topics of language and embodiment, issues that have been central in discussions in the anthropology
of Christianity. Juxtaposing religious language and embodiment with
an academically derived performance that takes its form (though not
its content) from the secular allows us to see not only what is distinctive about all these categories, but also how they are strung together by
a phenomenon that we will call *affect*. Intensities of affect, I will argue,
animate these forms and also in part drive the shuttling between them,
serving as a thread that runs through the secular and the religious, the
linguistic and the embodied. While we will see that affect is in no way
the exclusive reserve of Pentecostal/charismatic Christianity, we will also
see that there is something about the way that Pentecostal/charismatic
Christianity works with themes of control, spontaneity, and intimacy
(Csordas 1994) that makes this kind of religiosity a very good place to
think through the dynamic aspects of the affective (see also Pfiel 2011;

O'Neill 2013). In short, though affect is a universal category, affect's work has a centrality in Pentecostal and charismatic Christianity that allows the particular features of both affect and enthusiastic Christianity to come into relief.

Language, Body, Affect

Discussions of Christian language tend to be centered on how Christianity—particularly Protestant Christianity—makes a virtue of sincerity and spontaneity in speech. As opposed to other forms of religious language, in which using special, formulaic language indicates the divine alterity of what one is discussing (or whom one is addressing), properly Protestant speech is often understood as a transparent expression to an all-knowing yet personally invested God (Keane 2007; see also Bialecki and Hoenes del Pinal 2011). While there are some who see Pentecostal and charismatic speech as following essentially the same logic as Protestant Christianity, and while it is also true that Pentecostals and charismatics are often as suspicious of formally marked ritual as their Protestant brethren, it has been suggested that in this form of religiosity there are different aspects of language that become prized. For Pentecostals and charismatics, there are two aspects of ethically valued language that seem worth noting. First, there is a sensuous aspect of language, where it is circulated and treated as an almost material thing; exposure to certain words and discourses by pastors "build up" in the listener, like a physical accretion (Coleman 2006). Second, there are moments where it is not language's origins in an interior self that is valued, but rather the supernatural inspiration that animates language-acts like prophecy and tongues. Hence it is not always the aspect of language that is "sincere," in that it is self-motivated and transparent, that is emphasized, but moments of speech that a person may not create, control, or even understand (Bialecki 2011). These twin (but not unrelated) tendencies in Pentecostal/charismatic language at once point to the body, in the physical paroxysms that often (but not always) accompany it, yet also point to a beyond of the body, as it is the body's contact with incorporeal divine forces that is the source of both the paroxysms and the language.

It is these paroxysms that bring us back to embodiment, that other topic that has been so important in the anthropology of Pentecostal and charismatic Christianity. Again and again, for the same reasons that the sensuous aspect of its language has been stressed, it has been argued that bodily experience and action are central to Pentecostal/charismatic religiosity (Brahinksy 2012; Csordas 1994; Luhrmann 2004;). For these anthropologists, much as having to speak in a Protestant- or Pentecostal-endorsed way creates a certain kind of person, having certain kinds of bodily experiences as a believer (raising arms to worship, falling down when slain in the spirit, or having hands laid on her as her co-believers pray for healing) creates a certain kind of charismatic person as well.

The similarity between these interests in embodied and linguistic effects on subjectivity suggests that some kind of immediacy-foregrounding melding of the linguistic and the embodied is at the core of Pentecostal/charismatic Christianity. Natural enough as that might seem, there is a problem with that hypothesis. Put simply, there are moments where we have one without the other, where bodies and the sensations they garner are at work, but nothing is being spoken, or where language can circulate on its own, in the form of books, pamphlets, or signs, without any body being present. Even this observation doesn't quite get it right, of course; silence or physical gestures can communicate as well as words at times, and while you can have language sundered temporarily from bodies, there is a body that authors the text initially, and if that text ever finds an audience, that audience most likely will have bodies as well.

In this chapter, I'd like to suggest that the way to imagine the relation between embodiment and language in Pentecostal/charismatic Christianity is to think in terms of affect. Here, we will think of affect as the intensities and energies found in a particular moment or object that has consequences on others that it is in contact with in that moment. Affect would be defined as the preconscious movements and stillness of the body, the quickenings and slowings, the twitches and pauses, that others respond to often without even being aware of it (Massumi 2002). Affect, when it becomes consciously elaborated, is often called emotion, though speaking about emotion *as* affect is a mistake. It is better to think of emotion as that which follows affect once the moment is gone, and the "affected" person finally becomes aware of the experience, framing it discursively. By the time that this has arrived, the contagious nature of affect is to a degree spent; rather than a force quickly moving from person to person, it is now arrested, "owned" by the person "feeling" the emotion.

This harkening back to emotion might seem to bring us back to the body, and would seem to be vulnerable to the same complaint presented above regarding semiosis, except for the fact that language itself can be thought of as having at times captured a kind of affect as well: think of the prosody of written language, the rhythm, stress, and sound that it carries with it as a kind of acoustic shadow of the written form. Languages, both spoken and written, have their own speed and meter that parallel that of the body, and can work on those who are exposed to it. And affect—in the body, in speech, or in writing—begets affect in turn as a response (it is for this reason that affect has also been an important part of discussions of Pentecostal and charismatic music—see Oosterbaan, this volume).[1] Think of the way that two excited people can start to mirror each other in speed and enthusiasm, or alternatively, the way that a person can withdraw when confronted with an energy that seems off-putting or misplaced. By focusing on affect as a thread that runs through multiple bodies and between different kinds of language use, we can see how the linguistic and the embodied change and interact with one another, while still allowing bodies to be bodies and language to be language.

Because affects are qualitative states that engender other qualitative states, it would also be a mistake to equate affect entirely with Durkheim's "effervescence" ([1915] 1964). Durkheim's "effervescence" is always "collective," the thrill of people together misrecognizing the social as the religious. Affect has a role in this, but unlike effervescence, affect is present in smaller groups, in one-to-one conversations, and in texts and other media. Effervescence is either present or absent, like a flash flood; affect instead is like the always running murmur of water, or the continual motion of the air.

Empowered Evangelicals

This may give us a way to think about language and embodiment, but we still have some open strands to deal with. How does this help us understand Pentecostal/charismatic Christianity any better, and what in particular can it bring to the conference that we started out this chapter with? To deal with these questions, we need to know a little more about the Vineyard. The Vineyard is a worldwide association of churches that had its origins in Southern California, started in equal parts by people from the counterculture "Jesus People" movement of the sixties and by evangelical intellectuals who were interested in experimenting with more Pentecostal styles of worship that they had come in contact with in part through a greater familiarity with what is sometimes called "global Christianity." While the specific makeup of each church mirrors the communities that it is embedded in, generally Vineyard churches tend to skew white, professional, and educated; during fieldwork, I would regularly come across doctors, engineers, lawyers, and clinical psychologists, though I would come across handymen and construction workers as well. Vineyard believers present themselves as "empowered evangelicals," imagining themselves to be positioned in what they see as the tension-filled space between Pentecostalism and evangelicalism.

The Vineyard is generally reputed for two intertwined but distinguishable things: its style of worship and an intense dedication to the concept and practice of supernatural, Pentecostal-style gifts. The Vineyard was one of the first groups to pioneer a mode of emotionally intense worship set to a backdrop of popular music–derived, chorus- and hook-heavy catchy "praise songs" performed by rock band–like ensembles. While worship is going on, it is not uncommon to see people lifting their hands up over their heads, falling to their knees, crying, or otherwise seemingly taken away in the moment. Through classes, workshops, church conferences, video material, and books, the Vineyard has also been noted for its championing of the supernatural gifts that is common in much of global Pentecostalism, but relatively rare in the United States; it is not at all uncommon to hear Vineyard believers talking about supernatural healing, receiving prophecy from the Holy Spirit, or expelling a demon from someone (and even on very rare occasions to talk about trying to raise the dead). These two things, worship and gifts, are related because the former is often the setting of and catalyst for the latter; while prayer or revelation can occur anywhere, it most often occurs in church or conference settings, as the worship music plays.

Those conferences, intended primarily to train church leaders and provide peak experiences for lay members, are unlike the Vineyard *academic* conference that this chapter opened with. This conference was intended primarily for Vineyard believers and fellow travelers who also happen to (or aspired to) be academics, who wish to have an arena where they can present their scholarly work as it reflects on the movement and build a scholarly community. This was not a closed shop by any means, but it was a project that was very much supposed to be as much *for* the Vineyard and its members as *about* the Vineyard. This was signaled in several ways. The first was location. By not having the conference housed at an academic institution, but rather at a Vineyard church in suburban Seattle, it suggested that it was intended for the supporting (and housing) movement, rather than a broader academic world that it would have been embedded in had it chosen a campus site. The second signpost that this was an academic conference intended to build up the Vineyard was the attendance and paper-presentation policy. Attendance at the conference was open to anyone, and while the talks presented had to be vetted in advance by the steering committee (the usual procedure for academic conferences), it allowed presentations by individuals with a variety of qualifications, ranging from Ivy League professors to "bi-vocational" or part-time pastors. Paper topics ranged from the expected (theological essays, denomination and religious history, and both academic Christian commentaries on secular culture and critical reflections on the church) to surprising (biological science was particularly well respected, from a discussion of vaccines as a religious good to Christian critiques of intelligent design).

Delivered either by practicing academics or by those eager to engage in academic discussions, most talks at the Vineyard Scholars Conference held themselves up to the standards associated with the sort of speech and embodiment associated with professionals who engage in intellectual labor; that is, a certain kind of de-emphasis of the body that produces and performs this labor, and a kind of objectification of what is produced as a discourse that has a kind of abstract reality apart from the conditions of its production, performance, and circulation. Hence, it was often a space where a kind of carefully parsed language, a restrained use of a limited range of gestures, and a "calm" affective demeanor was what both speakers and audience members presented and expected (Boyer 2005), the kind of academic performance that in some ways tries to trace the subdued cadences and energy often found in academic writing. The future for many of the papers presented, after all, was some kind of further distribution, such as publication in theological journals or as parts of books. In these forms the papers presented would have to live on without their authors being present. But because this was also a space where the building of a sense of community around and for the Vineyard was the goal, and because there was a hope that this conference in some way was animated by and at the same moment serving God, this was not the only mode of speech or embodiment that could be found. Recognizably Christian modes of speech, and most importantly recognizably *charismatic* ones, as well as the invocation of those particular forms of embodiment, are thought to be the best indication of the presence of, and therefore the endorsement by, the Holy Spirit. This conference would be, therefore, an admixture of different types of language and different forms of embodiment.

"From Below, and from Above"

And it is here that we can see how multiple genres of speech and various regimes of embodiment are threaded through by qualitatively different affective states; we can see how two different modes of religious language—an evangelical Protestant sincerity and a Pentecostal ecstatic state—operate when they have to share space with another secular form, that of formal academic language. As our example, let's take a keynote talk presented on Thursday night. The speaker was a thin, grey-templed middle-aged man in a blue crew-neck sweater and wire-rim glasses. He had a quiet, academic, almost bookish aura to him, a fitting look for a doctor of theology from a respected French seminary who has gone on to author several books and articles. These academic *bona fides*, though, run against other aspects of his life: he also heads a church that has multiple ministries to groups such as gang members and economic refugees from Latin America, and serves as a part-time prison chaplain as well. Given that range of interests, the title of the talk ("Scholarship, the Holy Spirit, and the Poor: An Exhortation") perhaps wasn't that unexpected. His opening lines might be a little more surprising than the title; he started by hesitantly speaking into the mike the following words: "I guess I want to start out by just sharing a simple sentence I got when I was praying, Jesus, what do you want to tell this group of people?"

While those words are accompanied by a very slight head bob that gives it a beat of emphasis, they are said in a rather conversational tone, though there is an element of nervousness to it as well; after a momentary interruption (the space-filling "and, um" that serves as a syncopated diegetic pause in the narrative flow), the language changes, and a smile flashes on the speaker's face for just a second as he says that he "might as well start out with what, what I heard." At that second "what," his hands go up to just below ear level, quivering slightly for a beat; this is the first time that his hands have left his side since he's walked up to the podium. His eyes then fall to the pages on the podium he is speaking from, and his speech slows just a bit as he segues to reading the following lines: "I'm calling you and scholars of spirit and truth to pursue me with passion for the Kingdom of God is ours, it is within, among you." He only looks up three times while reading this sentence, at "truth," at "passion," and at "among you"; without looking up, he bobs his head hard at the first "you," at "Kingdom," at "ours," and at "within" as well. All these movements serve not only to emphasize the *content* of these words, but also to give a certain *velocity* to the reading, a sense of acceleration, as the ratio of head bobs to upward glances leans toward the former without breaking the rhythm of the latter. It is when he raises his head a third time without speaking, only to look down again and give one more "um," that the moment of what might be considered prophetic speech is over. His head bobs again slightly. Looking straight out to the audience after that brief but momentum-breaking pause, he states, "I've been about, um, pursuing the Kingdom of God, um, for a long time in my life." He then starts to recount his childhood, growing up evangelical, attending a private Christian school up until seventh grade, becoming disaffected at age thirteen when he switched to a public school, was "excluded" by the "Christian kids," and was "embraced" by the "dope smoking, partying rock and roll people." At this point he is speaking at a rolling, steady rate with scattered starts and stops, not the hesitant measured speech of the first moment, but not the constantly accelerating speech of the read divine message.

This all takes place in about a minute, but in that minute we have three shifts in what we might call genre, and two shifts in what we might call "stance," or the speaker's relation to the language (Shoaps 2002); from academic to inspired to evangelical, from extemporaneous speech to reading aloud, and back again. His first line is a sort of meta-commentary, saying what he will be doing and not doing in the talk, and while this is a common way to begin many performances, the closed-down body language and the context of a plenary talk make it seem at first like the starting moment of many academic papers. The shift in both genre and medium (and the first flash of what might be called either enthusiasm or an excess of nervousness) comes when he states that he'll be reading what he heard during prayer. For just an instant, he goes to a Pentecostal-style prophetic genre, and he is distanced from the words twice over, in that they are sourced not to him, but what he "heard" from Jesus, and in that they are read, not spontaneously uttered, therefore originating not then, but at a previous moment in time. Afterwards it goes to an autobiographical account, a familiar narrative of distancing oneself from faith and then finding it again during a course of spiritual development; this is an account of witnessing, of the speaker putting forward her life story to encourage others to change their own, a common Protestant and Pentecostal/charismatic mode of speech.

Given all these shifts, one might expect that aesthetically the talk would come across as rough or unsteady, but it does not. What keeps this talk from falling apart despite these hairline fractures is the building *rush of energy* as he speaks, an energy not specific to only his body movements, the interjective "ums," or the broader cadence of his spoken language, but also in the brief portion of the talk that is read, as shown both by this performance of it and in the meter of the written words themselves. This is not an unrestrained energy, not the exuberance that might be associated with the caricature of a television pastor, but one that is pressing all the same for being comparatively understated. This waxing and waning energy is what we are calling affect, and in transmitting subtle levels and kinds of enthusiasm it does as much work as anything else during this talk.

Of course, this is just the plenary's first moments; for about forty minutes or so, the speaker goes on to discuss his experiences as left-leaning, liberation theology–influenced missionary in the civil war–torn Guatemala of the 1980s, and to narrate his choice to get his doctorate from a French seminary so as to not be further enmeshed in what he presents as an imperialist United States; all this leaves him positioned as the kind of socially active, politically progressive Christian who would be skeptical of charismatic Christianity, thinking of it as a political sop for the disenfranchised. At the turning point of the talk he recounts how he was convinced by his then recently converted brother to explore the intense, Vineyard style of worship and charismatic gifts, and how he managed to do this in a way that left him feeling that it was not at odds with his abiding interest in a reading of the Gospel oriented toward the poor and marginalized, but in fact seemed to ratify those interests. He then brings the talk to its final point; based on a reading of John 1, of Christ as light, he claims that one of the most sizable challenges to an academic program like the one being put forward by the Society of Vineyard Scholars is the danger of getting caught up in "the enlightenment," used here as a stand-in for a kind of academically informed rationalism. There is a place for such light, but we much not mistake the "light of the Enlightenment" for the more hidden "light of Christ," that we not let intellectual light, which is the product of privilege, be a source of authority in contrast to the Gospel, an enlightenment that is available to all, and therefore legitimately democratic and empowering.

This of course marks another genre change, from witnessing, to again reading aloud, to a kind of homiletic speech, a didactic moment meant more to inform by instruction than by the example (as in witnessing). Just as soon as this is brought up, there is another lurch, a move to prayer. Like the opening message from Jesus, this is ex-centric, no longer a closed economy where the speaker addresses the audience, but one where God is breaking in to influence the unfolding of the speech act. "I just wanna, I want to to, I want to stop right now," he says, making a decisive downward chop with his right hand, "and just pray a prayer regarding this, because I feel like, um, God really wants to call us to be especially tuned, attuned to the light of Jesus, the true light of Christ, this humble, subtle, yet very powerful light, and not, not be distracted by the artificial. Let's pray." Gently, he starts rocking from side to side as he says this, only to close his eyes and with another hand chop constrict (for a spell) his body movements. In this gesture, combined with the sudden small bubbling hesitancies that can be found in the sentence, there is a yearning to go just a shade faster than the speed at which the language is produced, a sharp contrast to the relatively fluid prayer that follows, where he asks that those present be able to discern Jesus's light from the false light of the ruler of this world.

That prayer ends with this phrase:

I just bind right now, in the name of Jesus, the spirit of false enlightenment, the spirit of Lucifer, I bind it, and I, um, release in Jesus's name um just that um more of the light of Jesus, that of revelation, that it would come into, come into, come into our heart, into our minds, and that we'd be able to see, and to believe, and to receive, in Jesus's name.

A moment back to the homiletic based on the prayer (that authority is a gift of God), and then he states how he gets to see many people receive the Holy Spirit for the first time, but he feels that those present may need a refresher, and as he says so the speech starts interrupting itself in the same way, becoming almost a stammer. The speaker asks everyone to stand, and chords of music from the worship band are swelling by the time the speaker gets to his final phrase, a prayer request for more hunger for wisdom and fire from the spirit that would lead to a revolution "from below" and, after a pause, "from above."

Here is the moment when we can see affect working not just through one speaker's use of multiple forms of language and modes of embodiment, but between different speakers, through different actors. The music continues to climb, and people gather around the stage for prayer, in groups of two or three as they pray for one another, hands on bodies as those praying struggle to speak above the rising din, and those receiving prayer either kneel down in submission, or stand with arms up so as to receive. A line forms down the center of the church for those who want to be prayed over by the plenary speaker, who one by one is working his way up the line; his motions are larger, less hesitant now, though still traced by a sort of contortionist tension as he wraps his hands around people's heads while he prays for them; the people he prays over have a tendency to fall gently toward the ground, a condition called being "slain in the spirit." Around all this prayer a half circle forms, people searching for prayer or finished giving or receiving it, or simply those who are drawn to this scene but don't feel particularly moved to participate in it at the moment. A few people at times make brief announcements about a "word" that they have received that there is someone out there who has some emotional state, personal problem, or physical disorder that God wants to have prayed for tonight, but it is not always easy to hear these announcements, and people by no means stop engaging in prayer while these announcements are made.

Now, this is a moment recognizably different from the talk that preceded it, and I doubt that anyone present would have any difficulty identifying a moment of shift from central speaker to a series of decentralized hubs of prayer for renewal and physical and spiritual healing. With this opening up of activity, we have a multiplication of bodies, all of which now work not the register of small tics and gesture-like motions, but of larger arcs and big movements, and more intense trembling; with the din inevitably caused by the scene-setting music and multiple simultaneous speakers, we have language reduced mostly to its sonorous quality, where hearing what is said is at times a struggle. But this break is not total. Its tone was first set by the plenary talk, and it is as if people's own affects were liberated by and in resonance with that of the speaker.

Conclusion

Later on this evening, as the energy is spent and people's attention turns, people will fall back to more day-to-day modes of comportment, and no one will be unable tomorrow to give what are recognizably academic papers, with a more muted affective range, one that did not buckle like the evening's plenary talk did. And not everyone was swept away; as this particular worship period continued, for instance, I sat in the back, trying to have a conversation with a Vineyard veteran. But that is the point: that these affects build and fade, working up in intensities that are then usually dissipated. But not always. Much as the affective work done by body and speech in the plenary releases a larger wave of affect in the audience, there are instances when the energy liberated is greater than that which is exhausted; and in these moments, if there are channels through which that energy can be channeled, further transactions can be wrung from it. That this didn't happen that night is perhaps because many people were tired from travel, or nervous about papers that they would have to give the next day; or rather, that energy changed forms, a night's prayer used as the restorative to allow one to give a paper the next day. But the fact that this session of prayer happened at an academic conference at all (even if it was a denomination-sponsored one) gives us some interesting anthropological information; this kind of ecstatic religiosity cannot be reduced to ignorance, not in a crowd like this. Nor can it be seen as necessarily captive to any one political position. Vineyard members cover the political spectrum and are not all as left-leaning as this particular speaker, but there are a considerable number who would to substantial degrees agree with him.

This is important, I want to suggest, because it is not necessarily political position or sociocultural capital that is the engine of Pentecostal/charismatic Christianity; rather, I would argue it is this affective energy that often seems to stand at the center of the quickly moving, quickly changing religion. Indeed, as we can see from the common response to a particular political position, affect works to bridge divides in Pentecostal and charismatic Christianity (evidence also suggests that in other moments affect can work to bridge divides of class or race within Pentecostal/charismatic Christianity as well; see Bialecki 2010). We could look at this evening as a series of shifts from types of language and forms of embodiment that are about endorsement of personal and collective identity (the autobiographical witnessing, the homiletic portions of the speech) and portions in which identity is disrupted by words whose origins are elsewhere, where embodiment suggests a lack of control in the frenzy of the gestures, such as falling to the floor or throwing one's arms up as a display of openness. These are moments when Vineyard believers would say that the spirit is present; but they are also the moments when the affective energy built up seems to spill over, flowing from one person to another. Affect is not particular to either Pentecostal/charismatic Christianity or religion in general; in the sense that we've been speaking about it here, it is a category common to all humanity. However, Pentecostal/charismatic Christianity has been particularly successful in using heightened levels of affect to switch from identitarian to ex-centric, open modes of being. It is this pulsation-like dilation toward an openness that is used to expand, reinvigorate, and reconfigure individual and collective identities that the philosopher Henri Bergson ([1932] 1935) saw as being the primary work of religion. This may be going too far—but it may be true that Bergson's hypothesis tells us what it is that Pentecostal/charismatic religion does, and if that is true, then it seems that affect, running like a thread through Pentecostal/charismatic language and embodiment, is an important element in how it is done.

NOTE

1. To this extent, the approach taken here (seeing affect as present in texts and artifacts, even when they are not being animated by human actors) is a broader

reading of affect as a force that acts on other objects that have a capacity to be affected (Deleuze 1990), in contrast to accounts that would see it as limited to merely an aspect of subjectivity (compare Stewart 2007).

REFERENCES

Bergson, Henri. (1932) 1935. The Two Sources of Morality and Religion. London: Macmillan.

Bialecki, Jon. 2010. "Angels and Grass: Church, Revival, and the Neo-Pauline Turn." South Atlantic Quarterly 109 (4): 695–717.

———. 2011. "No Caller ID for the Soul: Demonization, Charisms, and the Unstable Subject of Protestant Language Ideology." Anthropological Quarterly 84 (3): 659–84.

Bialecki, Jon, and Eric Hoenes del Pinal. 2011. Introduction to "Beyond Logos: Extensions of the Language Ideology Paradigm in the Study of Global Christianity(-ies)." Special issue, Anthropological Quarterly 84 (3): 575–94.

Boyer, Dominic. 2005. "The Corporeality of Expertise." Ethnos 70 (2): 243–66.

Brahinksy, Josh. 2012. "Pentecostal Body Logics: Cultivating a Modern Sensorium." Cultural Anthropology 27 (2): 215–38.

Coleman, Simon. 2006. "Materializing the Self: Words and Gifts in the Construction of Charismatic Protestant Identity." In The Anthropology of Christianity, edited by Fenella Cannell, 163–84. Durham: Duke University Press.

Csordas, Thomas. 1994. The Sacred Self: A Cultural Phenomenology of Charismatic Healing. Berkeley: University of California Press.

Deleuze, Gilles. (1968) 1990. Expressionism in Philosophy: Spinoza. New York: Zone Books.

Durkheim, Émile. (1915) 1964. The Elementary Forms of Religious Life. London: Allen and Unwin.

Keane, Webb. 2007. Christian Moderns: Freedom and Fetish in the Mission Encounter. Berkeley: University of California Press.

Luhrmann, Tanya M. 2004. "Metakinesis: How God Becomes Intimate in Contemporary U.S. Christianity." American Anthropologist 106 (3): 518–28.

Massumi, Brian. 2002. Parables for the Virtual: Movement, Affect, Sensation. Durham: Duke University Press.

O'Neill, Kevin Lewis. 2013. "Beyond Broken: Affective Spaces and the Study of American Religion." Journal of the American Academy of Religion 81 (4): 1093–1116.

Pfeil, Gretchen. 2011. "Imperfect Vessels: Emotions and Rituals of Anti-Ritual in American Pentecostal and Charismatic Life." In Practicing the Faith: The Ritual Life of Pentecostal-Charismatic Christians, edited by Martin Lindhardt, 220–48. New York: Berghahn.

Shoaps, Robin. 2002. "'Pray Earnestly': The Textual Construction of Personal Involvement in Pentecostal Prayer and Song." Journal of Linguistic Anthropology 12 (1): 34–71.

Stewart, Kathleen. 2007. Ordinary Affects. Durham: Duke University Press.

5

Feminine Habitus

Rhetoric and Rituals of Conversion and Commitment among Contemporary South Korean Evangelical Women

KELLY H. CHONG

Beliefs, rituals, and language of spiritually oriented evangelical/Pentecostal religions have provided women with the unexpected means with which to exert power and influence within many such religious communities, power typically denied to them by these religions' conservative worldviews with regard to gender (Brusco 1995; Davidman 1991; Griffith 1997; Bartkowski 2001; Gilkes 1985; Lawless 1988; McLeod 1992; Stacey 1990). Although this "paradoxical" phenomenon had been observed for charismatically oriented religions in the American historical context, we need to pay attention to the empowering, or even subversive, effects of conservative religions in the contemporary world across different religious and cultural contexts by observing the ways women constitute self-understandings within religious frameworks and reinterpret the meaning of traditionalist rhetoric and rituals (Kaufman 1989; Mahmood 2001).

Focusing on the rhetoric and rituals of conversion and commitment among contemporary South Korean evangelical women, this chapter examines women's engagement with religious patriarchy in the South Korean evangelical setting. I attend especially to the ways women become constituted as new feminine subjects through the development of a new evangelical habitus, one that is constituted by new dispositions, both embodied and linguistic, and is developed through ritualized rhetorical, bodily, and spiritual practices (Csordas 1997; Harding 2000; Lindhardt 2011; Shoaps 2002; Keane 1997). My main argument is that in the Korean evangelical context, the classic tension between empowerment and submission, or agency and discipline, which is inherent in charismatically oriented religions, is resolved mainly in favor of the latter tendency, resulting in women's reintegration into the structures of social and religious patriarchy. This occurs even while the women actively appropriate the spirituality and charismatic connection to the divine for internal empowerment and resistance to patriarchal oppression. In the following sections, we will see in particular how Korean evangelical women, through the specific deployment and interpretation of evangelical languages of conversion and commitment, such as "sin," "surrender," "obedience," and "dying to self," construct their new evangelical feminine habitus.

Korean Evangelicalism, Women, and Charisma

Evangelical Protestantism first entered Korea in the late 1880s by way of American (particularly Presbyterian and Methodist) and European missionaries. In the narratives of how evangelical Protestantism has developed and flourished in Korea (Clark 1986; J. Kim 1996; T. Lee 2010; Suh 1982), one part of the story often goes underanalyzed: the way the Pentecostal/charismatic dimensions in Korean evangelicalism have been a significant part of the character of South Korean evangelicalism from its inception, and the role of women within the religion.

One of the origins of the charismatic dimensions of Korean evangelical beliefs and practices is the revivalistic orientations of earlier Western missionaries who sought to spread Christianity in Korea through spiritual awakenings. Developing in a syncretic relationship with native shamanistic beliefs and practices that have enabled Koreans to approach and appropriate Christianity in a particular manner, evangelical revivals in Korea have been from the inception characterized by a number of charismatic, Pentecostal-type features. These features, which include the baptism of the Holy Spirit, healings, miracles, fervent prayers, even exorcisms, have become an enduring part of the Korean evangelical tradition (J. Lee 1986, 169; Ryu 1982; Suh 1982; Yoo 1988).

In South Korea, however, the "experience-centered" evangelical traditions have coexisted uneasily with the more "rational"/"book-centered" mainstream conservative traditions because of the latter's suspicion of Pentecostal/charismatic movements from the early days.[1] Such suspicion has been accompanied by ongoing attempts by the Protestant establish-

ment to circumscribe Pentecostal practice and influence. The Pente-
costal/charismatic character of Korean evangelicalism, however, can no
longer be ignored because it has, since the 1970s, become an increasingly visible and accepted part of the Korean evangelical establishment,
due in large part to the phenomenal success of the Pentecostal Yoido
Full Gospel Church since the 1960s, one of the world's largest megachurches (Martin 1990, 146; Park 1993). Although the more Pentecostal
forms of charismatic expressions, such as glossolalia and exorcisms, are
practiced officially in a minority of churches, most of the churches in
South Korea—regardless of denominational affiliation—now incorporate some degree of Pentecostal/charismatic practices and beliefs into
their theology and ministry.

In South Korea, a common observation is that charismatic forms of
worship are more "feminine" and that they are embraced more enthusi-
astically by women than men. Part of this has to do with the purported
influence of Korean shamanism (a native religion based on the belief in
and worship of spirits and spirit possession that has evolved into a family cult monopolized by women) on the practices, beliefs, and style of
Korean Christianity, especially the acceptance of supernatural miracles,
healings, and exorcisms, as well as an "earthly blessing–focused" belief
system (*gibok sinhang*) (T. Lee 2010). Although this kind of gender connection is difficult to establish, what *is* clear is that in Korean evangelicalism, women, despite their unquestionably subordinate status within
the churches, have always been the most enthusiastic and devoted members, whose spiritual zeal has served as the driving force behind Protestantism's spectacular success.

In what follows, I describe some of the key disciplinary technologies deployed by the Korean churches—especially as observed in discursive, linguistic, and rhetorical practices of cell meetings—to facilitate
women members' development of new sacred feminine subjectivities. I
argue that a major motivation behind the female members' ardent participation in the evangelical church and the passionate nature of their
religiosity is an effort to cope with difficult domestic situations generated by the tensions within the contemporary Korean patriarchal family and gender system. Evangelical church involvement in many cases
represents a conscious attempt by the women to seek personal healing
and find viable ways to resolve their domestic situations. In this chap-

ter, I focus on both the discursive and spiritual processes by which the boundary-transgressing powers of the feminine are re-domesticated and proper Confucian-evangelical feminine subjectivities reconstituted in cell meetings.[2]

The observations and analyses presented in this chapter are based largely on ethnographic data and interviews gathered from a study of two large, middle-class evangelical churches in Seoul—one Presbyterian and the other Methodist (the two largest denominations in South Korea)—but incorporate my observations and studies of more than twenty evangelical churches in Seoul.[3] As I make clearer in the following pages, although South Korean evangelical churches are by no means monolithic in their beliefs, the ideologies of gender and family espoused by the vast majority of the churches and the patriarchally oriented institutional culture of these churches are, even across denominational lines, remarkably similar, as are their predominantly middle-class characteristics. Thus, although this study does not make claims of generalizability to all Protestant churches in South Korea, the study's findings do reflect an important set of core dimensions of middle-class women's experiences and encounters with evangelicalism and patriarchy in South Korea.

Cell Meetings and Quests for Healing

Although cell group–type gatherings exist in almost all societies, including the United States (see also Elisha, this volume), cell meetings have become particularly well developed and central to the organizational functioning of almost all Korean Protestant churches. A typical cell meeting in Korea, which is commonly gender-segregated, consists of about five to ten members, is held on a rotating basis once a week in the members' homes, and consists of a short Bible study session followed by a period of extended fellowship among the participants. One of the reasons that cell groups have become so central to the churches in South Korea is that they provide, especially in large churches, a venue for all-important small-group interaction, functioning as a kind of surrogate family for the members. Cell groups also serve a critical function as units for evangelization, mutual help, collective socialization, and monitoring, and represent the wider authority of the church. For female members, cell groups are one of the most important spaces for intimate fellowship within the church where private problems could be shared; they are also an important arena for autonomous female social interaction and locus of women's social lives.

One of the most notable aspects to emerge from the cell meetings I attended was the strikingly similar nature of women's personal problems. The middle-class women that I investigated were women in contemporary South Korean society who were subject to a distinctive set of domestic and gender-related dilemmas particular to the current historical moment in South Korea. These dilemmas were rooted in a sharp disjunction between the changing status and horizons of women and the powerful norms of the modern, neoconservative family and social structure that continue to uphold a number of central patriarchal principles and demands upon married women. These tensions have been particularly intense for well-educated, middle-class women, the major beneficiaries of the rapid rise in women's education and changes in the structure of the family (Cho 1986, 2002; Kendall 2002, 1996; Lett 1998; Nelson 2000).[4]

The problems described by women commonly focused on a few central themes: intense conflicts with patriarchal husbands, struggles with oppressive mothers-in-law, and the difficult burdens of housework and family caretaking in a society where the burdens of caring for kin still fall squarely on the shoulders of women (due to the inadequacy of the social welfare system). Furthermore, the traditional responsibilities of housework and mothering have been intensified by modern forms of "status production" work in an education/status-obsessed, economically hypercompetitive society (Papanek 1979).[5] For the majority of the women, experiences of intense domestic suffering or crises constituted the overriding motivation for church attendance and/or conversion, especially when attempts at other solutions, such as psychotherapy or shamanistic intervention, failed (cf. Burdick 1993).

Cell groups are thus first and foremost a kind of therapeutic community where women, through participation in ongoing ritual practices, sought healing for emotional injuries and a new empowered sense of self by cultivating a new relationship with the sacred.[6] Through the discursive "reframing" that situates women's plight in a God-centered framework, women also develop the appropriate religious habitus and dispositions necessary for attaining healing and domestic resolutions. In what follows, I analyze three specific ritual practices by which this often contradictory process is pursued in the cell meeting setting, focusing on the rhetorical aspects of the disciplinary practices embedded in the conversion process: the rituals of confession, surrender, and self-criticism.

Confessional Practices

As Michel Foucault (1988) correctly observes, Christianity is not only a salvation religion, it's a confessional religion. This means that Christianity does more than demand strict adherence to and acceptance of truth and dogma, but requires that one unceasingly demonstrate one's belief of these truths. But according to Foucault, Christianity demands yet another form of truth obligation: "each person has the duty to know who he is, that is, to try to know what is happening inside him, acknowledge faults, to recognize temptations, to locate desires; and everyone is obliged to disclose these thing either to God or to others in the community and hence to bear public or private witness against oneself" (1988, 40).

The first step in the conversion and the healing process in the cell meeting context begins with a ritual activity that is aimed at one central outcome: confession and self-revelation.[7] Every cell meeting opens with a Bible study session structured around a discrete topic from the Bible, and the cell leaders lead the group members to explicate its significance and meaning. But as the lesson progresses and the leader encourages the members to relate the topic to concrete events in their lives, the Bible study and the fellowship period that ensues are often transformed into an event of intimate sharing, opening the way for collective revelations and confessions.

In one meeting focusing on the topic of sin, for instance, the cell leader asked the group about the kinds of "habitual sins" the women find themselves committing in their everyday lives. After a heart-wrenching recounting of long-standing marital difficulties, one woman confessed, "I find that the most habitual sin I commit is to my husband. Out of frustration, I say things to hurt him all the time, so I repent this, and I vow every week that I will make sincere attempts to treat him with humbleness and obedience. But this doesn't last the week. So I keep repenting." Another woman offered woeful tales of her own troubled marriage and spoke of the "sinful" behavioral traits she developed toward her husband and to the world at large, which she described as the habitual sins of "negative attitudes," and the habit of "complaining about everything, being critical of everything, cutting people down."

In another meeting in which the main topic was the importance of intercessory prayers, the discussion on the need for praying for others generated many revelations about domestic difficulties. Describing prayers as a "spiritual battle," the cell leader spoke especially about the need to engage in sincere intercessory prayers as a way to overcome one's own hatred of one's "tormentors" in life, because praying for those individuals was the only way one can come to empathize with their pain, the first step toward forgiveness. Giving the example of her own lifelong marital conflicts with a difficult husband, whom she considered her main "tormentor," she nonetheless tried to understand whether her husband's own unhappiness was due in large part to his "misfortune" of having married her. She reiterated that the only way she can have the strength to deal with the cruelties of life was to be "seized" by God and to be obedient to him. Regardless of what kind of solution was proffered, what was evident was that the heartfelt confessions and self-revelations fostered in these meetings provide for the members an avenue for tremendous cathartic release and a sense of consolation from their domestic troubles. As an act of "opening up" of the inner self to God, and releasing of inner pain and suffering, this process often functioned as the first step in the conversion process.

During the meetings, cell leaders also fostered spiritual openness among the women by encouraging the practice of fervent prayer. Constant and impassioned prayer is seen as one of the most important means of deepening one's faith and fostering intense, experiential faith that would promote a powerfully close, emotional connection to God. The importance of such prayer in Korean evangelicalism is attested to by a remark by the pastor:

> A God's church is, first and foremost, a church that prays. You must pray without rest, pray without rest, as God commanded. . . . You will feel cold in your heart if you don't fervently pray. Accepting God into yourselves is not just calling out "Jesus" when you need help. You must always be ready, spiritually, to meet him, through constant prayer. . . . You must pray at

dawn, pray before meetings, pray all the time. You must pray whether there are others around or not. . . . Some people when they pray, words pour out like silk. . . . There is nothing outside prayer. It's the most important thing and the thing that'll make our church grow.

In line with such an approach, fervent praying, a ritual that is both linguistic and embodied, is consistently encouraged and promoted in the cell meetings as a way to experience the divine, especially the Holy Spirit, which would lead to a deepening of the women's spirituality, openness to God, and eventually to healing. Prayers in these meetings thus usually take the form of loud, highly emotional prayers in which the members are encouraged to make heartfelt confessions, again attesting to the centrality of language and articulation in the process of self-transformation. The role of the leader in these settings is not only to help guide the members toward a cognitive reinterpretation of their situations within the framework of the evangelical worldview, but also to aid them in learning the proper rhetorical techniques and methods with which to carry out such prayers, that is, teach them *how* to pray.

Ritual of Surrender

As women collectively and individually achieve greater spiritual openness to God and with each other, the next crucial step in the healing and conversion process is what I refer to as the ritual of surrender. In the evangelical view, the act of "surrender" is regarded as a crucial turning point in the conversion process; surrendering is considered a prelude to genuine commitment, a point at which a person, after admitting that she is a lost sinner, delivers herself up to Christ as savior, becoming "born again." For the women I studied, the ritual of complete and unconditional surrendering to the divine power has a particular significance in the healing process, most centrally as a paradoxical instrument of self-empowerment.

For the women, this movement toward total surrender begins with an understanding of the concept of sin. In Korean evangelicalism, the concept of sin is comprehended in two very contrasting ways: one, as something caused by an external force, namely, Satan, and two, a result of individual human moral transgressions and failings. Either way, understanding the concept of sin is critical to an overall reconstruction of one's worldview and identity as an evangelical, because it is only by first realizing and admitting one's utter helplessness as a sinner that one can invite God into one's life to be helped and saved.

Echoing the ideas of surrender described in various charismatic and sect-like groups in America (see Gordon 1984; Westley 1977), one of the most notable aspects of the notion of surrender in the Korean evangelical context is its exceptionally pronounced emphasis on the notion of self-abandonment and the total relinquishment of the self and will to divine control, along with unquestioning obedience.[8] The central idea here is that human beings, as helpless and inadequate sinners, are incapable of effecting any changes in their lives through their own ability and will; for any kind of change to occur, there must be a complete reliance on God's power. Only by letting God take control over one's life will one be able to attain peace, happiness, and freedom from the suffering and pain that plague people daily and be able to "go to heaven." As one pastor put it, "Believe in Jesus, surrender everything to God, simply do and obey as he wills, and be free from all your worries and pain."

For women, giving in to "surrender" helps the healing process in several ways. First, it begins to help women heal by enabling them to "unburden" themselves of their problems, which happens when they completely turn over their lives to God. The cell leaders tell the women that they can begin to be helped only by first turning everything over to God, because only this can free them from their suffering. Burdened by an overwhelming sense of domestic responsibility and tormented by conflicts that they feel helpless to solve or control, many women find this message appealing. The notion of total surrender is considered so important that in the Korean evangelical context it even comes to denote an attitude of childlike dependence of human beings on God where everything is "entrusted" to God. As described by one woman, "I think I am beginning to see why people seek God. I am beginning to understand the feeling of, okay, forget it, I'll just trust in God to watch over me and take care of everything, you know, the feeling of being a child throwing a tantrum at God to take care of things. I am beginning to feel like that."

The act of surrendering facilitates the healing process in another way: it serves as an important source of internal *empowerment* for the "helpless" believer, both by cleansing her of destructive emotions and by enabling her to gain a sense of renewed strength in God. In the very act of surrendering, one gains strength from the belief that God has taken charge of one's life and that one can accomplish things with "God's strength." Although Korean evangelicals in general are not likely to articulate this experience as a process of "regaining" self-control, as some other studies of evangelical conversion have found (see Gordon 1984), allowing God to take control seems to imply on the practical level the acquiring of freedom from the former sense of helplessness.

As in other arenas, surrendering, for Korean evangelicals, is generally expected to be a powerful experiential process, occurring particularly through prayer. As an experiential process, surrendering, ideally, is to be felt as both a physical and spiritual process as the Holy Spirit enters one's body; it is only by letting the Holy Spirit enter oneself and take total control that one experiences true "giving up." Indeed, when women recall moments when they have "surrendered" themselves to God, many remember these as key experiential events that are described in physical terms, such as feeling "hot" or having something enter their bodies, and as occasions for bodily healing.

Rituals of Self-Criticism: Egoism, Arrogance, and Impatience

Empowerment, especially through the experience of divine presence and intervention, is a central element in the development of a Pentecostal self. What must also be discussed, however, are the ambivalent and contradictory implications of this empowerment for women in the Korean evangelical context, that is, the ways women's appropriation of divine power, while providing women with the means with which to cope with their situations, also "empowers" women for renewed dedication to domestic service, by helping to channel their newfound powers for the purposes of domestic fulfillment and to reconstitute feminine identities. In this section, I examine the central linguistic and rhetorical technologies deployed by the church by which such "redomestication" of women is achieved in the cell group setting, which I refer to as rituals of self-criticism.

The "ritual of self-criticism" is a regularized practice of collective critique that is an important dimension of cell meetings, designed ultimately to foster the members' receptivity to the church's views on gender by assisting them to arrive at a "proper" understanding of their "wrong-doings" or "sins," especially regarding how these "wrongdoings" contribute to domestic disharmony. In addition to bringing about a group articulation of problems and orienting the members toward the acceptance of divine intervention for resolving these problems, a major part of a cell meeting agenda also consists of concerted efforts to engage the participants in a practice of intensive and repeated self-critique, which would pave the way for the members' acceptance of "correct" domestic solutions.

To effect changes in women's worldview, the churches employ a well-defined set of disciplinary strategies—both rhetorical and spiritual—that are designed to situate women's views within the evangelical interpretative framework and ultimately help them develop a new religious and gender-specific identity and habitus. The evangelical gender identity to be reconstituted, or restored, is one that approximates the traditional Confucian ideals of the virtuous female—the docile, obedient, forbearing, and self-sacrificing woman whose responsibility is first and foremost to her family, but whose deviations from or resistance to these ideals and behavioral norms have supposedly become the primary cause of the problems of the contemporary Korean family.

A central part of the churches' rhetorical strategy for assisting women to recapture the proper feminine identity from which they are seen to have strayed consists first of all in persuading women to recognize and accept their central role in and responsibility for their domestic problems and the need to rectify their wrongdoings. This process of penitence begins with redefining the variety of major and minor female domestic misconduct as terrible "sins" to be eradicated. Aside from disobedience, most of the "sins" to which women are most frequently led to confess and repent for are those thought to directly undermine the fundamental principles of the ideal gender and family order, male/female hierarchy, and proper gender roles, including all the "sins" that the churches view as arising particularly from female "egoism" and "arrogance" and, related to these, selfishness, willfulness, and pride. Women become particularly remorseful about their sins of willfulness, assertiveness, and inability to endure and forgive, which they come to believe are primarily responsible for marital discord and the alienation of husbands.

Another "sin" that is often a special cause of contrition for women is their perceived inability to endure difficulties, or "impatience." Agreeing with the church's diagnosis, women frequently express the belief that suffering in marriage may be inevitable but that it is their inability to endure these trials that is at the source of many domestic problems. The inability to forgive, in particular, is seen as a central source of conflicts. Women are also led to reflect harshly upon emotions of anger, resentment, and bitterness that arise from feelings of pent-up hatred and frustrated desires, feelings that are destructive not only to other family members but also, and most of all, to themselves. As a remedy, women, in one gathering after another, are continually reminded that proper feminine obedience and endurance, as well as the ability to forgive, are the bedrock principles of a social order that must be pursued because it is the first and primary means through which gender and family harmony can be restored.

In my observation, one of the most interesting aspects of the churches' discourse regarding these matters is the oft-repeated declarations about how difficult it is to actually achieve *genuine* internal transformation. According to this discourse, to recognize and repent for one's sins is one thing, but to truly reform one's behavior and thinking and fulfill the proper feminine virtues is quite another. Indeed, many of the committed women I have talked to will often state that proper obedience is not something that can be achieved without a sincere and deeply felt faith in God, especially without the experience of the Holy Spirit. As one woman put it,

> I don't think you can obey completely unless your heart is open with the Holy Spirit. The women who say they can't do this—well, I think it's because they haven't really been "awakened" properly yet. It's hard to go home and try to serve and wait on your husband totally. You must have faith to do this. But with faith, one can succeed in complete submission and obedience.

To help female members attain proper internal transformations, the churches pursue a program of behavioral, psychic, and emotional disciplining that is exceptional for its intensity. For instance, in one of the cell meetings, the task of transforming the self to approximate the virtuous feminine ideal involved attempts not only to change the members' beliefs regarding gender relations, but to thoroughly discipline the internal subjectivities of women by assisting them to repress and if possible eradicate all of the underlying "negative" desires and emotions deemed responsible for defiant or unruly female behavior.

In this effort to discipline and normalize women's subjectivities, the group, for example, consistently deployed the language and rhetorical strategy of the "dying" of self. To "die" to sin is a classic metaphor in evangelical conversion that is considered a prelude to rebirth. In the context of Korean evangelical women, the "dying of self," while referring to the conversion process, also carries another meaning—a process of eradicating the "sins" associated with gender violations, such as arrogance, egoism, or impatience. Dying of self, however, has an even more specific meaning in the context of Korean evangelical women: it refers to a process of more fundamental self-repression, which, involving the "death" of a person's "self" or "ego" (ja-ah), indicates the suppression of all the deep-down desires, emotions, and impulses considered responsible for generating the "sins" in the first place.[9]

Reflecting the influence of this discourse on church members, a number of women I talked to in both churches frequently used the related language of "killing of self" to refer to the repression of feminine desires and impulses, particularly the desire to try to have things one's way, the impulse to assert these desires, and desires or expectations regarding other people. As one cell leader, who had a large plaque with the phrase "I die every day" prominently displayed in her living room, repeatedly advised her members, "One of the things we have to do is to 'kill' (juk-i-da) ourselves every day. We keep coming back alive but that's no good. Every day, we must die with Christ."[10]

One church member, talking about how she learned to handle her domestic situation, confessed, "The most important thing I had to do in my marriage was to learn to 'die.' I had to 'kill' myself. Before, I used to talk back to my husband, get mad or upset, but now, I don't do that anymore. I always try to be happy even though I have difficult problems to contend with."

Indeed, for many, it appears that killing one's ego in such a manner is seen as the only way to be able to obey "properly," and therefore to accomplish the task of transforming others. Another member attested,

"I realized that only by totally 'getting rid' of myself and 'dying,' can I change the other person. If you try to do things by asserting your own temper and personality, it doesn't work. And that's how I deal with my husband, too."

Dying or killing of self, however, is not easy to achieve. Women often struggle mightily with a sense of anger and injustice at having to submit to such an extent of repression and self-denial. Another cell member acknowledged, "Despite all my training in the church, the most difficult thing about the life of faith is not being able to apply everything properly in life, and especially, still having a strong ego/self (*ja-a*)." When it becomes very difficult, it is again to prayer, of course, that women turn to aid them in this inner struggle. One cell member explained, "When I lowered myself before my husband, he softened. But still, you know, there are many times when anger just rises up within me. But I know I have to press down myself/ego. When this starts to happen, I just pray a lot." Although the degree of disciplinary success achieved by the churches is by no means uniform, prayer is, again, the primary vehicle through which women are expected to acquire the strength and inspiration needed to submit properly, that is, a key disciplinary instrument.

Conclusion

In existing literature on religion, the dual, contradictory aspects of religious power—power that has the capacity to both liberate and oppress, injure and heal—have been noted (Appleby 2000; McGuire 1983). While one of the central dimensions and foci of charismatic evangelical and Pentecostal religiosity lies in the pursuit and experience of empowerment through a spiritual encounter with the sacred, the religious engagement of South Korean middle-class evangelical women is a double-edged sword. Although it is a means of profound personal empowerment, healing, and uplift for women, it is, at the same time, a vehicle of women's resubjugation to the family/gender system, accomplished through a powerful reformation of women's consciousness, habitus, and subjectivity, which in turn is achieved through effective deployment of rhetorical and discursive strategies, and which leads to an effective circumscribing of the powers implied in their newfound religiosity.

In Korean evangelicalism, the contradictory operation of religious powers through the beliefs and practices of women is tied closely to a particular development of conflicting religious identities nurtured through evangelical conversion and faith experience. These are, on the one hand, the individually empowered self, generated through a personal, spiritual relationship with God, and on the other, the obedient, virtuous womanhood aimed at bringing about domestic healing and the reharmonization of women's relationship with their families. One major way that this restoration of the "virtuous" Korean feminine subjectivity serves to contain women's powers is, as we have seen, by facilitating the development of an obedient, forbearing, and accommodating feminine self whose willfulness and destabilizing desires will be kept within bounds for the sake of family harmony. That is, the feminine subjectivity centrally nurtured by the church is a role-defined, relational self-identity that ultimately reinforces the definition of a person in relation to the welfare and goals of the family, so that while women appropriate their faiths to seek healing, transcendence, and self-dignity, their domestically oriented self-conceptions and subjectivities also ensure that their powers are effectively suppressed for the goals of individual liberation, preventing the forging of new social power and boundaries by women.

Women's domesticated subjectivities, especially their obedient and dependent self-conceptions, contain implications for controlling and diverting female powers in other ways. For one, women's fundamentally submissive orientation toward authority, especially to male authority, often leads not only to a continued belief in their own fundamental inferiority, but to a belief that their newfound powers, seen as "borrowed" from God, are not their own, and thus cannot be used to assert themselves or their abilities, nor to challenge male authority. Reflecting their firm belief in the necessity of submission to men, women disown their own felt powers; if those powers are exercised, it is only for the purposes of serving others or God and to enable themselves to better obey, endure, and forgive. It is no wonder, then, that what we often find among evangelical women is a deeply conflicting sense of personal power and identity: a sense of an essentially powerless self existing alongside an image of an empowered self, mirroring their domestic self-conceptions as both strong and weak.

Furthermore, the churches' call for the fulfillment of other virtuous feminine qualities, such as self-sacrifice and endurance, also serves greatly to limit the impetus toward the pursuit of new social power and change on the part of women. The ideals of self-sacrifice and endurance, in general and for the family, clearly foster an attitude of forbearance toward difficult circumstances, discouraging active efforts to change the status quo, and effectively delegitimize any goals or actions that are interpreted as being oriented toward personal or individual gain and fulfillment, including seeking of personal freedom and equality. The submissive attitude is also fostered through the nurturing of a highly dependent self that must rely on the will of God, and others in positions of authority, producing a contradictory sense of self that is, while empowered, also devoid of a sense of agency.[11]

Recent studies of women and religious traditionalisms have highlighted the issues of women's agency and the strategic, empowering, or contestatory nature of women's religious engagement. Although these views have successfully challenged the simplistic views of women as "victims" of male domination, and of traditionalist religions as monolithic sources of oppression, the South Korean case helps us to refocus our attention to the more contradictory dimensions of religious power and the critical issue of patriarchal domination and power. While fully acknowledging the empowering, even subversive, possibilities of these believers' encounters with the sacred, in both the spiritual and domestic realms—including the ways women can "reform" or "domesticate" the behavior of men as discussed in other works (see Brusco 1995; Chong 2008; Stacey 1990)—I emphasize in this chapter the regulatory/disciplinary dimensions of women's religious experiences. I point particularly to the women's continued embeddedness in the family/gender regimes of South Korea, which underscores our need for critical engagements with religion that illuminate religion's complex and contradictory roles across different social and religious spaces in the contemporary world, its roles as a source of empowerment and a source of disempowerment and conflict.

NOTES

Some parts of the content of this chapter have appeared in modified form in *Practicing the Faith: The Ritual Life of Pentecostal-Charismatic Christians*, edited by Martin

Lindhardt (New York: Berghahn, 2011), and *Religion on the Edge: De-centering and Re-centering the Sociology of Religion*, edited by Courtney Bender, Wendy Cadge, Peggy Levitt, and David Smilde (New York: Oxford University Press, 2011).

1. See Riesebrodt (1993) and Riesebrodt and Chong (1999) for more details on the typological distinction between "rational" and "charismatic" fundamentalisms. Donald N. Clark (1986, 26) refers to the two main strains of Korean Protestant churches as "conservative and ultra-evangelical," with the latter exemplified, again, by the Yoido Full Gospel Church.

2. Confucianism is a both a political ideology and an ethical and religious code practiced in a patriarchal context, developed by Chinese scholars during the Sung dynasty (960–1279 CE). Although it is difficult to do justice to its complex philosophy, the principles of Confucianism stress a strict hierarchical order of human relationships based on age, sex, and inherited social status.

3. Presbyterians constitute about 73 percent of the Protestant population; Methodists make up about 11 percent of church membership. The women whose narratives are presented in this chapter are mostly married female congregants between the ages of thirty-five and fifty-five. The interviewees for the research also included female church members of varying age groups, a number of men, church leaders, and experts on Korean Christianity.

4. These contradictions, for instance, are evidenced by the acute discrepancy between the level of contemporary Korean women's educational levels and the rate of their labor force participation. South Korea currently has one of the highest educational levels in East Asia, including for women, but compared to neighboring Taiwan and Japan, South Korean women have the lowest rates of formal work participation at every age group. In South Korea, there is also an inverse correlation between the level of education and the rate of labor force participation (Brinton, Lee, and Parish 1995).

5. It is also worth mentioning that unlike what has been reported by some other studies, such as the study by Thomas Csordas (1994, 33), the kinds of problems reported by the two sexes and the kind and frequency of experiences undergone by men and women are highly specific and gendered in South Korea.

6. Although cell meetings fall outside what is typically considered charismatic healing events, and healing in this venue is approached in a collective manner—that is, through a collective access to the divinity through worship rather than through individual quests for divine mediation (see Csordas 1994, 38)—ritual engagements in cell meetings are clearly designed as vehicles for fostering personal as well as ultimately domestic healing.

7. See Omri Elisha's chapter in this volume regarding similar confessional practices observed in an American evangelical men's fellowship setting.

8. This emphasis on absolute or unconditional obedience to God in Korean evangelical churches has been amply documented in a number of studies, even studies on Korean immigrant churches (A. Kim 1996).

9. This theme of "dying" in conversion has been observed in studies of American evangelical conversion as well. For example, Gordon (1984), in his discussion of Jesus

People groups, talks about "dying to self" in the process of surrendering and "letting go," which ultimately leads to rebirth and reconstitution of a more empowered self.

10. My findings regarding the rhetoric of "killing" of self in evangelical women's discourse is corroborated clearly by Ai Ra Kim's (1996) study of first-generation Korean evangelical immigrant women in America, suggesting that this rhetoric is a central part of Korean female evangelical discourse.

11. Understandably, most husbands were not averse to their wives' participation in these cell meetings (even if they were skeptical at first), as they came to understand the domesticating agenda of these meetings. Indeed, I have not participated in one cell meeting where collective self-criticisms about domestic situations did not occur.

REFERENCES

Appleby, R. Scott. 2000. *The Ambivalence of the Sacred: Religion, Violence, and Reconciliation*. New York: Rowman and Littlefield.

Bartkowski, John P. 2001. *Remaking the Godly Marriage: Gender Negotiation in Evangelical Churches*. New Brunswick: Rutgers University Press.

Brinton, M. C., Y. Lee, and W. L. Parish. 1995. "Married Women's Employment in Rapidly Industrializing Societies: Examples from East Asia." *American Journal of Sociology* 100 (5): 1099–130.

Brusco, Elizabeth E. 1995. *The Reformation of Machismo: Evangelical Gender and Conversion in Colombia*. Austin: University of Texas Press.

Burdick, John. 1993. *Looking for God in Brazil: The Progressive Catholic Church in Urban Brazil's Religious Arena*. Berkeley: University of California Press.

Cho, Haejoang. 1986. "Male Dominance and Mother Power: The Two Sides of Confucian Patriarchy in Korea." In *The Psycho-Cultural Dynamics of the Confucian Family: Past and Present*, edited by Walter H. Slote, 277–98. Seoul: International Cultural Society of Korea.

———. 2002. "Living with Conflicting Subjectivities: Mother, Motherly Wife, and Sexy Woman in the Transition of Colonial-Modern to Postmodern Korea." In *Under Construction: The Gendering of Modernity, Class, and Consumption in the Republic of Korea*, edited by Laurel Kendall, 165–96. Honolulu: University of Hawaii Press.

Chong, Kelly H. 2008. *Deliverance and Submission: Evangelical Women and the Negotiation of Patriarchy in South Korea*. Cambridge: Harvard University Asia Center; Harvard University Press.

Clark, Donald N. 1986. *Christianity in Modern Korea*. Lanham, MD: University Press of America.

Csordas, Thomas J. 1994. *The Sacred Self: A Cultural Phenomenology of Charismatic Healing*. Berkeley: University of California Press.

———. 1997. *Language, Charisma, and Creativity: The Ritual Life of a Religious Movement*. Berkeley: University of California Press.

Davidman, Lynn. 1991. *Tradition in a Rootless World: Women Turn to Orthodox Judaism*. Berkeley: University of California Press.

Foucault, Michel. 1988. "Technologies of the Self." In *Technologies of the Self: A Seminar with Michel Foucault*, edited by Luther H. Martin, Huck Gutman, and Patrick H. Hutton. Amherst: University of Massachusetts Press.

Gilkes, Cheryl Townsend. 1985. "'Together and in Harness': Women's Traditions in the Sanctified Church." *Signs* 10 (41): 678–99.

Gordon, David F. 1984. "Dying to Self: Self-Control through Self-Abandonment." *Sociological Analysis* 4 (1): 41–56.

Griffith, R. Marie. 1997. *God's Daughters: Evangelical Women and the Power of Submission*. Berkeley: University of California Press.

Harding, Susan Friend. 2000. *The Book of Jerry Falwell: Fundamentalist Language and Politics*. Princeton: Princeton University Press.

Kaufman, Debra. 1989. "Patriarchal Women: A Case Study of Newly Orthodox Jewish Women." *Symbolic Interaction* 12 (2): 299–314.

Keane, Webb. 1997. "Religious Language." *Annual Review of Anthropology* 26:47–71.

Kendall, Laurel. 1996. *Getting Married in Korea: Of Gender, Morality, and Modernity*. Berkeley: University of California Press.

———, ed. 2002. *Under Construction: The Gendering of Modernity, Class, and Consumption in the Republic of Korea*. Honolulu: University of Hawaii Press.

Kim, Ai Ra. 1996. *Women Struggling for a New Life: On the Role of Religion in the Cultural Passage from Korea to America*. Albany: State University of New York Press.

Kim, John T. 1996. *Protestant Church Growth in Korea*. Belleville, Ontario: Essence.

Lawless, Elaine J. 1988. *Handmaidens of the Lord: Pentecostal Women Preachers and Traditional Religion*. Philadelphia: University of Pennsylvania Press.

Lee, Jae Bum. 1986. "Pentecostal Distinctives and Korean Protestant Church Growth." PhD diss., Fuller Theological Seminary.

Lee, Timothy. 2010. *Born Again: Evangelicalism in South Korea*. Honolulu: University of Hawaii Press.

Lett, Denise. 1998. *In Pursuit of Status: The Making of South Korea's "New" Urban Middle Class*. Cambridge: Harvard University Asia Center.

Lindhardt, Martin, ed. 2011. Practicing the Faith: The Ritual Life of Pentecostal-Charismatic Christians. Oxford: Berghahn.

Mahmood, Saba. 2001. "Feminist Theory, Embodiment, and the Docile Agent: Some Reflections on the Egyptian Islamic Revival." *Cultural Anthropology* 16 (2): 202–36.

Martin, David. 1990. *Tongues of Fire: The Explosion of Protestantism in Latin America*. New Haven: Yale University Press.

McGuire, Meredith. 1983. "Discovering Religious Power." *Sociological Analysis* 44 (1): 1–10.

McLeod, Arlene Elowe. 1992. "Hegemonic Relations and Gender Resistance: The New Veiling as Accommodating Protest in Cairo." *Signs* 17 (3): 533–57.

Nelson, Laura. 2000. *Measured Excess: Status, Gender, and Consumer Nationalism in South Korea*. New York: Columbia University Press.

Papanek, Hanna. 1979. "Family Status Production: The 'Work' and 'Non-Work' of Women." *Signs* 4:775–81.

Park, Sung-Ja. 1993. "A Feminist Theological Study of the Faith Patterns of Korean Church Women: Emphasis on the Religious Psychopathological Phenomenon." PhD diss., Ewha Woman's University, Seoul.

Riesebrodt, Martin. 1993. *Pious Passion: The Emergence of Modern Fundamentalism in the United States and Iran.* Berkeley: University of California Press.

Riesebrodt, Martin, and Kelly H. Chong. 1999. "Fundamentalisms and Patriarchal Gender Politics." *Journal of Women's History* 10 (4): 55–77.

Ryu, Dong-Shik. 1982. "The Korean Church and the Pentecostal Movement." In *A Study on the Pentecostal Movement in Korea.* Seoul: Korea Christian Academy.

Shoaps, Robin A. 2002. "'Pray Earnestly': The Textual Construction of Personal Involvement in Pentecostal Prayer and Song." *Journal of Linguistic Anthropology* 12 (1): 34–71.

Stacey, Judith. 1990. *Brave New Families: Stories of Domestic Upheaval in Late-Twentieth-Century America.* New York: Basic Books.

Suh, David Kwang-Sun. 1982. "The Study of Seung-rak and the Full Gospel Church." In *A Study on the Pentecostal Movement in Korea.* Seoul: Korea Christian Academy.

Westley, Frances R. 1977. "Searching for Surrender: A Catholic Charismatic Renewal Group's Attempt to Become Glossolalic." *American Behavioral Scientist* 20 (6): 925–40.

Yoo, Boo-Woong. 1988. *Korean Pentecostalism: Its History and Theology.* Frankfurt am Main: Peter Lang.

6

Mobility

A Global Geography of the Spirit among
Catholic Charismatic Communities

THOMAS J. CSORDAS

In the introduction to *Transnational Transcendence* (Csordas 2009),
I endeavored to outline a framework for anthropological research on
religion and globalization. This framework includes four modalities in
which the globalization of religion is taking place, each of which suggests a somewhat different problematic for research. The first is that in
which the local religious imagination takes up the encroachments of
global economy and technology. Perhaps the classic image in this modality is found in *The Gods Must Be Crazy*, a film in which a Coca-Cola
bottle littered from an airplane becomes an object of religious specula-
tion for the Kalahari Bushmen who pick it up. A second modality of
religious development in the context of globalization and global culture
is one that we could call pan-indigenous. It results in some surprising
juxtapositions, such as the existence of a Hopi Indian reggae society as
residents of the ancient mesas embrace a kindred Rastafarian spirituality, while from another direction the Dalai Lama visits Hopiland with
the implicit message that shared origin in a high mountain homeland
predisposes Tibetans and Hopis to a kindred spirituality. Of course, the
transcendence of local boundaries by indigenous religious traditions is
not limited to contacts among third and fourth world peoples, and a
third modality includes the increasing likelihood of religious influence
extending in a "reverse" direction, from the margins to the metropole.
The global spread of Yoruba religion is the prime example of this third
modality of religious globalization. Fourth, we come to the so-called
world religions and their trajectories within the cultural space of globalization. The question is of the "newness" of globalization: certainly there

is nothing special in talking about the globalization of Catholicism, Buddhism, or Islam when these are religions that have been globalized for many centuries. A pressing issue is to identify both similarity and difference between these premodern globalizations of religion and the postmodern globalization we are studying today.

The case I will discuss is an instance of the latter phenomenon, a kind of re-globalization of a world religion. I will proceed by invoking the idea of geography, which is appealing to think with in part because it can be used both literally and metaphorically. It can refer to a figurative conceptual terrain as well as to the physical features on the face of the earth. I am going to use both senses here, beginning with the metaphorical question of how to situate Catholic Pentecostalism, also known as the Catholic charismatic renewal, within the landscape of contemporary Christianity. The larger Pentecostal movement that began in the United States at the beginning of the twentieth century is based on the experience of "baptism in the Holy Spirit" and exercise of the "spiritual gifts" that are the fruits of this experience. It has spread throughout the world in a variety of forms and has generated an extensive literature (Hollenweger 1972; Synan 1987, 1997; Poewe 1994; Csordas [1997] 2012; Coleman 2000; Robbins 2004).

Catholic Pentecostalism as a branch of this movement within Roman Catholicism began in 1967, when students and young faculty at Catholic universities experienced baptism in the Holy Spirit under the tutelage of Protestant Pentecostals and neo-Pentecostal evangelists. While adherents exercised a full range of gifts of the Spirit, it was soon observed that charismatics tended to be more middle-class and university-educated than their classical and neo-Pentecostal counterparts, exhibiting a more restrained, domesticated spiritual style. By the 1990s the theologian Harvey Cox could write, "If Jimmy Swaggart is the Mick Jagger of Pentecostalism, the charismatic movement is its Guy Lombardo" (1995, 152)—a musical comparison associating charismatics with both the elderly and the insipid. Yet the Catholic movement grew rapidly, more rapidly and dramatically than charismatic renewal movements within mainline Protestant denominations such as the Episcopalian, which had already been extant for more than a decade.

If we were to focus on understanding the Catholic charismatic renewal in itself, it would suffice to say that it is a synthesis of Catholicism and Pentecostalism with respect to theology and ritual practice. How-ever, when it comes to the Catholic charismatic renewal, two comple-mentary and closely interrelated questions are of even greater interest and significance. First, how deeply has the Pentecostal movement pen-etrated the socio-spiritual fabric of the Roman Catholic Church? Sec-ond, what place does the Catholic movement hold in the socio-spiritual mosaic of Pentecostalism? I use the metaphors of "fabric" and "mo-saic" intentionally: despite its diversity, the Catholic Church is a tightly woven, hierarchical entity; despite its uniform emphasis on the Holy Spirit, organizationally Pentecostalism is a loosely arranged pattern of distinctly shaped fragments. Because of this fundamental difference, the movement's orientations toward the Catholic world and the Pentecos-tal world have of necessity been correspondingly different. The goal of Pentecostalism as a movement within Catholicism has been literally to renew the spiritual life of the Church. For Pentecostalism as a form of Protestantism, the goal has been to cultivate an ecumenical sensibility in relation to its multiple forms.

We can clarify part of what is at stake by observing that in 1977 the consensus at the General Conference on Charismatic Renewal in Kansas City was that the Pentecostal world was constituted by three streams: classical Pentecostalism, Protestant neo-Pentecostalism, and Catholic Pentecostalism (Synan 1997). This consensus persisted until 1983, when a new model was proposed by C. Peter Wagner of Fuller Theological Seminary, in which Pentecostalism was described as composed of three waves. The first was classical Pentecostalism, the second was the char-ismatic renewal, and the third was neo-charismatic or Signs and Won-ders (the latter led primarily by Wagner and colleagues John Wimber and Paul Cain). The effect of adopting the Fuller three-wave model is to collapse the Protestant neo-Pentecostal stream and the Catholic Pente-costal stream into one charismatic wave, with the third wave adopting a kind of post-charismatic identity that embraces the Pentecostal gifts of the Spirit without calling itself either Pentecostal or charismatic. In the three-stream model, on the other hand, Signs and Wonders Christianity would be regarded as a form of Protestant neo-Pentecostalism. It would hardly be of great consequence except that it not only alters the status of the Catholic Pentecostal movement within Pentecostalism, but also masks and diminishes it in a way that is concordant with the position that casts doubt not only on whether Catholics can also really be Pentecostals, but whether Catholics are really Christians in the first place. To the extent that the metaphor of three streams is washed away by the metaphor of three waves, there is a revision of Pentecostal history that should be taken into account rather than taken for granted.

The Catholic charismatic renewal has since the beginning been characterized by lay leadership and by an orientation that is simultaneously ecumenical and communitarian (Csordas 1997). Both the attribution of authority to lay leadership and a movement-initiated conception of ecumenism have at times created delicate political situations for the Renewal vis-à-vis the Church hierarchy, for example, with respect to jurisdiction of local bishops and the depth of collaboration with Pentecostals and Protestant charismatics. It is, however, to the communitarian dimension of Catholic Pentecostalism that I want to direct our attention in the present discussion. Whereas Catholicism is at the grassroots level organized into parishes and Pentecostalism into congregations or fellowships, Catholic Pentecostalism's grassroots organization is of two kinds: prayer group and community. The charismatic prayer group typically is parochially based, but includes a minority of parishioners or charismatics from a number of parishes, and often conducts a weekly prayer meeting with occasional ancillary activities. The charismatic community is typically somewhat larger and composed of members who have a greater degree of commitment to sharing a "life in the Spirit," often through a greater degree of authoritative structure, commitment of time and resources, and shared living situations as well as worship. Membership usually requires a trial period followed by formal commitment to a written "covenant" that binds members together. Given the greater degree of commitment, it is not surprising that there are substantially fewer communities than prayer groups. Currently in the United States, the National Service Committee's Chariscenter website lists 1,983 prayer groups and 89 covenant communities.[1]

I am going to focus on these communities, particularly on several global networks of communities. In this context the history of the relation between prayer groups and communities is relevant. In the movement's first decade, it was thought in some quarters that committed and disciplined life in intentional communities was the preferred goal for all charismatics, and that prayer groups were a preliminary stage in the development of communities. In 1977 a split occurred between those who held this position and those who maintained that prayer groups and the level of spiritual growth they fostered were acceptable forms of charismatic life in themselves. The communitarians by this time had already taken a step further and determined that in an era defined by the threats to the Church identified in the Rome prophecies, it was necessary to develop a "community of communities." The principle was that, just as in a single community each member is thought to be granted a charism or spiritual gift that contributes to the collective life of the community as a "body" or a "people," so each community had a particular gift or mission that would collectively contribute to building the Kingdom of God. Accordingly, an Association of Communities was founded in 1976.

By 1980–1981, however, the principal communities had developed irreconcilable differences with respect to the nature of collective life, particularly the degree of centralized authority to be exercised on the level of the network as a whole. The most militant and centralized group rechristened itself the Sword of the Spirit (SOS) in 1982 and adopted a kind of federal government of communities that each retained its own name. A group of communities more inclined toward confederacy came to consider themselves all semi-autonomous branches of a single community, taking on the name of the leading community among them, People of Praise. An even more loosely structured group eventually became known in 1990 as the Catholic Fraternity of Charismatic Covenant Communities and Fellowships. Meanwhile, in 1976 the Emmanuel Community (EC) was founded in Paris by Catholics exposed to the charismatic renewal in the United States, and it rapidly added branches throughout France and subsequently in other countries, including the United States in 1992. Finally, within the past decade a European Network of Communities was established, the president of which says in an interview on the network's website that freestanding charismatic communities that developed in the 1970s sometimes collapsed in the 1990s due to crisis or doubt in the context of postmodernism and post-Christianity. He and some others determined that "if there is not something to collect those communities out of their diaspora, we will lose them. So we felt a strong call from God to call those individual communities to form something like a family of communities together."[2]

Each of the networks and supercommunities has a distinctive history and relationship both to the institutional structure of the international Catholic charismatic renewal and to the Church hierarchy. What piques the imagination with respect to a global geography of the Spirit, however, is the cartographic self-representation of these communities. Websites of the communities exhibit a vivid sense of international presence and progress toward world evangelization, global Pentecost, and the Kingdom of God. The Sword of the Spirit site shows a white world map against a dark red background. Entitled "World Communities 2008,"[3] it has the names of each branch by country printed in white letters in the red oceanic spaces among continents. The Emmanuel website features an interactive world map with continent-wide provinces each presented in a distinctive color.[4] Clicking on each continent highlights that province, with countries in which the community has a presence presented in orange and those in which it does not presented in beige. Clicking on a country will reveal the website of the local branch or contact information for that country. The People of Praise site shows the distribution of communities in Google Map format, with each branch represented by the characteristic inverted teardrop pointer.[5]

I want now to briefly elaborate on this geography of the Spirit with respect to (1) what it means for the practice of everyday life among members; (2) the axes of variation of language and habitus (a system of taken-for-granted dispositions) in the communities; and (3) the phenomenological or experiential transformation of geographical space created in their transnational activities.

The Geographies of Everyday Life

Everyday life in these charismatic supercommunities is affected by transnational governance and transnational mobility. Community governance is organized at local, regional, and international levels. Leaders meet periodically at each of these levels, sometimes with separate meetings for male and female leaders. As one Sword of the Spirit coordinator says, "We try to do as much as possible at the local and regional levels— doing everything internationally is unwieldy and expensive." In addition, each member community receives a "visitation" from a team composed of delegates from other branches that gives a report to the community and its leaders on whether community life is going well, whether members are content, whether they are adhering to commitments made on joining the community, ideas and suggestions for improvement, and encouragement of strengths.

The circulation of members is even more pronounced among youth. A community leader who has been a member since the 1970s reported that many college-age young people travel to another community to serve there for a year, recounting the experiences of two of his own children in Glasgow and London. Young people also attend regional conferences, perform mission work, and make friends across international community branches. A college service program has become so institutionalized that it has generated a kind of "pastoral slang" (Csordas 1997). Twelve to fourteen years ago, when community youth programs began to grow, the North American regional youth director devised a plan to ask college students to spend a year serving in youth outreach, filling the "gaps" in the youth program. Since then the term "gapper" has applied to those who take on this service, and the program has "grown from an informal beginning into a powerful experience of Christian service for our youth. Most of our gappers, in addition to the service they perform, receive training, Christian formation, and have an opportunity to live in a residential Christian household." They have a strong tendency to remain active in community life as they grow older. In addition to the college-age gappers, there are also popular mission trips for high school students, regional and international conferences, "On Holiday" (taking a vacation with other SOS members), a fairly active informal flow of youth visiting communities for various lengths of time, and exchange students taking college language classes. One local branch in the United States reports that over the past two decades it has hosted at least a hundred such students who come for a school year or longer.

Patterns of travel and visiting among adult members of the Emmanuel Community appear to be similar to those in the Sword of the Spirit. However, the symbolic center of spiritual life for Emmanuel is Paray-le-Monial in France, a traditional site of pilgrimage in devotion to the Sacred Heart of Jesus. Paray has been literally adopted by the community, members of which have physically renovated the site and use it as a center for annual summer sessions that attract nearly twenty thousand people annually. For community youth, the most important activities are the annual International Youth Forums in Paray-le-Monial and smaller-scale youth days in various localities. The community has five schools of mission in European cities, which offer undergraduate programs for one or two years. Emmanuel also runs an international youth center in Rome, and maintains guest houses in France, Germany, Italy, Portugal, Israel, and Rwanda. Finally, Emmanuel runs Fidesco, its own NGO devoted to development and humanitarian aid projects in Africa, Asia, and Latin America. In 2009, 109 young volunteers were dispatched to such projects worldwide.

Variation in Language and Practice

Charismatic communities exist so that their members can share a collective spiritual life and a collective mission of evangelization for the sake of renewing the Church. Action toward these goals exhibits both commonalities and differences, however, and to illustrate this I outline a comparison of language and practice in the Sword of the Spirit and the Emmanuel Community. First and foremost, both communities are charismatic, in the specific sense that they are founded on the Pentecostal baptism in the Spirit and practice the spiritual gifts. Basic features of community organization are held in common, though often with slightly different names. The differences between the two are subtle but telling. The American community was founded in 1969 by Ralph Martin and Steven Clark, two young men who were college students in the culturally volatile post–Vatican Council 1960s, and who had participated in founding the Catholic Pentecostal movement two years before, in 1967. The French community was founded in 1976 by Pierre Goursat and Martine Lafitte, an older man in his fifties who was director of the French Board of Catholic Film Censors, and a younger woman in her thirties who was a hospital intern, and who had been baptized in the Spirit in 1972 after being exposed to the movement from people who had encountered it in the United States. The Sword of the Spirit (SOS) has been and remains predominantly composed of laypeople, while the Emmanuel Community (EC) advertises that its members include 223 priests, 95 seminarians, and at least two bishops. The EC is exclusively Catholic in membership, while the SOS is explicitly ecumenical in the sense that a substantial number of its communities include members representing multiple denominations.

If in one sense these differences suggest that the two communities fall at different points along a continuum between more Pentecostal and more Catholic in orientation, it is equally the case that this is a difference in self-conception and sense of mission of the Catholic charismatic renewal per se. The very names of the communities indicate this difference, with "Sword of the Spirit" conveying a relatively more militant sense of divine presence and "Emmanuel" (meaning "God with us") conveying that presence in a relatively more contemplative sense. The EC defines its underlying charism and mission in the threefold formulation "adoration, compassion, evangelization," with adoration of God understood as leading directly to compassion for others and from compassion to active evangelization of others. The SOS understands itself in threefold form as a bulwark to defend people in a time of spiritual warfare, a prophetic people proclaiming Christ, and a servant people working to stem the tide of evil and promote holiness. The communities' respective magazines are titled accordingly: the SOS publishes *Living Bulwark*, while Emmanuel publishes *Il Est Vivant* (He is alive).

An additional contrast is in accord with the foregoing comparison. First is that the relatively greater sense of militancy in the SOS is reflected in a gender ethos that has been relatively more masculinist and even macho. This is most easily seen in another shared community institution, the celibate brotherhoods and sisterhoods within each community. In the SOS a young adult can decide to live "single for the Lord" and in the EC to live in "celibacy for the Kingdom," and in both cases they commit themselves to lives of continuous availability for service within the community. The gender balances of members choosing this lifestyle option are dramatically different. In the EC they are referred to as brothers leading the consecrated life and sisters leading the consecrated life. The women, who clearly predominate in numbers, adopt the common clothing of blue skirts and white tops, in light imitation of the habits of nuns. In the SOS the brothers belong to a group called the Servants of the Word, while the sisters are members of the Bethany Association. The Servants of the Word, established and led by the community founder Steven Clark himself, has been a powerful force since the community's beginning. A parallel sisterhood remained in existence for only a few years in the face of a powerful commitment to "male headship" within the community, and was dissolved in 1990. The current Bethany Association was instituted only in 2009, with individual women living single for the Lord in local branches having in the meantime had no collective institutional recognition.

Transforming Space

In thinking about religion and globalization, and returning finally to the literal sense of geography, we cannot say that a "global religious phenomenon" ever starts out as global. It begins somewhere, and globalizes. The initial research questions then have to do with the historical and social conditions that facilitate or impede global expansion, and the characteristics of the religious phenomenon that allow it to travel well, or not, across social settings and cultural boundaries (Csordas 2009). There is, however, a second level of question that is more subtle and subjective: Does the globalization of a religious phenomenon effect a qualitative transformation? This might be thought of as a form of the transformation of quantity into quality insofar as a phenomenon grows as it spreads, assuming that the new locations remain in vital contact with their places of origin and continue to consider themselves part of the same enterprise. It could also be thought of as the transformation of extension into quality in two senses. First, the quality of relationships would be affected by the introduction of distance, especially with respect to the possibilities for intimacy and the exercise of authority. Second, the phenomenological quality of space qua geographical space would be affected, especially when the space in question is the space of the entire globe.

The ritualization of life and development of a spiritualized habitus in Catholic Pentecostalism (Csordas [1997] 2012)—to a degree characteristic of Pentecostalism in general—includes the transformation of interpersonal, domestic, civic, and geographical space. For present purpose I direct our attention specifically to geographic space and sense of place. Catholic charismatics have renewed interest in pilgrimage to traditional sacred sites of Catholicism such as Rome, Jerusalem, Lourdes, and Paray-le-Monial, and have been among the most enthusiastic visitors to the site of the Marian apparitions that began in the early 1980s at Medjugorje in Croatia. Especially in the first two decades of the movement, the charismatic map of the United States was also transformed, with destination cities like Ann Arbor, Michigan, and Pecos, New Mexico, replacing vacation sites like New York or San Francisco.

In examining mobility and circulation of members among local community branches, we have glimpsed the possibilities for transformation of relationships by creating intimacy across vast distances. Especially for community youth, members inhabit a literal global village that is not virtual or dependent on technological media but based on face-to-face encounters and always potential copresence. This is not to say that the Internet is not enlisted to enhance interaction among community branches. Skype technology is readily and comfortably used across far-flung Emmanuel Community households. An issue of the People of Praise community magazine *Vine and Branches* in 2006 had a cover with the title "Technology: Building Unity, Defeating Distance." The article described a videoconference project run by a new communications division of the community's small publishing house, in which a series of talks was tapped into by forty-eight computers at five community branches accompanied by the capacity for simultaneous "chat" interaction by participants. The article mentions that topics of the talks included cell phones, web cameras, high-speed Internet access, friendship with Jesus, and the history of the People of Praise. The president of the communications division observed that the Internet can provide "more ways for us to communicate and be present to one another." Dorothy Ranaghan, a founding member of the community, said, "When we had our twenty-fifth anniversary as the People of Praise, it became clear that, as much as we wanted to, we could not get the whole community together in one place. But with technology like this, well, maybe we can for our fiftieth!"

The transformation of geographical space achieved by the establishment of networks of communities is also both literal with respect to how space is used by participants in these communities and phenomenological insofar as the mode of dwelling in and inhabiting the world is transformed for those participants. In a more extensive study we could consolidate this insight by appealing to the intersection of two relevant bodies of literature that have taken shape in the past two decades, contemporaneous with concern with globalization as a social process and the role of religion in it. These are the anthropology of space and place (Feld and Basso 1997; Gupta and Ferguson 1997; Low and Zunigais 2003; Cieraad 2006) and postmodern or post-structuralist geography (Soja 1989; Doel 1999; Minca 2001; Murdoch 2006). The former invites us to think in terms of the importance to people of place and identity, dwelling and inhabiting, landscape and landmark, contestation of space and place, public and private, pilgrimage and mobility. The latter invites us to conceive of our environment using an analytic of geography and the simultaneity of spatiality as an alternative to history and sequentiality of temporality, rethinking the urban and regional in the context of globalization and problematizing the relationship between the local and the global, and the relation among geography, ecology, policy, and politics.[6]

We can illustrate how these considerations might augment our analysis by observing that in the Sword of the Spirit, it is taught that a motto for women should be "Make a space" and a motto for men should be "Seize the territory." These mottoes are intended to prescribe distinct gender roles for women and men. The verbs in the contrasting mottoes suggest ideal behavioral modes of creation and generativity for females, aggression and conquest for males. The female space is one of domesticity and Christian family morality, while the male territory is one of engagement with the world via Christian evangelism. Rethinking these in terms of geographical space and place allows us first to recognize their complementarity as three-dimensional habitation and two-dimensional expanse, a zone of nurturance and a zone of domination. More than this, it allows us to see a layer of cosmological meaning superimposed on both the household and the globe, along with a complementarity between them, working together to effect a wholesale phenomenological transformation that is henceforth self-confirming. Presence of one's brethren in branch communities around the world is immediate proof of the reality of the divine kingdom, and the simultaneous existence of multiple nurturant community spaces is evidence that the divine presence is indeed global. Seen in this way, the maps we have seen are not merely convenient means of keeping track or even of advertising success, but disclosures of a transformed mode of experiencing the world.

The value of the recent literature on place and geography in facilitating this kind of interpretation should not prevent us from recognizing a tension in some of this work between a theory-driven impulse toward reconceptualization of space and territory and the pragmatic manner in which space and place are generated by people engaged in specific types of social practice and ritual activity. The case we have been examining is valuable because it engages both sides of this tension: it is an indigenously generated transformation that in fact becomes more discernible as such in light of the theoretical work. Perhaps most interesting is that it offers a concrete instance of the re-enchantment of the world in terms of a specific kind of relation between history and geography. The history that is at stake is "salvation history," which in order to be complete requires that everyone be saved and that the divine word be heard everywhere in the world. The geographical dimension of this is a form of enchantment that is in essence experienced as a movement of the Spirit to transform the face of the earth. This is critical to the goals of the charismatic renewal, whether or not it be conceived on a continuum of grandiosity as preparing for the final judgment and second coming of Christ, as building the Kingdom of God on earth, or more prosaically as ensuring that the global Catholic Church is spiritually renewed by being initiated into the Pentecostal gifts of the Spirit.

Conclusion

Spiritual renewal of the church and evangelization of the world constitute the eschatological end point. Being able to represent one's home by means of a world map evokes a condition of a world that is already sanctified through its geographical extension/expanse by means of the presence of community branches that can be thought of as nodes in a network, hot spots, safe zones, or high points—high points in the sense of plateaus, a thousand of them if we can be allowed to poach on the metaphor of Deleuze and Guattari (1987). However, this network of Pentecostal plateaus is not interconnected in anonymous rhizomatic fashion, but as a system of distinct places, distinct destinations each with its characteristic charism and identity. In this sense the outlines of the Kingdom of God are already in place, traceable in a preliminary sense. Not only are individual members nestled in the security of their communities, but the communities are nestled securely in a worldwide web. At the same time there is dynamism in movement, sharing resources and talent, engaging in global evangelism and even in global humanitarian work. Moving corporeally about in this world in conjunction with the capacity for instant Internet communication transports participants beyond representation to habitation, presence, and copresence in the sacred geography. In this way our study is not only about religion in relation to processes of political and economic globalization, and not only about the global spread of religious practices and organizations, but about the re-enchantment of a world.

+ funneling

NOTES

This chapter is an abridged and adapted version of my article "A Global Geography of the Spirit: The Case of Catholic Charismatic Communities," *International Social Science Journal* 209–210 (2012): 171–84.

1. Chariscenter USA, "Renewal Database," 2013, http://www.nsc-chariscenter.org/search.asp.

2. European Network of Communities, "ENC Interview," 2013, https://sites.google.com/a/e-n-c.org/members/.

3. Sword of the Spirit, "Worldwide Communities 2008," 2008, http://www.swordofthespirit.net/sosmap508.pdf.

4. Emmanuel Community, "Emmanuel in the World," 2013, http://en.emmanuel.info/country.

5. People of Praise, "Our Branches," 2008, http://www.peopleofpraise.org/our-branches/.

6. The chapter on moral geography by Kristine Krause in the present volume takes a somewhat different approach by examining transnational linkages within Pentecostalism broadly speaking, while my discussion has emphasized the transformation of space within intentional communities concretely dispersed around the globe while concretely linked to one another.

REFERENCES

Cieraad, Irene, ed. 2006. *At Home: An Anthropology of Domestic Space.* Syracuse: Syracuse University Press.

Coleman, Simon. 2000. *The Globalization of Charismatic Christianity: Spreading the Gospel of Prosperity.* Cambridge: Cambridge University Press.

Cox, Harvey. 1995. *Fire from Heaven: The Rise of Pentecostal Spirituality and the Reshaping of Religion in the 21st Century.* Cambridge, MA: Da Capo.

Csordas, Thomas J. (1997) 2012. *Language, Charisma, and Creativity: The Ritual Life of a Religious Movement.* New York: Palgrave.

———, ed. 2009. *Transnational Transcendence: Essays on Religion and Globalization.* Berkeley: University of California Press.

Deleuze, Gilles, and Felix Guattari. 1987. *A Thousand Plateaus: Capitalism and Schizo-phrenia*. Translated by Brian Massumi. Minneapolis: University of Minnesota Press.

Doel, Marcus. 1999. *Poststructuralist Geographies: The Diabolical Art of Spatial Science*. New York: Rowman and Littlefield.

Feld, Steven, and Keith Basso, eds. 1997. *Senses of Place*. Santa Fe: School of American Research Press.

Gupta, Akhil, and James Ferguson, eds. 1997. *Culture, Power, Place: Explorations in Critical Anthropology*. Durham: Duke University Press.

Hollenweger, Walter. 1972. *The Pentecostals*. London: SCM Press.

Low, Setha, and Denise Zunigais, eds. 2003. *The Anthropology of Space and Place: Locating Culture*. Chichester, UK: Wiley-Blackwell.

Minca, Claudio, ed. 2001. *Postmodern Geography: Theory and Praxis*. Oxford, UK: Blackwell.

Murdoch, Jonathan. 2006. *Post-Structuralist Geography: A Guide to Relational Space*. London: Sage.

Poewe, Karla, ed. 1994. *Charismatic Christianity as a Global Culture*. Columbia: University of South Carolina Press.

Robbins, Joel. 2004. "The Globalization of Pentecostal and Charismatic Christianity." *Annual Review of Anthropology* 33:117–43.

Soja, Edward W. 1989. *Postmodern Geographies: The Reassertion of Space in Critical Social Theory*. London: Verso.

Synan, Vinson. 1987. *Twentieth Century Pentecostal Explosion*. Lake Mary, FL: Strang Communications.

———. 1997. *The Holiness-Pentecostal Tradition: Charismatic Movements in the Twenti-eth Century*. Grand Rapids, MI: Eerdmans.

SECTION 3

Transmission and Mediation

7

Mediating Money

Materiality and Spiritual Warfare in Tanzanian Charismatic Christianity

MARTIN LINDHARDT

An important trend within the anthropology of religion, and a trend to which the study of Pentecostal/charismatic Christianity has a good deal to offer, is what Matthew Engelke has recently described as "the move to materiality" (2011, 209). Increasingly, scholars are beginning to revisit disembodied, dematerialized definitions of religion in which most emphasis is put on belief, meaning, and worldview and focus more attention on the ways relations to the divine are constituted and nourished through bodily practice, social interaction, and the handling of material objects (Morgan 2010). The move to materiality does not imply a dismissal of questions of belief as irrelevant to the social scientific study of religion; rather, it inspires a careful consideration of the material cultures in which beliefs are shaped.

The focus on religious material culture is intrinsically related to a view of religion as mediation, by which is meant a set of practices, objects, and ideas that bind together and establish a relationship between the world of humans and the world of gods and spirits (see Engelke 2010, 374). The problem of mediation, that is, of making the divine tangible in the immanent, is also a problem of presence (Engelke 2007). Most definitions of religion include an orientation to an immaterial, spiritual realm beyond the grasp of everyday sensual perception. However, in order for religious people to have a meaningful relation to and engagement with spiritual beings, the latter need to be made present *in some way*. In other words, commitment to an immaterial force always requires some material form for its expression. "Materiality," Engelke writes, "is the stuff through which 'the religious' is manifest and gets defined in the first place: how

God, or the gods, or the spirits, or one's ancestors can be recognized as being present and/or represented" (2011, 213).

A glance at the scholarly literature on Pentecostal/charismatic Christianity indicates that to a large extent the rise and global spread of this religious movement in the twentieth and early twenty-first centuries can be ascribed to some of the solutions it offers to the problems of presence and mediation. Finding inspiration in phenomenology (Csordas 1997) or in the German philosopher Alexander Baumgarten's concept of aisthesis (Meyer 2010a), scholars have demonstrated how participation in Pentecostal/charismatic worship produces experiences of divine power as a physical bodily presence. Drawing on linguistic theories that emphasize the material, acoustic qualities of words and sounds, others have noted how for some charismatic Christians, sound (for instance, the sound of the name of Jesus when spoken out loud) can in itself convey sacredness (Lindhardt 2010; Engelke 2007). In addition, a booming field of scholarship on Pentecostal use of the mass media has produced some stunning insights into the abilities of media technology to engage the senses and produce powerful experiences of actual contact with other-worldly forces (see Pype 2012).

Based on long-term fieldwork in Iringa, a regional capital in south central Tanzania, where Pentecostal/charismatic ministries have grown and proliferated significantly in the last three decades,[1] this chapter is intended as a contribution to the literature on Pentecostal/charismatic Christianity and mediation. The particular focus lies in the ways Pentecostals/charismatics relate to divine power and, equally importantly, confront the powers of darkness through their careful handling of money. As do other Pentecostals/charismatics in Africa, Iringa's born-again population see themselves as engaged in an ongoing spiritual warfare against diabolic forces. Spiritual warfare is closely connected to—and provides a language for speaking about—this-worldly concerns, as the Devil and his agents are held responsible for different kinds of hardship such as illness, death, failure in school, poverty, inequality, and so forth. In Pentecostal/charismatic understandings, the players on the Devil's team include humans and spiritual beings associated with "African tradition" such as witches, traditional healers (who, according to Pentecostals/charismatics and others, also rely on the power of witchcraft), and ancestral spirits as well as spirits associated with Islam (*ma-*

jini). But while the Devil is believed to have human agents working for him, spiritual warfare rarely takes the form of open confrontations with traditional healers or presumed witches, but mostly consists in combating and neutralizing their powers by activating the power of God. Such an endeavor makes the problems of presence and mediation compellingly relevant as it requires diabolic powers to be detected and located in some tangible form, other than its human agents. And it requires divine power to be directed at those same forms. Existing scholarship on Pentecostal/charismatic Christianity has demonstrated how the human body serves as the main material form in which spiritual powers reside (for instance, in demonic possession and being filled with the Holy Spirit) and sometimes clash with each other, as in healing and exorcism/deliverance (Csordas 1994). But with the notable exception of Meyer's important work on the power of pictures (Meyer 2010b), little light has been shed on the ways spiritual warfare is fought through the handling of physical objects.

Pentecostals/charismatics in Iringa do not see spiritual power as being intrinsic to particular objects, but they do believe that it can be imbued in them, at least temporarily. It follows that the engagement with objects can in some cases also be a way of relating to the invisible world. Responding to Meyer's call for a closer dialogue between the study of Pentecostalism and the anthropology of things and material culture (2010b), this chapter explores the semiotic ideologies (Keane 2007) that organize Pentecostals'/charismatics' experiences and perceptions of relations between persons, things, and the spiritual world. I argue that money is a particularly important object of mediation and that its importance is related to widespread associations of the generation of wealth to the spiritual world. There is, of course, nothing new in stating that for African Pentecostals/charismatics, spiritual warfare is connected to this-worldly economic concerns. All over Sub-Saharan Africa, Pentecostal/charismatic preachers are delivering the message of prosperity and performing rituals that aim at breaking the diabolic/spiritual bondages that keep people trapped in poverty (see Gifford 2011). But while perceptions of a close relation between wealth, or lack thereof, and the spiritual world are well documented in the literature (see also Haynes 2013), I suggest that more careful attention be focused on how Pentecostals/charismatics try to influence this relation through their handling of money.

An important legacy left by Marcel Mauss (1954) to subsequent generations of anthropologists is the fundamental insight that relations between humans and material objects are always historically and culturally figured. Even within the same society, the meaning of objects is often underdetermined, allowing them to move in and out of distinct spheres of value (see Keane 2001). In an intriguing attempt to account for the ability of objects to defy their material stability and be different things in different scenes, Bill Brown proposes that we imagine things as "that which is excessive in objects, as what exceeds their mere materialization as objects or their mere utilization as objects—their force as a sensuous presence or as a metaphysical presence, the magic by which objects become values, fetishes, idols, and totems" (2001, 5). In her study of Pentecostalism and pictures in Ghana, Meyer picks up on this proposal and uses it as a point of departure, from which she goes on to demonstrate how religion can play a crucial role in "creating the possibility of excess by enveloping people and things . . . in a structure of (mutual) animation" (2010b, 126).

The analysis that I pursue below follows a similar path. What I hope to demonstrate is that looking at money through the lens of the anthropology of things, that is, as a permeable material object with unstable statuses (Keane 2001), as an object with changing relationships to its human possessors, and not least as an object whose possibility of excess can be created through religious practice, will provide new insights into Pentecostal/charismatic ways of addressing the problems of presence and the mediation of spiritual warfare.

The Presence and Concentration of Spiritual Power

Pentecostals/charismatics in Iringa conceive of divine and diabolic powers (*nguvu*) as substances that can reside and be concentrated, not only in human bodies and spoken words, but also in places and objects.[2] One elder Pentecostal woman, who suspected her sister of being a witch, told me that the latter sometimes brought her clothes as presents. The old woman never dared wear any of the clothes but always donated them to her church, trusting that the pastor would cleanse them through prayer before passing them on to someone else. In a similar vein, a person who is unable to come to church to receive prayers for healing may send a piece of cloth so that participants in a service may pray over it, thereby investing it with the divine power of healing. At open-air revival meetings, new converts are asked to bring all their *vitu vya uchawi* (witchcraft items), referring among other things to medicines and protective amulets provided by traditional healers, which are then burnt during a ritual where the power of God is also invoked through praying. On one occasion a visiting preacher in the Lutheran church asked members of the congregation to bring a little bit of soil from their yards to church. After a ritual during which the preacher and the congregation prayed intensively over the soil, the participants brought it back home and sprinkled it out in their yards again, so that the divine power invested in it would bring blessings to their homes. Pentecostals/charismatics also insist that praying over a glass of water will actually turn it into the blood of Jesus (even if it still looks and tastes like water) and that drinking it will therefore have healing and empowering effects. A witch who sees such water will instantly detect the power of God imbued in it and will avoid drinking it.

When Pentecostals/charismatics wish to protect a house, a shop, or a stall against the powers of witchcraft, they do so by walking around in those same places, "placing prayer" (*kuweka maombi*) or "placing the blood of Jesus" (*kuweka damu ya Yesu*) with the imposition of hands. This ritual resembles the practices of traditional healers who protect houses and shops by "placing medicines" (*kuweka dawa*), usually in the form of a powder, in corners, doors, and openings.

Many further examples could be added, but hopefully the ones provided here will suffice to establish the point that spiritual warfare involves a specific stance to materiality and is fought through the religious engagement with places and objects. For Pentecostals/charismatics, the human body is not just a container of divine power but a channel from which it can be externalized and transmitted to objects, thus turning them into things that exceed their own materiality. One particular object in which both divine and diabolic powers can be made to materialize is money, or—to be more precise—coins and bills.

Wealth, Money, and Spiritual Warfare

The concern of Pentecostal/charismatic Christians with coins and bills as objects particularly prone to be imbued with spiritual powers should be seen in relation to more widespread concerns with the generation of wealth as connected to an occult dimension. In Tanzania, as in other African countries, the "occult economies," consisting on the one hand in the quest for magical means for attaining wealth and, on the other, in the demonization and condemnation of people held to have accumulated wealth by such means (Comaroff and Comaroff 2001), have been on the increase in recent decades. Nowadays, most traditional healers provide clients with business medicines (*dawa za biashara*), usually in the form of a powder that must be spread out in shops or market stalls in order to attract clients. In addition to the use of such medicines, there has been an increase of rumors about rapid accumulation of wealth through witchcraft. Like the business medicines, the witchcraft of wealth can be used to attract clients to a shop or stall, but also to extract money from people's pockets or purses. According to popular belief, wealth acquired through witchcraft is haunted by ambivalence and comes with problematic conditions such as restrictions on the use of money. It may be that a person who has become rich through occult means is not allowed to sleep in a proper bed or eat certain kinds of food. The death or mental retardation of a close relative is another common sacrifice that must sometimes be made by persons who use witchcraft in order to gain wealth. A deceased victim may be used to feed witches and their assisting spirits (*majini*) who hunger and thirst for human flesh and blood. Alternatively, prosperous witches or persons allied with them may keep their victims as zombies (*misukule*) in their homes and put them to work in fields, shops, or market stalls. Others will believe that the person kept as a zombie is dead and buried, but what has really been buried is a doll that looks like the victim.

The use of business medicines and the rumors about the witchcraft of wealth are paralleled by the increasing impact of the Faith Gospel, also known as the Gospel of Prosperity, in both Pentecostal ministries and the charismatic revival groups of mainline churches. Central to this gospel is an outspoken conviction that every saved Christian has the right to receive divine blessings of health and wealth as well as the duty to pay tithes and make donations of money to God through a ministry. As I have argued in more detail elsewhere (Lindhardt 2009), the Faith Gospel is more than just another market option for the consumer who is shopping around for spiritual assistance in economic affairs. Pentecostals/charismatics are concerned not only with finding miraculous means of attaining wealth but also with the moral and potentially dangerous aspects of wealth acquired through alliance with spiritual forces. Many Pentecostals/charismatics readily recognize that witchcraft is far more efficient than divine power in terms of generating fast wealth, but they insist that wealth given by God has the advantage of being legitimate and long-lasting and that it does not require sacrifices.

Pentecostals/charismatics pray for money a lot. Not only do they ask God to grant money, but once they have it, they pray over coins and bills with the laying-on of hands. The purpose of such praying is to cleanse money of potential dangers, prevent it from being stolen through witchcraft, and invest it with divine power so that it may last and be used constructively. Praying for money to be donated in church is also a strategy for personalizing the exchange relationship between believers and God. Before donating coins and bills, Pentecostals/charismatics hold them in their hands and pray intensely, telling God what kinds of blessings or counter-gift they desire. Some informants described such praying as an act of placing (*kuweka*) their request in the money. A big request, made to God, for instance for a job or a scholarship, should always be accompanied by—or placed in—a donation of money. Through the act of praying, coins and bills are turned into inalienable gifts, invested with a part of the donor's essence (Mauss 1954, 12). If this essence is impure, Pentecostals/charismatics insist that the gift will produce no counter-gift. Money acquired through theft, corruption, prostitution, or the use of witchcraft is immoral, and while it may be donated to a church and cleansed through praying, its immorality sticks with the donor, who will receive no divine blessings (cf. Shipton 1989, 28).

We can see how Pentecostals/charismatics handle a widely shared concern with wealth as connected to a spiritual and potentially dangerous dimension through the ritual engagement with money (see also Lindhardt 2009). In addition, this engagement provides a measure against the alienating effects of money, as it prevents the relationship between believers and God from turning into an impersonal market exchange in which money, acquired by whatever means, could be used to buy blessings as if they were goods on a supermarket shelf. Money in its most concrete form, tangible coins and bills, becomes an object of mediation in and through which human qualities, hopes, and requests merge with transcendental powers.

While a range of noncommercial attributes is ascribed to money through religious, ritual processes, it never fully loses its status as cash value. First of all, the material stability of coins and bills makes it difficult to forget that they could also be used in the commercial sphere. Besides, a main purpose of ritual donations is to receive material, economic blessings in return, and donations do follow certain market principles. A big request made to God requires a large donation. And a note that is too damaged to be used in the commercial sphere is also considered unfit for a ritual donation. In an intriguing study of the use of money in ritual exchanges among the Sumbanese people in Indonesia, Webb Keane argues that money that circulates in ritual contexts is viewed as a symbolic, inalienable token removed from the cash sphere. But at the same time, he adds, the irreducible materiality of money always makes it vulnerable to slippage back into a commercial, nonritual regime of value (2001, 68–69). In the case of Pentecostal/charismatic ritual donations, I argue that the potential slippage not only represents a risk or vulnerability but also a possibility of mediation between ritual/spiritual and commercial spheres. It is exactly by being both money (cash value) and at the same time something more than just money that donated coins and bills can serve as a point of transfer of spiritual powers into everyday economic affairs.

The multifaceted nature of money as, on the one hand, a crucial resource and medium of exchange in worldly economies and, on the other, an object that can be imbued with spiritual powers and with the powers and qualities of its human owners/donors, makes it an important weapon in a spiritual warfare that is often connected to this-worldly economic affairs and conflicts. A few ethnographic sketches will serve as further illustrations of this point.

Case 1

On an evening in late November 2011, the house of Mama Mbilinyi was attacked by an angry crowd, which threw stones through the windows. Mama Mbilinyi herself suffered some severe beatings from members of the crowd, and when the police arrived they had to escort her to the hospital for treatment. Mama Mbilinyi was a successful businesswoman who had built a big house in a middle-class neighborhood. She was also a prominent member and lay preacher of the charismatic revival movement within the Lutheran church. But rumor suggested that her success in business should be ascribed to witchcraft. It could hardly be a coincidence that one of her sons died in a bus accident (according to some informants a very unusual accident in which nobody else got hurt) at about the same time as her business started flourishing. Besides, her husband started to become retarded and now spent most of his time at home doing nothing. Many people suspected that the fates of her son and husband were sacrifices Mama Mbilinyi had made in order to become rich and that her born-again Christian identity was merely a facade she put up to conceal her occult activities.

The attack at her house was caused by the revelation that Mama Mbilinyi kept zombies in her home. Supposedly a house girl who knew nothing about the zombies living in the house had suddenly seen them while she was cooking. She ran out of the house in fear, and afterwards the zombies, equally scared by the encounter, came out and were seen by passersby and neighbors, who then attacked the house and were soon joined by others. It was reported that some spectators identified Mama Mbilinyi's late son, a late driver who used to work for her, and a late neighbor among the zombies.

A few days before the zombie incident, the nationally known revivalist preacher Christopher Mwakasege visited Iringa. Mama Mbilinyi attended a big open-air revival meeting in which Mwakasege was preaching and decided to donate a large sum of money to his ministry. She handed over the money to him herself and he insisted on praying for it right away. As he was praying over the money with the imposition of hands, Mama Mbilinyi fell to the ground, which indicated that she was being slain in the Holy Spirit. The fact that this occurred when Mwakasege was praying over the money and not over Mama Mbilinyi herself was not surprising. As previously explained, born-again Christians believe that the qualities of a person can be invested in his or her money. Praying over already donated money is also supposed to result in the blessing of a donor. But after the zombie incident, a different interpretation of the interaction between Mwakasege, Mama Mbilinyi, and her money was proposed by several people. Apparently Mwakasege had sensed that the money she donated was imbued with evil powers and had to be purified immediately. By purifying the donated money through prayer, he also started combating the powers of the donor. This was what caused Mama Mbilinyi to fall to the ground. And since her witchcraft powers were reduced, the secret that she kept zombies at home came out a few days later.

Case 2

Mama Jimy, a Pentecostal woman, owned a small hair salon in a suburb of Iringa. As she and her husband, who ran a successful business, were relatively prosperous by local standards, they were concerned about potential witchcraft attacks, not only by less fortunate relatives but also by unrelated people from their suburb who resented their success and who might try to extract some of their wealth by use of occult means.[3] One of Mama Jimy's regular customers was a local old lady, Mama Justin, who would usually come in to get her hair done in the morning. Mama Justin would pay and then say, "You will get many customers today" before leaving the saloon. Whenever that occurred, Mama Jimy would indeed get many customers, but despite receiving payment from all of them, she would have only a small amount of money in her purse at the end of the day.

There was no history of animosity between the two women; on the contrary, they had a friendly customer-client relationship and usually chatted cheerfully when Mama Justin was getting her hair done. But a local rumor suggested that Mama Justin was a witch who had at one point been responsible for the illness of the children of an unrelated neighbor, and though Mama Jimy was unfamiliar with the details, she often felt uneasy around the old lady and sensed that a good deal of envy was hidden behind the friendly facade. At one point Mama Jimy dreamt that Mama Justin was a witch who wanted to kill her. Mama Jimy felt that God was trying to warn her and further started suspecting that Mama Justin was practicing a kind of witchcraft known as *likipa* in the local *kihehe* language. This witchcraft consists in stealing people's money by mixing it with the money of a witch. When Mama Jimy received payment from Mama Justin in the morning, she would put the money into her purse, and as the day went by add the money she received from other clients. By having her own coins and bills, imbued with the powers of witchcraft, placed in the same purse as Mama Jimy's other coins and bills, Mama Justin was able to extract the latter.

The day after Mama Jimy had the dream, Mama Justin showed up at the hair salon. Mama Jimy started doing Mama Justin's hair but suddenly felt like someone was sticking a knife into her stomach. She asked her assistant to continue with the work and then went into the back room of the shop and prayed, asking God for power and protection. When she came out, Mama Justin was sweating and seemed upset and insisted she had to leave in a hurry. Mama Jimy now felt that her suspicion was confirmed, but nevertheless Mama Justin kept coming back to get her hair done, acting as if nothing had happened. At one point Mama Justin asked Mama Jimy for a loan of forty thousand shilling (approximately twenty-five US dollars). Mama Jimy decided to bring Mama Justin fifty thousand shilling, insisting that it was not a loan but a gift. But before handing over five ten-thousand-shilling bills, Mama Jimy held them in her hand and prayed intensively over them. A few weeks after receiving the money, Mama Justin again came to see Mama Jimy and started complaining about lack of strength and energy. She further explained that her economic situation was worse than ever. There was little doubt in Mama Jimy's mind that the fifty thousand shilling, filled with divine power through the act of praying, had reduced the witchcraft powers of Mama Justin and made her unable to continue extracting other people's money.

Mama Jimy's decision to give Mama Justin the money instead of lending it to her points to a complex process of mediation, in which human and divine qualities and powers are, to some extent, conflated—and must indeed be conflated—in order to produce effects. Mama Jimy explained that it would not have been possible for her to invest the bills with divine power if they had been a loan. She was unsure why this was the case, but her explanation clearly suggests that divine power can reside only in personalized money. Though still a personal favor, a loan, which should be repaid at a later point, would also have been an impersonal transaction. Being a born-again Christian, Mama Jimy considered herself to be a battery and transmitter of divine power. It was only by giving the money as a gift that her "personal" spiritual qualities and powers could be transferred to it.

Conclusion: Money That Mediates

For some time, scholars have been arguing that classical understandings of Protestantism as an essentially immaterial religion that privileges content over form and tends to employ signs and symbols as mere vehicles for underlying meanings fail to stand up to empirical scrutiny (Keane 2007; Lindhardt 2009; Meyer 2010a, 2010b; Engelke 2007, 2011). As both Keane (2007) and Engelke (2007) have forcefully demonstrated, the problem of presence and the inescapability of some material form through which the divine can be accessed are intrinsic to Protestantism. But while these problems are not a Pentecostal/charismatic peculiarity, they become particularly acute and compelling for Christians who perceive themselves as involved in a continuous spiritual warfare, which is intimately and causally connected to this-worldly concerns such as social conflicts, health and illness/death, or poverty and prosperity. As spiritual warfare cannot be fought simply by confronting presumed witches (who are believed to be human servants of the Devil and have access to his powers), it requires the immaterial forces involved to be mediated and directed in some other way. The two cases I have presented above are intended to illustrate how a close associational link between spiritual warfare and this-worldly economic affairs and conflicts inspires a particular stance to and religious engagement with money. In fact, a certain parallel can be observed between the handling of money and the Pentecostal/charismatic stance to another material form in which spiritual powers are known to reside and sometimes clash with each other, namely, the human body. Pentecostals/charismatics frequently pray over sick and demon-possessed persons, demanding that all evil powers leave them alone in the name of Jesus. And they pray for the continuous uploading of the body with the power of the Holy Spirit, which they experience as a pleasant, sometimes ecstatic bodily presence.

In a similar vein, we have seen how money can be cleansed of diabolic powers (including witchcraft) and imbued with divine power through the act of praying. For Pentecostals/charismatics in Iringa, participation in spiritual warfare involves an orientation to some tangible form. When people's engagement in spiritual warfare is focused on illness and physical well-being, this form tends to be the human body. When what is at stake is wealth and the ambiguity and potential immorality associated with it, what better object of mediation can be imagined than coins and bills?

NOTES

1. Pentecostal denominations in Iringa include a few missionary churches (the Elim Pentecostal Church, the Assemblies of God) and a large number of Tanzanian churches, usually founded as offshoots of missionary churches or as offshoots of offshoots. In addition, charismatic revival movements can be found within the Evangelical Lutheran Church and the Catholic Church. Pentecostal churches and charismatic revival movements share an emphasis on personal salvation (being born again), on the manifestations of the Holy Spirit, on spiritual warfare, and, increasingly, on prosperity. Research for this chapter was conducted in the Lutheran revival movement and the Pentecostal ministry New Life in Christ, which is an offshoot of the Lutheran revival movement.

2. Here, I speak in general terms. While different Pentecostal/charismatic ministries differ in the extent to which they emphasize healing, deliverance, and prosperity, and in their views on (infant and adult) baptism, I have observed no notable differences in their perceptions about the ability of spiritual powers to reside in material forms.

3. In Tanzania, as elsewhere in Africa, witchcraft accusations have traditionally circulated between family members. However, many people believe that contemporary urban witchcraft is more anonymous and that "modern" witches are able to attack different people. More than half of the actual witchcraft accusations or suspicions I have heard of were directed at unrelated neighbors or business rivals. Envy of others who are doing well is believed to be the most common motive of witchcraft attacks directed at unrelated others. Witches who kill others or keep them as zombies in order to become rich will mostly, but not exclusively, choose their own relatives.

REFERENCES

Brown, Bill. 2001. "Thing Theory." Critical Inquiry 28 (1): 1–22.
Comaroff, Jean, and John Comaroff. 2001. "Millennial Capitalism: First Thoughts of a Second Coming." In Millennial Capitalism and the Culture of Neoliberalism, edited by Jean Comaroff and John Comaroff, 1–56. Durham: Duke University Press.
Csordas, Thomas. 1994. The Sacred Self: A Cultural Phenomenology of Charismatic Healing. Berkeley: University of California Press.

———. 1997. *Language, Charisma and Creativity: The Ritual Life of a Religious Movement*. Berkeley: University of California Press.

Engelke, Matthew. 2007. *A Problem of Presence: Beyond Scripture in an African Church*. Berkeley: University of California Press.

———. 2010. "Religion and the Media Turn: A Review Essay." *American Ethnologist* 37 (2): 371–79.

———. 2011. "Material Religion." In *The Cambridge Companion to Religious Studies*, edited by Robert Orsi, 209–29. Cambridge: Cambridge University Press.

Gifford, Paul. 2011. "The Ritual Use of the Bible in African Pentecostalism." In *Practicing the Faith: The Ritual Life of Pentecostal-Charismatic Christians*, edited by Martin Lindhardt, 179–97. New York: Berghahn.

Haynes, Naomi. 2013. "On the Potential and Problems of Pentecostal Exchange." *American Anthropologist* 115 (1): 85–95.

Keane, Webb. 2001. "Money Is No Object: Materiality, Desire, and Modernity in an Indonesian Society." In *The Empire of Things: Regimes of Value and Material Culture*, edited by Fred R. Myers, 65–90. Oxford: James Currey.

———. 2007. *Christian Moderns: Freedom and Fetish in the Mission Encounter*. Berkeley: University of California Press.

Lindhardt, Martin. 2009. "More Than Just Money: The Faith Gospel and Occult Economies in Contemporary Tanzania." *Nova Religio: The Journal of Alternative and Emergent Religions* 13 (1): 41–67.

———. 2010. "'If You Are Saved You Cannot Forget Your Parents': Agency, Power and Social Repositioning in Tanzanian Born-Again Christianity." *Journal of Religion in Africa* 40 (3): 240–72.

Mauss, Marcel. 1954. *The Gift*. London: Cohen and West.

Meyer, Birgit. 2010a. "Aesthetics of Persuasion: Global Christianity and Pentecostalism's Sensational Forms." *South Atlantic Quarterly* 109 (4): 741–63.

———. 2010b. "'There Is a Spirit in That Image': Mass-Produced Jesus Pictures and Protestant-Pentecostal Animation in Ghana." *Comparative Studies in Society and History* 52 (1): 100–130.

Morgan, David. 2010. "Materiality, Social Analysis and the Study of Religions." In *Religion and Material Culture: The Matter of Belief*, edited by David Morgan, 55–74. London: Routledge.

Pype, Katrien. 2012. *The Making of the Pentecostal Melodrama: Religion, Media and Gender in Kinshasa*. New York: Berghahn.

Shipton, Parker. 1989. *Bitter Money: Cultural Economy and Some African Meanings of Forbidden Commodities*. Washington, DC: American Anthropological Association.

8

Mediating Culture

Charisma, Fame, and Sincerity in Rio de Janeiro, Brazil

MARTIJN OOSTERBAAN

The crowd in the *favela* in the northern zone of Rio de Janeiro applauds loudly when the gospel singer Elaine Martins takes the stage. Just as will several other renowned gospel singers present, she will perform some of her popular gospel songs during this *cruzada evangelista*.[1] Martins is a tall black woman from Rio de Janeiro whose powerful voice is as imposing as her height. As she brings the microphone to her mouth and starts to sing, the notes pierce the air and leave the audience in awe.

Between the second and third song, Martins addresses the crowd and assures them that this event is not for her but for the people of the *favela* community. It is so they may receive the Holy Spirit so God can do for them what He has done for her in the *favela* where she grew up:

> It was on a day like this that God pulled me from the Complexo de Alemão, astray from the Lord's presence, a brother dead because of the drug trade, . . . [another] brother four years in prison because of the drug trade. They spoke to my mother: is this what God has intended for Elaine, roaming the *favela* up and down? No, this was not what God had written about me, this was not what the Lord had spoken to my mother, who kept praying. And that is why I am here on a Saturday like this.

The crowd responds with hallelujahs as she finishes her testimony and starts her next song, which echoes through the *favela*.[2]

The performance of Elaine Martins can be read as a blueprint for successful gospel performances in Rio de Janeiro. Martins's texts echo common evangelical lyrics that praise the Lord, and her style of singing is relatively uncontroversial in Pentecostal circles. Her songs can generally be typified as romantic ballads bordering on soul and contemporary R&B. Equally important, Martins regularly makes clear that she is a faithful Christian by redirecting the praise she receives from the audience to the Lord, expressing her humility in front of the enthusiastic crowd. Furthermore, she reveals instances of her past to convey that she once led a sinful life until she was saved from the harsh and potentially dangerous *favela* life and was able to bloom and grow into a respected gospel artist.

This chapter aims to contribute to the debates about the worldwide spread of Pentecostalism and charismatic Christianity and to the debates about the relation between religion and media. The analysis of Pentecostal music contributes to these debates because it highlights that current mergers between Pentecostalism and electronic media constitute new and often larger audiences, yet underscores that new circuits of transmission regularly invoke theological and normative conflicts about the borders between the sacred and the profane. In this chapter specifically, I hope to show that Pentecostal musicians struggle with the potential gain *and* loss of charisma in "the age of mechanical reproduction" (Benjamin 1968) and that they attempt to guard themselves against possible denunciations as insincere *crentes* (believers) by including testimonies in their performances, CDs, and DVDs. Before doing so, I will briefly say something about Pentecostalism in Brazil and gospel music in daily life.

Pentecostalism in Brazil

Coinciding with Brazil's return to democracy in the late 1980s, Pentecostal churches expanded rapidly. The growth of Pentecostal churches in Brazil largely corresponds to its success in most other parts of the world. In Latin America Pentecostalism has grown substantially since the eighties (Boudewijnse, Droogers, and Kamsteeg 1998; Garrard-Burnett and Stoll 1993), and in various parts of Africa it has become one of the most popular types of Christianity (Meyer 2004). Indeed, as several authors have noted, the spread of Pentecostalism runs markedly parallel to other well-known forms of cultural globalization (Coleman 2000; Csordas 2009; Droogers 2001; Martin 2002; Robbins 2004).

The Brazilian census of 2010 showed that 22 percent of the population described itself as *evangélico* (evangelical), a rise of approximately

61 percent in ten years. In Brazil, the term *evangélicos* is used to denote the broader collection of Protestant Christians in Brazil. Nevertheless, the majority of Brazil's 42.3 million *evangélicos* can be identified as Pentecostal. Interestingly, the evangelical denomination that displays the biggest rise in affiliates according to the 2010 census is the Assembléia de Deus (Assemblies of God), one of the oldest Pentecostal denominations of Brazil (from 8.4 to 12.3 million in ten years).[3]

The popularity of Pentecostal churches in Brazil should be understood in light of the harsh conditions that many inhabitants of Brazilian cities face (Antoniazzi 1994; Montes 1998) in combination with the Pentecostal appropriation of modern mass media (Birman and Lehmann 1999; Corten 2001; Novaes 2002; Oro 2003). Especially the neo-Pentecostal Igreja Universal do Reino de Deus (Universal Church of the Kingdom of God) has become known for its use of communication networks. Over the last twenty-five years, the church has obtained one of the six national public television broadcast networks, Rede Record, mounted a professional Internet site, and started its own publishing house and record company. It publishes the weekly newspaper *Folha Universal*, and it owns several radio stations. Meanwhile, older Pentecostal denominations such as the Assembléia de Deus have also become much more visible and audible in the public domain.

Here, as in earlier work, I argue that to understand the appeal of Pentecostalism in Rio de Janeiro (and beyond), we have to pay close attention to how Pentecostal media correspond with the "structures of feeling" (Williams 1977) and thus examine the relations between the aesthetic of popular Pentecostal media and the structural life conditions and cultural backgrounds of the people involved. Such an endeavor not only helps us to explain the emotional involvement of the people with (the content of) these media but also demonstrates the particular "glocal" form Pentecostalism acquires in Rio de Janeiro.

Music and Pentecostalism in the *Favelas* of Rio de Janeiro

Pentecostal movements have been highly successful in spreading a relatively coherent religious form across the world, and nearly all scholars interested in Pentecostalism confirm that music is an essential element of its appeal (Cox 1995; Hackett 1998; Miller and Yamamori 2007; Meyer

2010). If one looks at the contemporary Brazilian context, for example, music is the cultural form par excellence through which Pentecostal messages are remediated. Moreover, successful radio and television programs, magazines, or Internet sites are often related to the Brazilian gospel music industry (Mendonça 2008, 229).

In earlier work I have discussed the important role of gospel music in the reproduction of collective Pentecostal identity in the context of *favela* life, and I have argued that the transmission of gospel music is experienced as the circulation of the redemptive powers of the Holy Spirit. Such an experience of gospel music is closely related to the social conditions of the *favelas* of Rio de Janeiro (Oosterbaan 2008, 2009). Here I briefly want to emphasize once more how gospel music intersects with *favela* life and popular Pentecostal notions concerning the technological transmission of the Holy Spirit and its bodily reception.

Cruzadas evangelistas are public Pentecostal events intentionally held to reach as many *favela* inhabitants as possible through loudly amplified music and prayer. During *cruzadas*, artists and preachers regularly deliver elaborate *testemunhos* (testimonies) of personal suffering.[4] Testimonies are highly structured accounts of the encounter with God that generally follow a clear narrative pattern. Many testimonies offer dramatized accounts of a (wretched) life leading to a moment of catharsis when the narrator decides to accept Jesus as personal savior. In the context of the *favelas*, these testimonies frequently contain personal accounts of the violence related to the *tráfico* (drug trade).

Though *tráfico*-related violence is by no means the only or principal social circumstance that provides meaning to Pentecostal events in the *favelas* of Rio de Janeiro, it belongs to the more intrusive life experiences around which collective stories of suffering in the *favelas* are organized (Machado da Silva 2008). Though clearly there are differences between innocent victims and willful perpetrators of *tráfico*-related crime, young men are fairly vulnerable to the structural persuasions that lead to a dangerous life of crime. Accounts of former drug gang members during *cruzadas* speak both to the young men still involved in the *tráfico* and to the wider public who understands that it takes extraordinary powers to keep youngsters (neighbors, brothers, boyfriends, sons) from pursuing such a path.

Not infrequently, a *cruzada* has a decisive impact on the life of a young *favela* inhabitant. Two weeks after the *cruzada* with Elaine Martins, I interviewed Emerson, an inhabitant of the *favela* where the *cruzada* was held. Seven years earlier, Emerson had been head of a *bonde* (gang) of a large criminal faction operating in the *favela*, until a *cruzada* led him onto the path of transformation.

> EMERSON: It was during a *cruzada* like that one that I offered my life to Jesus. . . . I was with the *bonde*, everyone was armed. We were close to the event, listening. And at that moment those gospel music songs were reaching me, entering my heart. At the end of the *cruzada* they called people to come forward and pray and I went. I pulled off my backpack and laid down my weapons and I went to receive a prayer. At that very moment I received the Holy Spirit; total remission. Nothing had been able to fulfill me till then, not the drugs, not the *baile funk* [popular dances in the *favelas*], the liquor, the flirting, nothing had fulfilled me the way the presence of God did at that moment.
>
> MO: What is the role of music according to you?
>
> EMERSON: If you put on this music and transmit it to the boys who are involved in the *tráfico*, when they hear it, . . . ahhh [*indication of being overwhelmed*]. And not just them, it speaks to everyone. When you are in pain or in a moment of commotion, people whose child is using drugs or imprisoned. When this music is transmitted, people start to cry. Impressive, the impact. Do you understand? The impact changed my life, when I heard it I said, "What is this?" It is heavier than a *ponta* 30 [30-millimeter bullet]; it is like throwing a grenade of glory, a tremendous effect. Seven years ago it was. And Elaine Martins was pulled out from a community [*favela*], there in the Complexo de Alemão, she was also rescued. Today God uses her primarily for worship music, impressive; she has a gift [*dom*]. God gives people gifts to use. He gave her this gift and blessed her.

Emerson's praise of Elaine Martins exemplifies her role as a charismatic gospel singer who, by means of her gift, is able to save youngsters involved in the drug gangs. Her testimony provides confirmation of the redemptive powers of the Lord, who granted her a life as a successful artist and firmly anchors the story of her own transformation in the sociocultural background of the people present at the *cruzada*. However, as I will argue in the remainder of this chapter, her testimony also serves other purposes. To reach potential converts with the help of media technology, singers have to deal with the Janus-faced consequences of its appropriation, and testimonies play a pivotal role in their efforts.

Charisma and Mechanical Reproduction

Since the beginning of the 1990s, the gospel music industry has developed into a professional arena with large revenues. Large evangelical companies, such as the Rio de Janeiro–based MK, sustain a total production and distribution network. MK has its own FM radio station (93 FM), a publishing house, and Internet sites where the artists and their records are advertised. Nowadays, gospel music can also be bought in regular music stores in Rio de Janeiro, and the gospel radio stations Melodia FM and 93 FM are ranked as the second and third most popular FM radio stations in the city.[5]

The professionalization of the gospel music industry in Brazil during the eighties and nineties has opened up new avenues for the distribution and dissemination of gospel music throughout the country. Gospel singers not only perform throughout Brazil, they also record CDs and DVDs and try to get their music played on radio and television channels. In Pentecostal circles, the growing popularity of evangelical radio stations is understood as a great step forward in bringing the gospel to Brazilians. Pentecostal singers are seen as important instruments of the Lord to reach and convert people, as we have seen in the case of Emerson. Pentecostal audiences generally consider Brazilian gospel singers charismatic people who have received the gift (*dom*) of God to transmit His spiritual powers by means of their music. Charisma should be understood here as the recognition of the extraordinary capabilities of particular individuals to mediate between supernatural powers and an audience (Csordas 1997). According to Thomas Csordas, while charisma is generally perceived as a personal attribute beyond human agency, in fact it is the result of skilled performance.

Where Csordas focuses on the rhetorical features and ritual language of such performances, Marleen de Witte (2008) argues that charisma also relies upon the carefully crafted (and edited) representation of persons in/through modern media. According to her, "charisma operates at the interface between the technological and the religious" (88). Such a conception of charisma allows us to unravel its contemporary manifestation as the fusion of bodily techniques, religious language, and media technologies (see also Schulz 2003) and also gives us insight into how "affect" operates at the interface of technology and charismatic Christianity (for a discussion of affect, see Bialecki's chapter in this volume). However, as I argue, this fusion carries a number of tensions and can also generate a corrosion of charisma as a result of the ambivalent Pentecostal appraisal of mass adoration and stardom.

Fame and Sincerity

As gospel musicians enter the arena of popular consumption, they have a chance to become known throughout the country, yet they also face several pitfalls. Media technologies have changed and expanded the reproduction of charisma, but have also generated controversies about the authenticity and sincerity of the performers. With the appropriation of mainstream media techniques, boundaries between Pentecostal performers and other kinds of pop singers in Brazil are increasingly blurred. Staged performances of Pentecostal artists generally expand the similarities between them and so-called worldly artists who try to make it in the music industry. Moreover, in recent years, a number of professional singers with non-Pentecostal backgrounds, whose careers were not very successful, publicly converted and started making gospel music, supposedly to boost their record sales.[6] Among Pentecostal audiences this has led to doubts about the ulterior motives of these performers, and questions were raised as to whether they were sincere and whether they converted out of "real" spiritual desire or to earn money and fame (see also Cunha 2007, 93–99).[7]

Doubts about the sincerity of a person's conversion potentially annihilate charisma. The general acceptance of a performer's charisma stands or falls with his or her credibility as a Christian whose genuine motive is to reach out and convert people by means of the music. Becoming famous is desirable because it enlarges one's reach, but, according to the general Pentecostal opinion, it can also lead artists to forget that unlike "worldly" performers, they serve a higher purpose. Even those gospel singers who have a Pentecostal background run the risk of losing their status as extraordinary channels of God if they do not make clear that they are different from "worldly" musicians. Performers who do not clearly state that they are singing in the service of the Lord run the risk of being regarded as "ordinary" celebrities who are in it simply and purely for the fame, status, and wealth.

Pastor Roberto of an evangelical church in the same *favela* where Elaine Martins performed had sung for a considerable time in a gospel band that was becoming moderately famous when he quit. When I asked him how at the time he dealt with fans who adored him, he replied,

> I always tried to hide from those things. . . . I had learned that if we want to go to heaven we should not sin, sin separates man from the presence of God. Those who stand with the microphone in their hand become the center of attention. If you don't know who you are and for whom you are singing, you will not resist, you will drown. The biggest problem is forgetting your mission. Fame is a marvelous thing. You have to know how to control these things. A friend of mine is pastor of Fernanda Brum [very popular MK gospel singer]; another is pastor of a church of ten thousand members. They haven't changed at all. A[nother] pastor is responsible for a church with fifty-two thousand members but every time his church grows, he thanks God that He has made it possible. He couldn't have done it otherwise. The same things are happening in gospel circles, people think that they are stars. They are stars, all right, but what is their mission? Is it the same as Ivete Sangalo or Roberto Carlos [very famous Brazilian pop singers]? No, their mission is to bring the truth, and that means you can't lie. That is why you can't separate these things. Rede Globo has recently opened up Som Livre [record company] for gospel music, because of the market.

As the last sentences demonstrate, Pastor Roberto connects the apparent threats to the sanctified status of Pentecostal artists to recent changes in the gospel music market in Brazil. Recognizing the potential benefits of investing in gospel music, influential record companies have started to employ gospel musicians. Rede Globo, the most influential media network in Brazil, contracted a number of renowned Brazilian gospel singers by way of its company Som Livre in 2008; and Sony Music, one of the world's largest record companies, followed in 2010. The involvement of these record companies acknowledges that Brazilian gospel music has become part of mainstream culture, yet has also encouraged debates among Pentecostal adherents.

The problems related to the public image and performances of gospel singers who enter the domain of mass consumption and stardom are not particular to Brazil, nor reducible to the recent commercialization of gospel music. As Webb Keane has argued, Protestant Christianity heavily influenced moral understandings of the distinction between outward behavior (words, gestures) and inward feelings (thoughts), which subsequently elevated the problem of sincerity. In response to the suspicion of alleged religious behavior as possibly fraudulent—as not "truly" reflecting what a person thinks or feels—sincerity became a key trope in evaluating whether people really experienced divine presence. As Keane states, "To be sincere . . . is to utter words that can be taken primarily to express underlying beliefs or intentions" (2007, 209). Since for most Protestant Christians baptism by itself is not a sufficient mark of a transformation into a *crente* (believer), "adults must confirm their true faith in public performance, one of an endless series of socially grounded affirmations" (216).

Keane convincingly argues that the particular Calvinist notion of sincerity became an important index of modern notions of the self and of interiority and helped to drive a conceptual wedge between utterances and thoughts. Moreover, as the words of Pastor Roberto indicate, questions about sincerity—"knowing for whom you are singing"—have become part of the moral evaluations of contemporary Brazilian evangelical movements. Nevertheless, we should keep in mind that Keane analyzes a particular branch of Protestant Christianity (Calvinism), and that the relations between piety, words, and behavior cannot be transposed to Brazilian charismatic Christianity straightforwardly.

Affirmations of divine presence in Brazilian Pentecostalism involve more than the evaluation of words, and Brazilian Pentecostals arguably hold a different semiotic ideology than the Calvinist one that Keane describes. In charismatic Christianity, the confirmation of divine presence generally involves a scheme of bodily gestures and experiences. Some of these practices and experiences are very specific to Pentecostalism and thus markedly different from the "sensational forms" (Meyer 2009) of other Christian traditions. This also holds for the "language ideology" (Keane 2007) of most Pentecostal adherents, for example. Pentecostals generally value other aspects of language besides the meaning of words and, contrary to most other forms of Protestantism, they recognize "the supernatural inspiration that animates language-acts like prophecy and tongues" (Bialecki this volume).

As in the case of Elaine Martins and other Brazilian gospel performers, speaking in tongues (*glossolalia*) and other acts performed during gospel shows generally help to confirm the sanctity and authenticity of the Pentecostal musician and his or her music. Nevertheless, this does not do away with the problem of sincerity. The question of whether and when gospel music songs transmit "affective energy," as Bialecki calls it (this volume), cannot be entirely separated from the question of whether the people who mediate such energies are perceived as sincere, because Pentecostal audiences generally feel that the spiritual status of the medium (singer) and of the content (the sound) influence each other.

Sincerity operates at multiple levels, and evaluations of it involve not only the actual performances of gospel musicians onstage, but also their (presumed) behavior offstage. Fame specifically heightens discussions about the motives of Pentecostal celebrities, as it elevates their status to exceptional people in service of the Lord, yet supposedly also lets them taste of the "worldly" gratifications of mass admiration. This potentially makes them forget what their mission was, as Pastor Roberto put it. It is thus at the particular junction of evangelical expansion, technological innovation (the microphone/the record), and capitalism (the gospel market) in Brazil that sincerity is brought to the forefront as part of the question of who and what is sanctified or not. As a result, Pentecostal musicians are pressed to demonstrate that they are trying to become recognized for the right reasons.[8] As I argue, Pentecostal singers attempt to cancel out the corrosive effects on charisma by adding other features to their (mediated) performances: personal testimonies, prayers, emotional confessions, and other (bodily) expressions that have become part and parcel of contemporary gospel styles and that (ought to) confirm they are genuine.

Gospel Music, Testimony, and Idolatry

As in the case of the performances and CDs and DVDs of Elaine Martins, gospel music is regularly accompanied by testimonies of the singers in question. Some CDs and DVDs even have a separate track or menu category called *testemunho*. Mediated testimonies of Pentecostal performers help to build and maintain charisma in the face of commercialization and mass admiration because they potentially do a number of things simultaneously. They first and foremost demonstrate that the Pentecostal artist in question should not be confused with a regular "worldly" artist. Surely, as most singers and admirers will confirm, the lyrics of gospel songs remain one of the most important characteristics that separate gospel songs from their worldly counterparts (see Oosterbaan 2008), yet testimonies are important practices that help to distinguish gospel music from worldly music.

Testimonies can also demonstrate that the artists' acceptance of Jesus as savior was not the result of a superficial image change, made to benefit from a growing niche in the music market, but that such an acceptance followed some form of genuine spiritual experience, generally related to personal trauma in the past. As Elaine Martins's condensed testimony and Emerson's words exemplify, testimonies are persuasive narratives that identify singer and audience as coming from or belonging to identical life worlds. Such identifications can help to create a strong sense of intimacy with the performer. It allows audiences to identify with the performer who experienced comparable personal torment but who was (also) saved by the almighty God.

Interestingly, this mechanism comes surprisingly close to the way celebrity culture is reproduced in general, as Jo Littler (2004) has insightfully shown. According to Littler, "intimacy, reflexivity and dramatising the 'grounded' moment of pre-fame are key tropes through which current celebrity culture is reproduced and maintained" (23). While testimonies reproduce an apparent "closeness" to gospel stars in much the same way proximity to "ordinary" celebrities is produced, Pentecostal testimonies generally also serve to authenticate the performers as sincere and pious Christians who can therefore function as mediums of the powers of the Lord and conductors of the Holy Spirit.

Identification with gospel performers can help to sustain the experience that singers and audience members are equals under God. Such an experience is important because the question of hierarchy between performers and audience is related to controversies about the alleged idolization of Pentecostal celebrities. Pentecostal adherents in Rio de Janeiro occasionally expressed their worries about the dangers of "fandom" when "proper" worship of the gifts of God turns into an idolization of the singers in question. As Keane has shown, there is a recurring problem regarding worship and media in Protestantism. Doctrines and ideologies can be transmitted only with some type of semiotic embodiment—some kind of material form that carries meaning (words, signs, pictures, sculptures, etc.) (Keane 2007, 81). For most Protestants this entails a recurring danger that the material form is revered instead of the transcendent power it is meant to transmit. In that case the material form becomes idolized. Even though there is a perpetual effort in Christianity to purify doctrine and separate the "true meaning" from its material form, every medium introduced to replace the "fetish" runs the risk of becoming fetish itself (Keane 2007, 76–82).[9]

In relation to contemporary Brazilian gospel music, this worry has risen as a result of the growth of the gospel music market and in particular as a result of the mass mediatization of representations of Pentecostal performers. Arguably, as in "ordinary" celebrity culture, the musical skills and the representations of performers reinforce each other and potentially coproduce a sense of intimacy with a performer. Yet it is particularly in relation to the (image of the) performer that worries among Brazilian Pentecostals arise (I never encountered a discussion concerning the dangers of adoring the sound of the music).[10] As Marleen de Witte has argued, charismatic performers in Ghana are regularly treated as "living icons" as a result of their exceptional capabilities to mediate the sacred (de Witte 2009). However, as I witnessed in Rio de Janeiro, such iconization might potentially also be detrimental to the charismatic status of a performer when doubts arise about the targets of the worship energy of the audience.

Inclusion of testimonies in (recorded) performances partially eradicates the suspicion that worship is in fact idolatry because it allows gospel singers to clarify that any adoration (of them) is in fact worship of the Lord. As I described in the opening of this chapter, Elaine Martins reassured the crowd that the *cruzada evangelista* was not about her but about the marvelous things God could do for the people of the *favela*. The phrase *bate palma para Jesus* (clap your hands for Jesus), regularly yelled during gospel shows throughout Rio de Janeiro, is also indicative of this eradication mechanism. As audience member, one applauds the gift that God has given the artist and celebrates the surrender of the artist and audience to His divine plan to use them as channels for the spiritual powers. Recounting their own testimonies onstage allows artists to clarify that they are shining onstage by the grace of God and that any similarity between worshipper and fan or gospel artist and ordinary celebrity is harmless.

NOTES

1. *Cruzada evangelista* (evangelical crusade) is the popular name for public evangelical events in Rio de Janeiro.

2. The force of her testimony is enlarged by the fact that the *favela* where she grew up—the renowned Complexo de Alemão—regularly appears in broadcast media as the (former) fortress of the infamous drug-trafficking gang Comando Vermelho (Red Command). Just months before her performance at this *cruzada evangelista* in 2011, the Brazilian military spectacularly invaded the Complexo de Alemão to rid the *favela* of its heavily armed traffickers.

3. Instituto Brasileiro de Geografia e Estatística (Brazilian Institute of Geography and Statistics), http://www.ibge.gov.br/home/estatistica/populacao/censo2010/ caracteristicas_religiao_deficiencia/caracteristicas_religiao_deficiencia_tab_pdf.shtm (accessed July 24, 2012). See also "Assembleia de Deus atrai 3,9 milhões de novos evangélicos," *Folha de São Paulo*, June 30, 2012, http://www.folha.uol.com.br/fsp/ poder/51844-assembleia-de-deus-atrai-39-milhoes-de-novos-evangelicos.shtml (accessed July 24, 2012).

4. *Testemunhar* is Portuguese for witnessing. For an elaborate description of the relation between conversion and witnessing in evangelical culture, see the work of Susan Harding (2000).

5. For the ranking of FM radio audiences in Rio de Janeiro in 2012, see "Audiência RJ: Com mercado em baixa apenas as rádios 93 FM, JB e Rádio Globo apresentara crescimento no 'top 10,'" Tudoradio.com, September 11, 2012, http://tudoradio.com/ noticias/ver/7925-audiencia-rj-com-mercado-em-baixa-apenas-as-radios-93-fm-jb-e-radio-globo-apresentara-crescimento-no-top-10 (accessed December 8, 2012).

6. In contrast to their "worldly" counterpart, the Pentecostal public is generally known to consist of faithful buyers of CDs, and the potential earnings in the gospel industry are thus relatively high.

7. Recently, Heather Hendershot has suggested that the ambivalent border between Christian and non-Christian music in the United States provides the basis for the

access of religiously inspired music into the secular market (Hendershot 2004). Joêzer de Souza Mendonça (2008) makes a similar argument about Brazil. While I certainly think that such crossovers are taking place in Brazil, there is also widespread concern among Pentecostal adherents about the possible dilution of Christian music.

8. Whereas doubts concerning the sincerity of gospel performers run markedly parallel to discussions about their authenticity, as for instance James S. Bielo (2011) has described, authenticity in my opinion can be regarded as an overarching concept that involves more than the notion of sincerity. Someone could be regarded as sincere but still can be found lacking authenticity, for example. The other way around would be somewhat unlikely.

9. Matthew Engelke (2007) has also analyzed this Protestant "problem of presence" insightfully.

10. While the relation between the adoration of gospel music and that of gospel performers deserves much more attention than I can grant here, it is arguable that the strong emphasis on the dangers of worshipping the (representation of the) artists is related to the historical role that images and statues played in the European Reformation and the perceived materiality of the image versus the supposed "immediacy" of speech and song (Eisenlohr 2009; Engelke 2007).

REFERENCES

Antoniazzi, Alberto. 1994. "A Igreja Católica face a expansão do Pentecostalismo." In *Nem anjos nem demonios*, edited by Alberto Antoniazzi, Avelino Grassi, Cecília Loreto Mariz, and Ingrid Sarti, 17–23. Petrópolis, Rio de Janeiro: Editora Vozes.

Benjamin, Walter. 1968. "The Work of Art in the Age of Mechanical Reproduction." In *Illuminations: Essays and Reflections*, edited by Hannah Arendt, 217–51. New York: Schocken.

Bielo, James S. 2011. *Emerging Evangelicals: Faith, Modernity, and the Desire for Authenticity*. New York: New York University Press.

Birman, Patricia, and David Lehmann. 1999. "Religion and the Media in a Battle for Ideological Hegemony: The Universal Church of the Kingdom of God and TV Globo in Brazil." *Bulletin of Latin American Research* 18 (2): 145–64.

Boudewijnse, Barbara, André Droogers, and Frans Kamsteeg, eds. 1998. *More Than Opium: An Anthropological Approach to Latin American and Caribbean Pentecostal Praxis*. Lanham, MD: Scarecrow Press.

Coleman, Simon. 2000. *The Globalisation of Charismatic Christianity: Spreading the Gospel of Prosperity*. Cambridge: Cambridge University Press.

Corten, André. 2001. "Transnationalised Religious Needs and Political Delegitimisation in Latin America." In *Between Babel and Pentecost: Transnational Pentecostalism in Africa and Latin America*, edited by André Corten and Ruth Marshall-Fratani, 106–23. Bloomington: Indiana University Press.

Cox, Harvey. 1995. *Fire from Heaven: The Rise of Pentecostal Spirituality and the Reshaping of Religion in the Twenty-First Century*. Cambridge, MA: Da Capo.

Csordas, Thomas J. 1997. *Language, Charisma and Creativity: The Ritual Life of a Religious Movement*. Berkeley: University of California Press.

———. 2009. "Introduction: Modalities of Transnational Transcendence." In *Transnational Transcendence: Essays on Religion and Globalization*, edited by Thomas J. Csordas, 1–29. Berkeley: University of California Press.

Cunha, Magali do Nascimento. 2007. *A explosão gospel: Um olhar das ciências humanas sobre o cenário evangélico no Brasil*. Rio de Janeiro: Mauad.

De Witte, Marleen. 2008. "Spirit Media: Charismatics, Traditionalists, and Mediation Practices in Ghana." PhD diss., University of Amsterdam.

———. 2009. "Modes of Binding, Moments of Bonding: Mediating Divine Touch in Ghanaian Pentecostalism and Traditionalism." In *Aesthetic Formations: Media, Religion, and the Senses*, edited by Birgit Meyer, 183–205. New York: Palgrave Macmillan.

Droogers, André. 2001. "Globalisation and Pentecostal Success." In *Between Babel and Pentecost: Transnational Pentecostalism in Africa and Latin America*, edited by André Corten and Ruth Marshall-Fratani, 41–61. Bloomington: Indiana University Press.

Eisenlohr, Patrick. 2009. "Technologies of the Spirit: Devotional Islam, Sound Reproduction and the Dialectics of Mediation and Immediacy in Mauritius." *Anthropological Theory* 9 (3): 273–96.

Engelke, Matthew. 2007. *A Problem of Presence: Beyond Scripture in an African Church*. Berkeley: University of California Press.

Garrard-Burnett, Virginia, and David Stoll, eds. 1993. *Rethinking Protestantism in Latin America*. Philadelphia: Temple University Press.

Hackett, Rosalind I. J. 1998. "Charismatic/Pentecostal Appropriation of Media Technologies in Nigeria and Ghana." *Journal of Religion in Africa* 28 (3): 258–77.

Harding, Susan. 2000. *The Book of Jerry Falwell: Fundamentalist Language and Politics*. Princeton: Princeton University Press.

Hendershot, Heather. 2004. *Shaking the World for Jesus: Media and Conservative Evangelical Culture*. Chicago: University of Chicago Press.

Keane, Webb. 2007. *Christian Moderns: Freedom and Fetish in the Mission Encounter*. Berkeley: University of California Press.

Littler, Jo. 2004. "Making Fame Ordinary: Intimacy, Reflexivity and 'Keeping It Real.'" *Mediactive* 2:8–25.

Machado da Silva, Luiz Antonio. 2008. Introduction to *Vida sob cerco: Violência e rotina nas favelas do Rio de Janeiro*, edited by Luiz Antonio Machado da Silva, 13–26. Rio de Janeiro: Nova Fronteira.

Martin, David. 2002. *Pentecostalism: The World Their Parish*. Oxford: Blackwell.

Mendonça, Joêzer de Souza. 2008. "O Evangelho segundo o *Gospel*: Mídia, música *pop* e neopentecostalismo." *Revista do Conservatório de Música da UFPel* 1:220–49.

Meyer, Birgit. 2004. "Christianity in Africa: From African Independent to Pentecostal-Charismatic Churches." *Annual Review of Anthropology* 33:447–74.

———. 2009. Introduction to *Aesthetic Formations: Media, Religion, and the Senses*, edited by Birgit Meyer, 1–28. New York: Palgrave MacMillan.

——. 2010. "Pentecostalism and Globalization." In *Studying Global Pentecostalism: Theories and Methods*, edited by Allan Anderson, Michael Bergunder, André F. Droogers, and Cornelis van der Laan, 113–30. Berkeley: University of California Press.

Miller, Donald E., and Tetsunao Yamamori, eds. 2007. *Global Pentecostalism: The New Face of Christian Social Engagement*. Berkeley: University of California Press.

Montes, Maria L. 1998. "As figuras do sagrado: Entre o público e o privado." In *História da vida privada no Brasil* 4, edited by Lilia Moritz Schwarz, 63–171. São Paulo: Companhia das Letras.

Novaes, Regina R. 2002. "Crenças religiosas e convicções politicas: Fronteiras e passagens." In *Política e cultura: Século XXI*, edited by Luís Carlos Fridman, 63–98. Rio de Janeiro: Relume Dumará.

Oosterbaan, Martijn. 2008. "Spiritual Attunement: Pentecostal Radio in the Soundscape of a Favela in Rio de Janeiro." *Social Text* 26 (3): 123–45.

——. 2009. "Sonic Supremacy: Sound, Space and the Politics of Presence in a Favela in Rio de Janeiro." *Critique of Anthropology* 29 (1): 81–104.

Oro, Ari Pedro. 2003. "A política da Igreja Universal e seus reflexos nos campos religioso e político brasileiros." *Revista Brasileira de Ciências Sociais* 18:53–69.

Robbins, Joel. 2004. "The Globalization of Pentecostal and Charismatic Christianity." *Annual Review of Anthropology* 33:117–43.

Schulz, Dorothea E. 2003. "'Charisma and Brotherhood' Revisited: Mass-Mediated Forms of Spirituality in Urban Mali." *Journal of Religion in Africa* 33 (2): 146–71.

Williams, Raymond. 1977. *Marxism and Literature*. Oxford: Oxford University Press.

9

Mediating Miracle Truth

Permanent Struggle and Fragile Conviction in Kyrgyzstan

MATHIJS PELKMANS

Introduction

The miracle occurred on a cold Sunday morning in March, in a poorly lit basement, actually a restaurant, which doubled as church hall for a chapter of the Church of Jesus Christ[1] in southern Kyrgyzstan. The service had started with the usual worship songs, but soon everyone's attention rested on one of the congregants. Venera, a Kyrgyz woman in her twenties, had not spoken a single word in her life, and was about to be cured of her speech impediment. The prayers of the approximately seventy congregants waxed and waned; their sound joined outcries for divine intervention, producing a rhythm that made the air heavy with anticipation and full of energy. This was the kind of atmosphere in which one would expect the Holy Spirit to descend. Pastor Kadyrjan stood right in front of Venera and pressed his hand on her forehead. The tension in the air was palpable, and anticipation peaked. The phrase "Help her, Jesus" came from everywhere. Still nothing happened. Venera stood trembling in the middle. Then, when some started to give up hope, the Holy Spirit descended upon Venera, and she started to speak. She spoke hesitantly and barely audibly to most congregants, but those who stood closest reported that the first word she uttered in her life was "Jesus" (isus).

Given this chapter's title, the reader may wonder about my position regarding miracle truth. Will I proceed by affirming the miracle's divine nature, and potentially be accused of having lost the critical distance deemed indispensable for analysis? Or will I instead deny the possibility of divine intervention, and possibly be blamed for positivistic reductionism and atheist bias? If the former were the case, I might marvel at God's inscrutable ways and suggest that the miracle demonstrated the power of prayer. That view is what Bakyt, one of the congregants, expressed to me after the service had ended and we were having lunch in a nearby *chaikhana* (tea house). If by contrast I adopted a secular perspective, then I might analyze how the building up of momentum produced merely the illusion of a miracle. To prove this point I could have stressed that those who had suggested that Venera called out "Jesus" later mentioned that they were not sure and that perhaps it had only been a grunt. In fact, this is what Bakyt—the same Bakyt—told me a couple of weeks after the events, when it turned out that Venera had not made further progress in learning to speak.

Despite their centrality in Pentecostal churches, miracles have rarely featured as an *analytical* theme in studies of Pentecostalism. This is partly due to the awkwardness of the truth question; so even when the scholarly gaze has rested on miracles, it has tended to evade the issue of truth. Thus, one prominent writer has argued that "analytically there is no observable difference between true and false miracles" (de Vries 2001, 27). Bruce Kapferer, moreover, suggests that there is no need to engage with the truth question because the significance of miracles is in their effect and affect (2003; see also Ewing 1994). Such approaches rightfully reject positivistic reductionism, but in this rejection they risk excluding more productive engagements with the truth question. That is, by not examining how truth is produced, they leave important analytical opportunities untouched. As Charles Hirschkind argues, attention needs to be paid to how people distinguish between true and false miracles (2011, 94). *Pace* Kapferer, one cannot understand effect and affect without addressing the truth question, especially when the reality of miracles—their truth—is not taken for granted by the involved, such as was often the case in Kyrgyzstan. Bakyt's shifting perception regarding the miracle's truthfulness profoundly influenced how he spoke about the event and potentially affected his relationship with the church. This underlines the importance of analyzing the trajectories of miracle truth.

A focus on miracles is intellectually productive precisely because the mysterious and unstable qualities of miracles (and their truth) resonate with the unstable nature of conviction, as can be seen in the Pentecostal advance in post-Soviet Central Asia. This resonance can be illustrated with reference to the term "charisma." Charisma is a quality of the present, revealed in the here and now, which cannot be durably transposed across time or space. Charisma as divine gift is what makes Pentecostalism both effervescent and transient. But understood in a secular Weberian sense, charisma is also the key source of authority "at times of distress," when legal structures have collapsed and tradition has been uprooted, as was the case in post-Soviet Kyrgyzstan.[2] That is, the sociopolitical context in which the miracle occurred was itself unstable. As I will go on to discuss, the unstable Pentecostal mission on the "post-atheist" Muslim-Christian frontier offers a stark illustration of the effervescent as well as fragile qualities of Pentecostal conviction.

Pentecostal Truth in a Post-Soviet Muslim Context

Zamira had moved to the provincial city of Jalalabad in southern Kyrgyzstan a couple of years before we met. Her marriage had ended, meaning that she had to leave her in-laws' village house and move with her two daughters to the city. She was lucky to find a new job as a teacher, but surviving on an inadequate salary in a city where she had no direct relatives was an uphill battle. The battle became an imminent crisis when her five-year-old daughter fell seriously ill. "I didn't have any options left. I had taken my daughter everywhere, to the mullah [here: Islamic healer], the hospital, but all they did was take my money. That's when I accepted [my colleague's] offer to take me to her church. For a whole night I didn't sleep, I stayed up and prayed. I gave myself over to God, asked Jesus for forgiveness. And by the next day my daughter started to feel better!" Zamira joined the church's home group meetings straightaway, meanwhile keeping her conversion hidden from her relatives. When they found out several months later, they were shocked. Her brothers, one of whom had been involved in an Islamic piety movement, accused her not only of apostasy but also of betraying her Kyrgyz-ness (*kyrgyzchylyk*). Her parents also responded negatively, but they increasingly "took it for what it was. They knew how I had suffered from the sickness of my daughter." Zamira stressed that since then she has continuously witnessed to others "about the healing of my daughter through Jesus Christ, and that He has completely transformed my life. I have witnessed to my acquaintances, my relatives, my colleagues."

***

This story is one of many that I collected among members of the Charismatic-Pentecostal Church of Jesus Christ, the largest evangelical-Pentecostal church in Kyrgyzstan, with ten thousand members and forty-five congregations. Zamira's account has many parallels with Pentecostal conversion stories from other parts of the world. The swiftness of conversion, the discourse of discontinuity, the importance of witnessing, and the centrality of divine intervention (such as in healing) are elements that feature prominently in Pentecostal discourse and practice worldwide. These familiar themes, however, unfolded in a context that is relatively new to Pentecostalism and rarely covered in the literature. As in any Muslim context, conversion to Christianity was controversial, but seventy years of Soviet anti-religious modernization had eroded the position of Islam and made conversion a possibility.

Although several underground Pentecostal churches had been active in Soviet Kyrgyzstan, these were referred to as "traditional" and "legalistic," which catered only to a narrow circle of Russians. It was only after the collapse of the Soviet Union that Pentecostal churches started to attract larger numbers of people, including Muslims. By the early 2000s approximately twenty-five thousand Muslim Kyrgyz had converted to evangelical-Pentecostal Christianity (ethnic Kyrgyz made up approximately 50 percent of these churches, alongside Russians, Koreans, Tatars, and others). This section discusses the process of conversion, and asks how Pentecostal conversion, with its characteristics of rupture, charisma, and intensity, articulated with the post-Soviet Muslim geography in which it unfolded.

Given that conversion from Islam to Christianity is exceptional, it is relevant to ask how and why conversion became an option for some Kyrgyz, that is, how its conditions of possibility had emerged historically. This is particularly significant because Christian missions in the pre-Soviet period had failed miserably. To the Kyrgyz, the idea of conversion to Christianity had been inconceivable; in the early 1900s evangelization instead reinforced the notion that Christianity was a religion of alien Europeans and that Kyrgyz were Muslim by definition (Pelkmans 2009a,

3–4). Seventy years of anti-religious campaigning and Soviet moderniza-
tion profoundly altered the playing field. The anti-religious policies that
kicked off in the late 1920s destroyed Islamic institutions, curtailed the
circulation of religious knowledge, and "domesticated" Islamic practices
(see Khalid 2006 for a good discussion). This did not mean that Islam
was completely eradicated. In fact, Soviet rule ironically affirmed the
connection of ethnic and religious identities by "folklorizing" Islam.
The implicit contradiction in the Soviet attempt to repress religion while
promoting culture, while in fact the two cannot be easily disentangled,
had the result that many "religious" practices were incorporated into
a standardized "cultural" or Kyrgyz repertoire. The resulting "cultural
Islam" was largely devoid of Islamic knowledge and religious effervescence, and therefore vulnerable to subsequent post-Soviet challenges
(McBrien and Pelkmans 2008). In short, Soviet secularism had relegated
religious expression to the domestic sphere while contributing to the
objectification of religion, which enabled Kyrgyz actors to consider their
position vis-à-vis Islam.

Reflecting this complex history, Zamira's story both illustrated the
controversial nature of conversion to Christianity and demonstrated that
conversion had become a conceivable option. This condition of possibility coincided with the Kyrgyz government adopting the most liberal
religious policies of all post-Soviet Central Asian countries, which in
practice meant that missions and churches faced few state-imposed obstacles. The destabilization of Islam and the liberal policies of the Kyrgyz
government created an environment in which evangelical-Pentecostal
churches could be active and relatively successful. Although this background sketch suggests why conversion was conceivable, we now need
to look at the appeal of Pentecostalism in the post-Soviet context.

The attractiveness of evangelical-Pentecostal churches was partly
constituted through the general appeal that "the West" had in the wake
of the Soviet collapse. They represented "the modern," understood here
as the promise "to reorder society by applying strategies that have produced wealth, power, or knowledge elsewhere in the world" (Donham
1999, xviii). Moreover, although Kyrgyzstan is a Muslim-majority country, negative sentiments toward Islamic renewal movements prevailed.
Many associated such movements with backwardness and fanaticism,
in doing so invoking Soviet anti-religious rhetoric while connecting

to globally circulating discourses about Islamic radicalism (McBrien 2006). The association with "the West" thus proved advantageous to the position of Pentecostalism, but it is important to note that the most successful churches in Kyrgyzstan were not foreign missionary churches but rather those that were run by Kyrgyzstani citizens of various ethnic backgrounds (see also Pelkmans 2007). The Church of Jesus Christ is a case in point. It did boast its connections to charismatic churches in the United States and elsewhere, but the church had been led by local pastors, with the senior pastor being an ethnic Russian (born in Kyrgyzstan) and the pastor in Jalalabad (like most pastors outside the capital) an ethnic Kyrgyz. The church cherished its modern and transnational image, while its homegrown leadership ensured that it was plugged into the realities of Kyrgyz society.

Beyond "image," it was the church's message that proved attractive: it offered not only salvation, but also access to prosperity, health, and success by faithful prayer. This problem-solving dimension met a receptive audience in Kyrgyzstan. The economy had crashed in the early 1990s, the Soviet welfare system was dismantled, unemployment soared, and circular mass migration (mostly to Russia) took off. The end of the welfare system resulted in people relying increasingly on their kinship networks, but mass migration and high divorce rates meant that many people, especially women, fell through the cracks. These factors were reflected in the overrepresentation of marginalized groups in the church's demography. The Jalalabad congregation consisted of 75 percent women, slightly more than half of whom had lost a husband through divorce or death (based on a survey among 121 congregants; see Pelkmans 2009b for details). Although I cannot provide percentages, it was quite common for congregants to have suffered from addictions before they came to the church. The church acknowledged such patterns, and in the capital proactively engaged with them, for example through its elaborate outreach programs to prisoners and the homeless. When asked, church representatives explained these characteristics with reference to Jesus's teaching that "the last will be first and the first will be last" (Matt. 20:16).

It is easy to see the attractions of the Pentecostal message to people living in a state of "post-Soviet chaos" (Nazpary 2002), who are struggling with the effects of an unravelling welfare state in which life became more difficult and less predictable, especially for those who found themselves at the margins. Pentecostalism offers hope and direction to shattered lives, and concrete answers for dealing with the multifaceted existential uncertainty of post-Soviet life. Moreover, the idea that divine intervention can be invoked by prayer pushes people to assert their agency in dealing with an unruly world, that is, to tame the unpredictable forces of the post-Soviet chaos (see also Wanner 2007). However, the miracle occurrence was never completely naturalized, but in fact remained fragile.

The destabilization of fields of meaning and practice also meant that new religions were not always very firmly, or very permanently, embraced. Not all that long ago, the truths of the Soviet state and its communist ideology had been unmasked and denounced as propaganda. Even for those who had never been committed communists, the experience of having lived with official truths that were exposed as "merely propaganda" also meant that new truths were often approached with a dose of skepticism. This skepticism was the more pronounced because post-Soviet times were characterized less by an ideological void than by ideological excess in which spiritual and secular movements competed for the truth (see also Borenstein 1999, 447). In post-Soviet Kyrgyzstan, destabilized fields of meaning were recalibrating, creating an environment in which everything was potentially true, and everything was possibly a lie. Two kinds of uncertainty converge here: epistemological uncertainty (referring to knowledge) and existential uncertainty (referring to conditions of life). The centrality of miracles reflects this uncertainty, both in the sense that they work to overcome such existential uncertainty and in the sense that their epistemological status remained unstable.

Producing Miracle Truth

Pastor Kadyrjan saw proofs of divine intervention throughout the city of Jalalabad, where he had planted his congregation several years previously. "We prayed for civilization, and [this civilization] really arrived after we began our prayers.[3] Just look around the city. Nowadays people sell goods of [higher] quality at the bazaar, and we now have some shops like the ones they have in Bishkek. . . . After praying took up, people even started building new houses."

Almaz, a young man of twenty-four, told me, "For a long time I didn't have any work. Then, on January 19, 2004 I prayed to God, and asked for work. The following day when I was having lunch [in town], I was invited to work. I understood that God had heard me. I am grateful to God for that."

***

Possibly the most significant aspect of these examples of divine intervention is their narration. It is through their circulation that they gain status as miracles. To put it differently, central to the miracle business was the process by which people become cognizant of them, and start to recognize miracles in their own lives and in the world around them.

My acquaintances in the church saw evidence of divine power in many corners of life. It was seen in the slow and creeping changes in the cityscape as suggested above by Pastor Kadyrjan, and was just as likely to be detected in fleeting events, such as when during a service the worship leader ascribed the return of electricity (after a power outage that had lasted for an hour) to the Holy Spirit. Divine power was seen to be at work when people recovered from their illnesses, got rid of other physical problems, or were liberated from their addictions. It was evident when one received unexpected help from a neighbor, enjoyed an economic windfall, or received a job after praying, such as Almaz experienced.

For a happening to *be* a miracle, the decisive factor is that it is caused by divine intervention. But for such a happening to be *recognized* and *acknowledged* as having been caused by divine intervention, several ingredients need to be present. First of all, of course, there needs to be a *favorable* outcome: an addicted person who is liberated, an ill person recovered, a jobless person who receives a job, or indeed an electricity outage being restored. Second, this outcome should be *unexpected*: the addicted person had tried many times to quit drinking; the patient's medical doctors had given up hope of recovery; the jobless person had been jobless for a long time; the electricity returned at exactly the right moment. Two additional features are not indispensable, but are conducive to miracle status: the absence of an alternative explanation, and the happening having occurred after (i.e., in response to) the prayers of believers. Certain phenomena fit these criteria better than others, but the fit is always dependent on interpretation, influenced by presentation, and open to contestation.

The specificities of miracle truth production in the Church of Jesus Christ can be illustrated by a brief contrast with the institutionalized process of miracle validation in the Roman Catholic Church. There, putative miracles are tested against alternative explanations before the validity of the miracle can be (hesitantly) affirmed. In the Church of Jesus Christ, miracles are never formally tested. Instead there are powerful informal mechanisms by which truth is produced and generalized. The reality of miracles is affirmed in sermons, shared and communicated informally between congregants, and staged in public encounters.

As will have become clear, there was no deficit of miracles in the church. A seemingly paradoxical way of phrasing this would be to say that the miraculous was rather mundane—in the sense that the occurrence of miracles was routine and commonplace. Such an attitude was encouraged within the church. Sermons often focused on the occurrence of miracles, and congregants were encouraged to share their own experiences with divine intervention. The pastors often referred to the power of prayer and the need for committed prayer. Miracles were not to be questioned or scrutinized, but rather repeated and embellished.

Acceptance of miracle truth was facilitated by the links with existing cultural repertoires and the flexible adjustment to local realities. For example, while sermons in Bishkek often addressed the spirit of slavery (*dukh rabstva*) as evident in alcoholism and drug addiction, in Jalalabad the focus was on the spirit of magic (*dukh koldovstva*) seen in people's adherence to local Muslim traditions. And in the close-by mining town Kok-Jangak, where the church had only recently made its first entrance, it was the spirit of death (*dukh smerti*) which according to Pastor Kadyrjan could be detected in unemployment, lethargy, and illness. This vocabulary had significant similarities with local forms of spiritual healing, and demonstrated the manner in which the church adjusted to different contexts and addressed different sets of problems. In fact, there were remarkable similarities between the worldview promoted by Pentecostal churches and indigenous notions about spirits, as well as between Pentecostal faith healing and traditional "Muslim" healing. Kadyrjan once inadvertently commented on this when recollecting that he and his wife had initially often been mistaken for *koz-achyklar* (clairvoyants). Or, as one of the congregants who had previously been active as a (Muslim) spiritual healer told me, "I saw many miracles of Jesus. I believe that he is savior and healer because when I put my hands with the name of Jesus on ill people, they recover."

Ideas about miracles, propagated in sermons, made meaningful through their semiotic connections, achieved realness in the *domashka* (home church). Here, congregants exchange ideas and experiences, and thereby become more experienced in recognizing divine influence on events in their lives. That at least is what transpires from stories told by congregants. They referred to the *domashka* as a space of learning, where the confusing and mysterious aspects of the Pentecostal emphasis on the Holy Spirit became meaningful and understandable. As one congregant described her experience,

> My husband accompanied me to the *domashka* at the pastor's house. The atmosphere was cozy, everyone was uninhibited, they treated me as if they had known me for a long time. . . . Then the pastor and his wife prayed for me. . . . I accepted [Jesus] in my heart and that same day I was blessed with the Holy Spirit.

But it was not just about recognition. In fact, inclusion in the *domashka* often facilitated positive transformations, providing the mutual support necessary to overcome addictions and to deal with social and economic problems.

The surge of Pentecostalism across the post-Soviet landscape resembles in some ways the proliferation of magic. As Galina Lindquist has argued, "Magic deals with uncertainty, . . . neutralizing its destructive potential, and making hope, as a mode of existential orientation, once again possible" (2006, 21). Like magic, Pentecostalism is able to provide direction to agentive power, while it simultaneously embeds people in new solidarity networks. The miracles presented in sermons and embellished in more informal settings were all manifestations of the divine, and had the effect of transforming life: incurable diseases were cured, long-held addictions overcome, personal flaws repaired, jobs provided.

Miracles need to be *recognized* as miracles. This point implies that they need to be seen as not only positive and relevant, but also meaningful. On the one hand they need to be "miraculous," while on the other hand they need to be believable. There are several tensions at work here. First, miracles were most needed where they were least likely to occur. It is because of this that the *post factum* attribution of miracle status is much more likely to be successful than their anticipation through intentional prayer. Second, while the church's mundane approach to miracles allowed them to play a central role in everyday life, it also meant that miracles risked losing their enchantment.

Truth Decay

Aikan lived in the mining town of Kok-Jangak, located twenty-five kilometers from the provincial capital Jalalabad. Her conversion had been swift and complete. She became an active congregant immediately after her conversion, went out on evangelization trips, and was convinced that her prayers had not only cured her son, but also given her a job. She insisted that the church even positively influenced her marriage, especially when her husband also converted and started to take his role as provider more seriously. However, one year later Aikan's husband left her. Prayers to get him back were unsuccessful. And even though she still had her job, the abysmally low salary barely allowed her to survive. Meanwhile, some pious Muslims from her neighborhood started to make visits to her and other church members, trying to convince them that their conversion was a mistake. Although Aikan told me that she had not been convinced by their arguments, in the months thereafter she disengaged from the church, as did several of her friends. Like Aikan, they had become disillusioned or been pressured by Muslim leaders or their relatives to abandon their newfound faith.

***

On previous occasions, Aikan had vividly described to me the emotionally charged atmosphere in the church, in a way that reminded me of what Venera experienced when congregants collectively prayed to cure her speech impediment: a trembling pressure with a clear focal point that produced a momentary outburst of energy. What both stories also indicated was that although the church's mechanisms for generating miracle truth were effective in the short term, they faced difficulties in the long run. The example of Venera, who after two weeks was still unable to produce more than just a few sounds (and hadn't she been able to do that before anyway?), showed that miracles may stop being seen as miraculous. Meanwhile, Aikan's story illustrated that miracles that involved healing and employment may lose their gloss or even cease to be seen as miraculous.

The problem can be referred to as the "charisma paradox." While essential for generating temporary conviction, charisma is inherently unstable. The amazement, the temporary fascination will necessarily wear off. If the charisma is not to evaporate completely, either new miracles need to occur, or the charismatic needs to be connected to more permanent structures.[4] But in neither case will charisma remain what it used to be in the beginning. Whereas the former will produce problems of credibility, the latter is likely to result in a loss of effervescence.

Ironically, although economic hardship was conducive to the church's initial success, for prolonged impact it needed an environment in which it could demonstrate the fruits of prayer through the achievements of church members. In other words, the sustainability of new communities of faith also depended on the extent to which the church's promises—of health and wealth—continued to be convincing.[5] This was contingent both on the strength of the congregation within which success stories circulated and on actual possibilities of success. In the mining town Kok-Jangak—which lacked opportunities for economic as well as social advancement and thereby failed to produce success stories—disillusion quickly set in and the newly established congregation evaporated. In short, although conversion can be seen as an emancipatory strategy for those involved, its success depended on both the strength of and support provided by the congregation and the economic environment in which it operated.

While the destitute situation made it difficult to reproduce conviction over time, the sensitivities of the Pentecostal presence in a Muslim-majority situation had more unpredictable results. That is, the confrontation with opposing relatives and neighbors seemed to work in two opposing ways. In the case of Aikan, once the enthusiasm wore off and the experienced miracles lost their gloss, the confrontation with Muslim neighbors resulted in complete disengagement from the church. But the confrontation with disapproving neighbors and relatives could just as well have the opposite effect. Damira, who lived in Jalalabad and was part of a vibrant congregation, told me that her relatives, especially those on her husband's side, had strongly disapproved of her conversion: "They told him to divorce me, they called him to mosque, and an *ajy* [woman knowledgeable in Islam] visited me, but I told her that I wouldn't leave God." In fact, the agitation with which she told this story suggested that these challenges had strengthened her in her faith.

It is impossible to establish exactly whether these different outcomes were the result of personal characteristics, the deliverance of the fruits of prayer, or the strength of the congregations. But what is clear is that the dynamics of inclusion and exclusion can contribute to as well as erode the structures of faith. As was mentioned in the introduction, Pentecostal effervescence needed challenges to produce a sense of exclusivity, of belonging to a chosen group. However, when such external challenges worked upon an already weakened congregational structure and when prayer failed to produce success stories, they could easily lead to the erosion of conviction and to disengagement from the church.

Conclusion

[Church membership in Jalalabad] rose to 250 and then it fell again, then it rose again; it is a process we go through. If you would add up all the people who converted in our church, you would probably get to 800 people. It happens all the time. People join the church and then suddenly they say that they no longer have time. And that's the end of it. What happens is that the 'open' people come to our church, but then relatives and others start to put pressure on this person, trying to convince them that they should not go to the church, offer money so that they won't go, and if that doesn't help, they will exorcize them. It is the usual thing; persecution is part of Christianity.
—Pastor Kadyrjan, Church of Jesus Christ, Jalalabad

The preceding pages should have made clear that engaging with the truth question does not necessarily lead to either positivistic reductionism or a collapse of critical distance. As observers, we may not have the means to detect whether or not miracles are directly caused by divine intervention, but studying the production of miracle truth in relation to the effects and affects that miracles produce in the lives of believers is analytically productive. By taking seriously the empirical observation that miracle truth is unstable, and by analyzing how truth status is ascribed to and removed from specific incidents, we may uncover the working of Pentecostal conviction.

At its most concrete, this chapter has demonstrated that Pentecostalism, with its emphasis on prayer and divine intervention, encountered fertile ground in Kyrgyzstan. The dislocation of society and the unravelling of the welfare state had produced an environment receptive to Pentecostal promises. The chapter also showed that the portable nature of Pentecostal truths and the ways its message is contextualized ensured that it was in tune with local realities, engaging with it mostly through critique.

Miracle status was fragile partly because of the unstable characteristics of the post-Soviet condition. This highlighted that truth is often less about evidence than about the organization of information (cf. Hastrup 2004, 456). The specific manner in which this information was organized, and how it related to the larger social field, made miraculous happenings momentarily convincing. However, the invocation of the divine could fail to deliver results, and miraculous happenings could lose their charismatic gloss or run up against rival interpretations. People's assessment of miracles depended not only on their epistemological underpinnings, but also on the social relations that surrounded these miracles. The encouragement, repetition, and explication of unexpected happenings enabled the production of effervescence. But when these social relations eroded or a non-Pentecostal network asserted itself, the truth of miracles started to unravel. The risk of failure was largest in contexts where the need for miracles was greatest, because these were also the situations in which it was most difficult to produce success in the form of jobs, regained health, and reliable husbands. And when effervescence decreased, when doubt set in, the challenge posed by rival epistemological and existential points of reference loomed particularly large. Such processes not only underlined the effervescence of Pentecostal truth, but also highlighted the tension between Pentecostal Christianity and Islam, and the active steps undertaken by relatives and neighbors to dissuade Kyrgyz congregants from engagement with the church.

What needs to be stressed is that people actively engaged with the epistemological and social dimensions of different bodies of knowledge. As I have argued, Pentecostal truth was about gaining a hold over elusive forces, about asserting one's own agency. The notion that divine intervention can be invoked through prayer was empowering in and of itself. It gave people the motivation to try and overcome their addictions, the confidence to search for a job. It provided direction in a context of post-Soviet chaos, in a situation of ideological excess. This logic also holds true for the ascent of Pentecostal Christianity in Kyrgyzstan more generally. It was asserting its own presence by claiming to make an impact on society, by seeking challenges. As could be seen in Kadyrjan's commentary on the fluctuations of church membership, the Church of Jesus Christ was a forward-pushing movement, and could survive only by staying on the offensive. Numerous people fell by the wayside, but that was only to be expected because not everyone is chosen to be saved. In a sense, failure was part of the struggle between good and evil in this world, and it was through this struggle that a fragile conviction could be maintained.

NOTES

1. The official name is Full Gospel Church of Jesus Christ, but was commonly referred to as Tserkov' Isusa Khrista (Church of Jesus Christ).

2. In Weber's terms, at times of distress the "natural" leaders "have been holders of specific gifts of the body and spirit" (1948, 245).

3. Civilization (*tsivilizatsia*) here refers to a modern and "cultured" life.

4. The development of such stable connections can refer to institutionalization in the Weberian sense, meaning that miracle occurrence gains bureaucratic authority by becoming embedded in church structures. It can also refer to a deepening of personal relationships with the divine. A good example is Luhrmann's analysis of "new paradigm" Christians in California who described "spiritual maturity" as having developed a long-term friendship with God in which "the problem of unanswered prayer becomes the problem of why your good buddy appears to be letting you down" (2007, 95).

5. Haynes discusses the problem of disappointment with the Prosperity Gospel among Pentecostal Christians on the Copperbelt, showing how they adjusted their expectations to local economic and social realities, producing what she calls a "limited prosperity gospel" (2012, 127). Such adjustment of expectations also happened in the Church of Jesus Christ, but the differences between Jalalabad and Kok-Jangak also show the limitations of such adjustment and hence the fragility of the church in destitute contexts.

REFERENCES

Borenstein, Eliot. 1999. "Suspending Disbelief: 'Cults' and Postmodernism in Post-Soviet Russia." In *Consuming Russia: Popular Culture, Sex and Society since Gorbachev*, edited by Adele Marie Barker, 437–62. Durham: Duke University Press.

Donham, Donald. 1999. *Marxist Modern: An Ethnographic History of the Ethiopian Revolution*. Berkeley: University of California Press.

Ewing, Katherine P. 1994. "Dreams from a Sufi Saint: Anthropological Atheism and the Temptation to Believe." *American Anthropologist* 96 (3): 571–84.

Hastrup, Kirsten. 2004. "Getting It Right: Knowledge and Evidence in Anthropology." *Anthropological Theory* 4 (4): 455–72.

Haynes, Naomi. 2012. "Pentecostalism and the Morality of Money: Prosperity, Inequality, and Religious Sociality on the Zambian Copperbelt." *Journal of the Royal Anthropological Institute* 18:123–39.

Hirschkind, Charles. 2011. "Media, Mediation, Religion." *Social Anthropology* 19 (1): 90–97.

Kapferer, Bruce. 2003. "Introduction: Outside All Reason—Magic, Sorcery and Epistemology in Anthropology." In *Beyond Rationalism: Rethinking Magic, Witchcraft and Sorcery*, edited by Bruce Kapferer, 1–30. Oxford: Berghahn.

Khalid, Adeeb. 2006. *Islam after Communism: Religion and Politics in Central Asia*. Berkeley: University of California Press.

Lindquist, Galina. 2006. *Conjuring Hope: Healing and Magic in Contemporary Russia*. Oxford: Berghahn.

Luhrmann, Tanya. 2007. "How Do You Learn to Know That It Is God Who Speaks?" In *Learning Religion: Anthropological Approaches*, edited by David Berliner and Ramon Sarró, 83–102. Oxford: Berghahn.

McBrien, Julie. 2006. "Extreme Conversations: Secularism, Religious Pluralism, and the Rhetoric of Islamic Extremism in Southern Kyrgyzstan." In *The Postsocialist Religious Question: Faith and Power in Central Asia and East-Central Europe*, edited by Chris Hann and the "Civil Religion" group, 47–73. Berlin: Lit Verlag.

McBrien, Julie, and Mathijs Pelkmans. 2008. "Turning Marx on His Head: Missionaries, 'Extremists,' and Archaic Secularists in Post-Soviet Kyrgyzstan." *Critique of Anthropology* 28 (1): 87–103.

Nazpary, Joma. 2002. *Post-Soviet Chaos: Violence and Dispossession in Kazakhstan*. London: Pluto.

Pelkmans, Mathijs. 2007. "'Culture' as a Tool and an Obstacle: Missionary Encounters in Post-Soviet Kyrgyzstan." *Journal of the Royal Anthropological Institute* 13 (4): 881–99.

———. 2009a. "Introduction: Post-Soviet Space and the Unexpected Turns of Religious Life." In *Conversion after Socialism: Disruptions, Modernisms, and Technologies of Faith in the Former Soviet Union*, edited by Mathijs Pelkmans, 1–16. Oxford: Berghahn.

———. 2009b. "Temporary Conversions: Encounters with Pentecostalism in Muslim Kyrgyzstan." In *Conversion after Socialism: Disruptions, Modernisms, and Technologies of Faith in the Former Soviet Union*, edited by Mathijs Pelkmans, 143–61. Oxford: Berghahn.

Vries, Hent de. 2001. "In Media Res: Global Religion, Public Spheres, and the Task of Contemporary Religious Studies." In *Religion and Media*, edited by Hent de Vries and Samuel Weber, 4–42. Stanford: Stanford University Press.

Wanner, Catherine. 2007. *Communities of the Converted: Ukrainians and Global Evangelism*. Ithaca: Cornell University Press.

Weber, Max. 1948. *From Max Weber: Essays in Sociology*. Translated, edited, and with an introduction by Hans Heinrich Gerth and Charles Wright Mills. London: Routledge and Kegan Paul.

SECTION 4

The State and Beyond

New Relations, New Tensions

10

Politics of Sovereignty

Evangelical and Pentecostal Christianity and Politics in Angola

RUY LLERA BLANES

Concerning evangelical and Pentecostal Christianity, Angola occupies a somewhat peculiar place in the African continent. This is related to the country's unique positioning within the Atlantic and Lusophone (Portuguese-speaking) sphere (see Sarró and Blanes 2009) and to a religious landscape of "proliferation" (Viegas 2007), which has experienced dramatic changes in the last twenty-odd years. After a colonial period of what could be called "tripolarity" (including Catholicism, Protestantism, and local animist traditions), in the first years of independence (1975–1979, approximately) Angola experienced a period of fierce anti-religious policy, ideologically inspired by the importation of Marxist-Leninist ideologies (see Blanes and Paxe 2015). However, after a political transition to multipartisanship and a form of "pragmatic socialism" that merged into "state capitalism" throughout the 1980s and into the 1990s, the Angolan government progressively transformed its state-sponsored atheism into a policy of strategic alliance relationships with major religious institutions (Blanes and Paxe 2015). This move was made in order to benefit from their impact and outreach in terms of education, health, and social welfare (Blanes 2014) and simultaneously promote favorable public opinion and electoral grounds for the ruling party, the MPLA.[1]

As of 2010, there were eighty-three officially recognized religious institutions in Angola, and around 850 awaiting juridical recognition (INAR 2010). The country's capital, Luanda, is scattered with religious landmarks, from shiny new cathedrals in the main traffic arteries to makeshift healing places in the city's *musseques* (slums). The national media, official and private, make religion a major topic in their daily news production, including the nationwide broadcasting of religious services every weekend. Within this framework, a vast majority of religious institutions are Christian, ranging from evangelical and Pentecostal/neo-Pentecostal[2] churches to Catholic, mainstream Protestant (Presbyterian, Methodist, Baptist, etc.), prophetic/messianic (Tokoist, Kimbanguist, etc.), Adventist, Jehovah's Witnesses, Holy Spirit or revival churches,[3] and, finally, a range of movements that challenge the above categories. In this environment, if the Catholic Church has been able to recover (after the atheist period of the 1970s) and maintain a stable, hegemonic position, increasingly inserted within the texture of national identity and heritage politics, the situation of other religious movements such as those of the evangelical and Pentecostal type can be described as being of constant turmoil, with the accumulation of churches, protagonists, and events.

Today we can find several interesting examples in Angola of how Pentecostal and evangelical movements engage in aspects of governance and partisan policy in the public sphere, responding to shifting developments and evolving state-sponsored religious policies. As Adrian Hastings (1995) and Terence Ranger (2008) noted, such churches typically remained marginal during the decolonization period in Africa, withdrawing from the public sphere during the struggles for independence. The same could be said for the Angolan war (1961–1975). However, since the 1980s, they have become active agents in the processes of peace building (see, e.g., B. Schubert 2000; Neves 2012) and democratization,[4] establishing themselves as protagonists in the public sphere and addressing several sectors of governmentality such as social welfare and development (e.g., Gifford 1995, 1998; Freeman 2012). As Manuel Fernando, the current head of the INAR (National Institute of Religious Affairs), described to me in an interview in January 2012, the government's current policy is determined by an idea of "collaboration" and "partnership" with religious institutions. This stance has provoked interesting questions about how evangelical and Pentecostal churches in Africa have translated their transnational, universalizing ethos and narrative into specific, located engagements with national regimes, producing narratives that are equally able to be recognized as meaningful discourses within ethnic or national inscriptions (see Coleman 2000; Hackett 2004; and Griera 2013; for a comparative note with Central

America, cf. O'Neill, this volume). This coupling of religion and nation can be ascertained in specific ideologies and narratives that circulate in the public sphere, but also in processes of institutional framing within national settings. It also raises the question of how we might rethink models and methods of church expansion and mission today, especially in terms of its agents and directionalities.

But obviously, to think about "religion" and "nation" is to deliberately insert oneself into a multilayered phenomenon, involving several inter-connected dimensions—from questions of diplomacy and homeland security to legislative cultures and regulation (e.g., Kirsch and Turner 2008; Giumbelli 2013), heritage issues (Silverman 2010), social welfare (Freeman 2012), education (Eickelman 1992; Willert 2013), freedom and human rights (Hackett 2011), financial flow (van der Veer and Lehmann 1999), and so forth. The angle we are approaching here is concomitant to certain debates that have emerged in the social sciences of religion concerning sociopolitical processes of imagination (Anderson 1983) and boundary work that distinguish (or in turn couple) nation and creed, in reaction to processes of transnational circulation of people, ideas, and goods (see Mapril and Blanes 2013). Such boundary work may include processes of top-down state management of religious activity, and/or the promotion of nationalizing religious or secularized narratives in the public sphere. Following mainstream interpretations, such processes emerge within a nation-building dynamic (see Anderson 1983; Hastings 1992; Hobsbawm 1992); however, as the anthropological outlook I convey here will try to demonstrate, a bottom-up perspective reveals how, beyond the usually straightforward political narratives concerning religion, this boundary work is anything but linear.

Religion and Politics in Angola

In the religious landscape presented above, a specific feature observed in Angola is the "nationalization" of religion, a state-promoted strategy of not allowing religious creeds to claim any kind of economic or politi-cal allegiance to territories outside Angola. The country's constitution defines the state as being laic and recognizing religious freedom, "as long as [the churches] do not undermine the Constitution and public order, and conform to the law" (INAR 2010, 7, my translation). However, although it is not specifically stated in the Law of Religious Freedom,[5] religious institutions in Angola are inserted into the specific post-reform and postwar political and economic environment of Angola, where the MPLA government defines, supervises, and centralizes all sectors of business and enterprise, but also where capitalist models are encouraged in what has been described as "business Angola-style" (Oliveira 2007). For this reason, if business companies working in Angola, even when they are transnational or foreign, become Angolan, likewise it is not reasonable to talk about "foreign churches" in Angola, but rather of "Angolan churches of foreign origin." Economic and political sovereignties are thus at stake: by "nationalizing" churches, the government also nationalizes their economic activity and political allegiance, ensuring that appointed religious leaderships are Angolan nationals and not foreigners.[6]

One case in point that can be analyzed from this perspective is that of the Muslim community in Angola. The Comunidade Islâmica de Angola (CISA) has existed in the country for several years,[7] and has unsuccessfully tried to have its juridical status recognized by the government. Despite recurring complaints on behalf of local leaders in the media, the government has rarely, if ever, made a public statement on the issue. Recently, it was forced to deny its prohibition after several media reports denounced the forceful closure of mosques.[8] However, in my conversations with people close to government or involved in religious affairs in Angola, the comment is recurring: the government will not (or "should not," depending on the interlocutor) recognize Islam in Angola because it would challenge the country's "Christian identity." This statement, although historically speaking seemingly contradictory, characterizes the current sentiment in present-day Angola, where, as previously mentioned, the key word is "partnership."

Considering the portrait above, it appears that Christianity takes the better half of the religious cake in Angola. And indeed, it is demographically hegemonic and intrinsically connected to the country's colonial and postcolonial history. However, a closer look will reveal complexities that distinguish between certain Christian institutions and insert other, nonreligious elements into the equation beyond the nationalist imagination. As hinted above, one is the economic factor, and the other, the political/ethnic factor.

This point becomes evident when we look at the evangelical and Pentecostal field in Luanda, where we can distinguish four major groups in terms of geographical origin: (1) historical evangelical movements, the outcome of nineteenth- and twentieth-century missionary projects originating in Europe and North America; (2) transnational, southern Atlantic churches, mostly of Brazilian origin and frequently close to a neo-Pentecostal model; (3) Bakongo-based "Holy Spirit" churches, frequently originating from the Democratic Republic of Congo and loosely associated with the blending of evangelical and "traditional" elements;[9] and finally (4) locally initiated churches, sponsored by Angolan leaders who may or may not have belonged to other, originally foreign churches.[10]

The result of such a diverse scenario is the competition of multiple, diverse perceptions concerning evangelical and Pentecostal Christianity. For instance, in my interactions with religious folk in Angola, I noticed that there is a perception of foreignness regarding Brazilian churches that combines a certain suspicion with the acknowledgment of their entrepreneurial capacities—an idea that is undoubtedly associated with ongoing south-south economic connections between Angola and Brazil, involving business interactions (in the resources and construction sectors) as well as cultural and media exchange (music, soap operas, etc.). This combination may also be a by-product of the strategic silence that these churches promote in terms of public commentary on internal political affairs, making them either "good partners" or "accomplices" of the state (depending on the political positioning of the interlocutor).

Such a view contrasts with the more ambiguous (and in any case negative) image of Bakongo churches, which are frequently accused in the local media of illicit behavior—from witchcraft to adultery, smuggling, and exploitation. This in turn is associated with the complicated position of Bakongo ethnicity in Angolan culture, often framed as "foreign" to Angolan interests (see, e.g., Mabeko-Tali 1995; Pereira 2004). Such an environment may explain why many such churches remain, voluntarily or involuntarily, within the informal sector and in neighborhoods with a predominantly Bakongo ethnicity (Cazenga, Palanca, etc.). On the other hand, many local evangelical churches, such as the Assembleia de Deus Pentecostal do Makulusso, for instance, have initiated their own processes of transnationalization, working through the Angolan diaspora in their branching out of the Angolan territory.

Such a plurality becomes even more complicated when we attempt to make sense of the denominational histories of these churches. As noted by Angolan researchers (Viegas 1999, 2007), there is a history of dissidence, proliferation, and innovation within most major churches that challenges the classical distinctions between religious institutions and makes it difficult to map their journeys. From this perspective, the factors that distinguish evangelical and Pentecostal churches from other Christian movements are in most cases difficult to perceive, rendering them virtually useless in many cases.[11] The result of this is a complex mosaic of churches that respond diversely to the process of "nationalization" mentioned above.

From an anthropological perspective, the problem thus becomes one of how to address such a mosaic ethnographically. Since 2007, I have travelled to Luanda recurrently to conduct research on religious movements, and have struggled to make sense of these churches' complex denominational politics and their ambiguous positioning vis-à-vis the state. Perhaps a small vignette from my recent fieldwork illustrates the environment better: in November 2013, I was driving through central Luanda with the pastor of a Holy Spirit church. A very old man today, he was the prime actor in the establishment of this church, which I will not name here, in Angolan territory from the Democratic Republic of Congo in the 1980s. Today, he is the main pastor and leader of the church (which is officially recognized), and is revered by thousands of followers. On the other hand, he is also a terrible driver, and every car trip with him in the already chaotic capital of Angola became a tachycardiac experience for me, as wrong turns, near-certain crashes, bumps, insults from neighboring drivers, and getting stuck in muddy holes or whatnot were quotidian. On this occasion, he missed the expected left turn in one of Luanda's major arteries, and decided to correct this in the subsequent crossing, ignoring the road sign that forbade the move. And the sign was there for a good reason, since in his attempt to make the left turn, we realized that he did not have enough space to maneuver and needed a long time to remove his car from obstructing the lane, which eventually happened after a storm of honking and screaming all around us. Unfortunately for him, a transit police officer witnessed the operation and ordered him to stop the car on the side of the road as soon as he got out of the mess. The officer then proceeded to fine the pastor, but the latter protested, explaining that he was also a nurse by profession and that "you never know what can happen tomorrow; today you help me and tomorrow I can help you." The police officer was unmoved, as if not listening to the pastor at all, and continued to write down the fine. Eventually he gave him the fine, told him to go to a bank to pay it, and left in a hurry. But he kept no receipt of the fine himself and, unlike many transit officers in Luanda, demanded no immediate compensation or *gasosa* (bribe) money. To my knowledge, the fine was never paid.

This episode, apparently somewhat banal, illustrates some of the points I am trying to convey here: the juxtaposition (and often intermingling) of law-abiding and law-bending strategies that stem from the different actors involved in the relationship between churches and state. From this perspective, in the same setting, a predicament and its contradiction may coexist, in a relationship between government officials and citizens that is a "tapestry of webs"[12] based on interpersonal relationships with multiple and often diverging interests—what Jon Schubert (2014) called the "Angolan *sistema* (system)" (see also Tomás 2012; Faria 2013). Thus, a fundamental distinction is observed between official discourses on behalf of the state and the practical outcome of such discourses. Likewise, most churches in Angola, regardless of their origin, also accumulate state-building constructionist strategies with more informal practices that escape public knowledge, in order to "work the system" in their favor. From this perspective, the state's attempt to "nationalize" religion is part of a strategy of control, but also gives room for other kinds of strategies that provoke subsequent dynamics such as inter-church competition or voluntary clandestinity.

Moments of Tension and Revelation

Considering the complexities outlined above, in this section I will present three interesting examples that illustrate how categories of foreignness and sovereignty emerge in the intersection of government and religious institutions in Angola. They are representative of the tapestry of webs that characterizes such an intersection.

The first example occurred in 2007–2008. By then, the Igreja Maná, a transnational neo-Pentecostal church founded in Lisbon in 1984 by Jorge Tadeu, a Portuguese migrant in South Africa, was one of the biggest and fastest-growing religious institutions in Angola, with around four hundred churches throughout most, if not all, provinces of the country (see Smit 2012).[13] Its main temple, in the Golfe region in Luanda, was one of the largest, most-attended, and notorious in the city. However, in a surprising move, the government announced the Igreja Maná's immediate closure and forbade any kind of public manifestation on behalf of its leaders, leaving hundreds of thousands, if not millions, of believers without a church to attend. No official statement was ever disclosed to justify the government's decision, but word of mouth stated that it was related to embezzlement, the misuse of money donated to the church by governmental agencies.[14] Tadeu eventually accused the government of enacting the closure in order to create a schism in the church.[15] In any case, the Igreja Maná never opened again in Angola, and its main Angolan pastors eventually created new churches (such as the Josafat Church or the Arca de Noé Church), through which they have attempted to recover their patrimony. Today, the former Maná followers are dispersed throughout these churches and other neo-Pentecostal movements. However, there is a widespread assumption that the Josafat is, in fact, the "Angolan version" of the Igreja Maná, the only significant change being the substitution of its leadership for an Angolan bishopric.[16]

Considering that most of the data I am using concerning this case are based on media coverage and conversations with followers from other churches and people related to the government, it is clear that we do not have the full story behind the main decisions taken. However, what this case shows us is how, through what seems to have been a breach in political confidence, the Angolan government's decision provoked a process of "nationalization" of the Igreja Maná by removing its allegiance to a foreign leader and retaining its patrimony and heritage within Angolan borders.

A case that contrasts with that of the Igreja Maná involves the events that took place in late 2012 and early 2013 in the Universal Church of the Kingdom of God (UCKG), probably the most notorious neo-Pentecostal venture in the Lusophone world and beyond (see, e.g., Freston 2001, 2005; Mafra 2001; Almeida 2009; van de Kamp 2012). Founded by the pastor Edir Macedo in Brazil in 1977, the UCKG soon became a model of capitalist Christianity through its focus on a theology of prosperity and deliverance. This church arrived in Angola in the early 1990s and soon established a strong, visible presence through what has been described as its "cathedral politics" (Mafra 2007). Its flamboyant Catedrais da Fé (cathedrals of faith) in focal points around the city (such as the Alvalade neighborhood) made a strong impact, and its public image, unlike what happened in countries such as Portugal (Mafra 2001), was soon established as a positive one. Its role in the government-promoted electoral census campaign in 2006, using its churches as registration points, was one example of the partnership between church and government in the country. Furthermore, as Mafra, Swatowiski, and Sampaio (2012) point out, the UCKG's development of a "social welfare" strategy in Angola granted it a strong, favorable position in institutional terms. Therefore, its expansion throughout the territory was fast and successful, and it was able to combine a strong transnational circulation between Brazil, Africa, and Europe of pastors, media, and ideologies with their establishment in the local scene, for instance, through investment in church building construction in practically every neighborhood of Luanda.

However, on the New Year's Eve of 2012–2013, the UCKG organized a massive event, called Os Dias do Fim (The Days of the End, a tragically ironic title, as we will see below), in the national Cidadela stadium, in central eastern Luanda. The event was supposed to counterbalance the traditional Angolan custom of intense celebration of the New Year, usually involving the ingestion of significant amounts of alcohol. Hence it was widely publicized throughout the city, and hundreds of thousands of people showed up at the stadium. The overbooking was such that in a sudden stampede, several dozen believers lost their lives, a tragedy that became a huge scandal in subsequent weeks.

After these events, the government's immediate decision was to close down all church activities for sixty days and command the Ministry of Justice to open an investigation into what happened.[17] Arriving in Luanda just a few days after the incident, I witnessed how the believers I knew from this church were confined to "praying at home," and how various UCKG church buildings had their front doors locked. Rumors also circulated about the pastors asking their believers for money to endure the juridical process and the official closure. In the meantime, several

Angolan commentators questioned the government's decision, considering it to be a clear undermining of the country's judicial independence and a demonstration also that there is no de facto religious freedom in Angola, given that it is determined by the government through its control of the courts and judges.[18] An indication of such control is the fact that the INAR in Angola answers to the Ministry of Culture, while religious institutions seeking official recognition must submit their request to the Ministry of Justice.

In the subsequent weeks, however, the rumor mill shifted into producing the idea that the government was not just investigating the New Year's Eve event, but also looking into suspicious financial practices by the UCKG as well as by other Brazilian-originated churches present in the territory.[19] One such case was that of a dissident group of the UCKG, known as the Igreja Mundial do Poder de Deus (IMPD, World Church of the Power of God). This church, founded in 1998 by the Apostle Valdomiro Santiago, a former pastor of the UCKG, has also made an important impact in the Angolan religious scene in recent years. However, the financial scandals the church and its apostle were involved in in Brazil, and the intense rivalry between this institution and the UCKG, raised strong suspicions in Angola concerning its objectives, and therefore its juridical status has not so far been officially recognized.[20] This situation was later interpreted in Brazil as allowing for the UCKG's hegemony in the neo-Pentecostal field of Angola.[21] It was subsequently rumored that Valdomiro Santiago was not granted authorization to enter Angolan territory. Interestingly enough, however, his church's services and miraculous testimonies can be watched live on cable television in Luanda.

In any case, upon my return to Angola in September 2013, I observed how, unlike what happened with the Igreja Maná, the UCKG was indeed able to reopen its churches and continue with its usual functions. In contrast, a list appeared a few weeks later of over 160 churches whose official recognition request was denied, including the IMPD. It was also determined that these churches were not allowed to continue their activity, and in doing so would commit a crime of "qualified disobedience."[22] This illustrates what is one of the most common accusations suffered by the MPLA government concerning religious affairs: its imbalanced attitude regarding the different religious movements, offering different kinds of privileges to the more wealthy and well-known institutions, and not giving equal rights to the churches awaiting recognition. From this perspective, while some churches are able to build mega-cathedrals in strategic locales, others see their buildings torn down without prior notice due to, for instance, property issues.

These ambiguities surrounding the shifting place of evangelical and Pentecostal churches in Angola contrast with the more linear transformation of other Christian churches in Angola vis-à-vis the state. I am thinking specifically of autochthonous movements, such as the Tokoist Church, a prophetic/messianic church that emerged in late colonial Angola, around the following of a local leader, Simão Gonçalves Toko (1918–1984). As I describe elsewhere (Blanes 2014), the church's trajectory, as well as that of its founder and leader, Simão Toko, acts as a marker of the evolution of religious affairs in colonial and postcolonial Angola. Emerging in a period of heightened contestation of the Portuguese colonial project, Toko's movement became a cornerstone of anticolonial resistance, through independent preaching and staunch resistance to Portuguese persecution. Beginning as a local, ethnic (Bakongo) endeavor in the 1950s, the Toko's following soon expanded into the other regions of the Angolan province, as believers were imprisoned and sent into labor and detention camps from the north to the south of Angola. From this perspective, Toko's message, one of resistance and expectation, became as appealing to Angolans as that of the politico-military liberation movements—the MPLA, UNITA, and the FNLA. However, after independence, because of the anti-religious stance of the first independent Angolan government (led by the MPLA), as well as its concern over Toko's capacity to act as an opposition to its political project, the Tokoist movement was persecuted and pushed into a situation of hiding that would last until the prophet's death in 1984 (see Blanes 2013, 2014). Eventually, the situation improved for the church, as the MPLA policy evolved from a fervently anti-religious attitude into a more pragmatic pluralist laicism. In this framework, the Tokoist Church achieved official recognition in 1992, but its internal situation—of intense strife and schism owing to a dispute over the succession of Simão Toko in the church leadership—kept it in a situation of spiritual, institutional, and financial difficulty.

However, in 2000, after a new leadership took over one of its sections, the Tokoist Church began to experience a radical transformation that would bring it back to the spotlight, with a strong generational renewal, administrative innovation, and an adoption of the "cathedral paradigm," building what is today one of the largest Christian places of worship in Africa, in the Golfe neighborhood. The Tokoist Church would thus become *the* Angolan church par excellence, boasting privileged relationships with the Angolan government. While its leader, Bishop Afonso Nunes, enjoys personal and institutional growth in prestige, notoriety, patrimony, and financial situation, he is also criticized by marginal sectors of Tokoism, who see this new strategy as a form of spiritual corruption and "selling out" to politics and partisanship (see Blanes forthcoming). In any case, this association of the church with the government has fed into its new construction as a "national project," producing specific amnesias concerning the church's past—namely, its persecution by the same government that is now its partner—in order to proclaim a "victorious history" (Benjamin 1968; Blanes 2013) that adapts to the government's current policy regarding political affairs.

The case of the Tokoist Church illustrates another interesting dimension of Christian politics in Angola: the way local churches have struggled to respond to two concurrent phenomena. First, the Angolan state has developed a strategic collaborative agenda that undermines religious institutions' political and economic autonomy. Second, the active role of evangelical and Pentecostal churches in such a context has stimulated a competitive environment in the local scene, especially concerning their active participation in the education, social welfare, media, and culture sectors.

Concluding Notes

I started this chapter by portraying evangelical and Pentecostal Christianity in Angola as a peculiar case. This stemmed from an acknowledgment of the specific trajectory of religious affairs in this country and connections with wider political and economic processes. I identified a strong, but necessarily ambiguous, involvement of the Angolan government in religious affairs, to the point of determining the fate of different churches according to their willingness to engage in the "partnership" agenda it sponsors. Thus, in the different examples I discussed above, we observe different degrees of success and failure in the establishment of evangelical and Pentecostal churches of foreign origin in Angola within the process of "nationalization," as well as the emergence of an idea of autochthonous Christianity that competes within the same scenario.

However, we can also argue that the Angolan situation is only as peculiar as any other country can be when we observe the relationship between "state" and "religion." In fact, what we see is but one expression of how religious and political jurisdictions affect each other, producing concomitant permutations (see Kirsch and Turner 2008). From this perspective, comparatively speaking we detect a different trend than what is observed in, for instance, Brazil, where the political involvement of evangelical and Pentecostal churches has reached local and parliamentary politics (Mafra 2001, 2006); in Guatemala, where Kevin O'Neill (2010) describes the emergence of Christian models of citizenship and agency in the public sphere; or in Mozambique, where a separation of church and state has been maintained throughout different political transitions (Silva 2008). What makes the Angolan case peculiar, apart from its insertion within particular (Lusophone—see Sarró and Blanes 2009) routes, is, going back to Schubert, its local *sistema* of fracture and reconnection between government and religious institutions, one in which the official government narrative of nationalization is frequently overwritten by interpersonal logics. It also reveals the inexistence of an autonomous Christian political narrative (cf. O'Neill, this volume) in Angola, as it appears subsumed within the *sistema*.

I also argue that this kind of fracture can be appreciated in its complexity only through the ethnographic lens that attempts to understand the particularities of the *sistema* and the evangelical and Pentecostal churches' insertion within it. For this, a distinction between official, public discourse and other, more localized and often clandestine practical logics is required.

NOTES

1. Movimento Popular de Libertação de Angola (People's Movement for the Liberation of Angola) is a political party that has ruled Angola since its independence, led by Agostinho Neto (1975–1979) and José Eduardo dos Santos (1979–today).

2. By "neo-Pentecostalism" I refer to a specific type of Pentecostal churches—of which the UCKG appears as one of the most emblematic—in which demonology, deliverance, and prosperity are central theological aspects.

3. As we will see below, this category refers to a specific kind of religious movement in Angola, mostly of Congolese origin.

4. I acknowledge that the concept of "democratization" is not stable and deserves constant scrutiny, both as a concept that describes political processes in postcolonial Africa and as a more general description of Western politics.

5. See, e.g., Law no. 2/04 of May 21, 2004, *Diário da República de Angola*, I Série—no. 41, pp. 2, 825ff.

6. One exception, for historical reasons, is obviously the Catholic Church. Although it may appear somewhat subsumed in this text, the Catholic Church is a central player in Angolan post-independence history (see, e.g., Neves 2012).

7. The CISA has existed formally since 2007, as a merger between several previous smaller, unrecognized associations. But there are records of Muslim presence in the territory since colonial times.

8. See, e.g., Aristides Cabeche and David Smith, "Angola Accused of 'Banning' Islam as Mosques Closed," *Guardian*, November 28, 2013, www.theguardian.com/world/2013/nov/28/angola-accused-banning-islam-mosques/ (accessed November 30, 2013).

9. These are usually referred to as *Mpeve ya Nlongo* (Holy Spirit) churches, an umbrella term that covers several different religious expressions that combine Christian beliefs with local healing practices. But there are also more "mainstream" Pentecostal churches of Congolese origin in Angola. Perhaps the most visible and established one in Angola is the Igreja do Bom Deus (Church of the Good God), founded by the pastor Simão Lutumba in Angola in 1981.

10. Within the proliferated scenario of Angolan Christianity, obviously this systematization does not encompass the totality of the evangelical and Pentecostal universe. For instance, the Assemblies of God are known to have been present in the territory for several decades. Furthermore, during my research in the past years I recorded the presence of Portuguese evangelical missions in the territory, mostly structured around NGO-type work such as the construction of schools, health posts, and so forth, in rural areas.

11. Thus, I often find it more useful to think about charismatic movements—inasmuch as charisma is in most cases the central dimension of the church's work—shifting the focus from religious administration to theology "in praxis."

12. This expression was taken from the album of the same name by the alternative rock band Past Lives.

13. Very few churches, apart from the Catholic Church and the Tokoist Church, can claim a similar national outreach in Angola.

14. See "Angola: Igreja Maná fechada por decreto-lei," *Diario Digital*, January 31, 2008, http://diariodigital.sapo.pt/news.asp?id_news=316471 (accessed January 12, 2012).

15. Ibid.

16. See "Maná 'ressuscita' como Igreja Josafat," *Angonotícias*, August 7, 2009, http://www.angonoticias.com/Artigos/item/23249/mana-ressuscita-como-igreja-josafat (accessed February 2014).

17. See "Executivo responsabiliza e suspende actividade da Igreja Universal," *Agência Angola Press*, February 2, 2013, http://www.portalangop.co.ao/angola/pt_pt/ noticias/politica/2013/1/5/Executivo-responsabiliza-suspende-actividade-Igreja-Universal,dab06ce3-f644–4ba4–9f23–37f6833166e2.html (accessed February 10, 2013).

18. Such was the case of the writer, professor, and politician Nelson Pestana "Bonavena," who noted that the church's suspension was unconstitutional. See "Decisão de suspender a IURD é inconstitucional, diz analista angolano," *AngoNotícias*, February 5, 2013, www.angonoticias.com/Artigos/item/37465/decisao-de-suspender-a-iurd-e-inconstitucional-diz-analista-angolano (accessed March 6, 2013).

19. See "Governo angolano suspende igrejas 'Mundial' e Pentecostal Nova Jerusalém," *África 21 Digital*, February 6, 2013, africa21digital.com/politica/ ver/20030693-depois-da-igreja-universal-governo-angolano-suspende-igrejas-qmundialq-e-pentecostal-nova-jerusalem (accessed September 2, 2013).

20. See "IMPD: Congregação alastra-se por Angola," *Portal de Angola*, March 23, 2012, http://www.portaldeangola.com/2012/03/impd-congregacao-alastra-se-por-angola/ (accessed April 4, 2013).

21. See Patricia Campos Mello, "Medida do governo angolano assegura 'monopólio' à Universal," *Folha de São Paulo*, April 27, 2013, http://www1.folha.uol.com.br/ mundo/2013/04/1269734-medida-do-governo-angolano-assegura-monopolio-a-universal.shtml (accessed January 3, 2014).

22. See *Jornal de Angola*, November 9, 2013, 42–44.

REFERENCES

Almeida, Ronaldo de. 2009. *A Igreja Universal e os seus demônios: Um estudo etnográfico*. São Paulo: Terceiro Nome.

Anderson, Benedict. 1983. *Imagined Communities: Reflections on the Origin and Spread of Nationalism*. London: Verso.

Benjamin, Walter, 1968. "Theses on the Philosophy of History." In *Illuminations*, edited by Hannah Arendt, 253–64. New York: Schocken.

Blanes, Ruy Llera. 2013. "Extraordinary Times: Charismatic Repertoires in Contemporary African Prophetism." In *The Anthropology of Religious Charisma: Ecstasies and Institutions*, edited by Charles Lindholm, 147–67. New York: Macmillan.

———. 2014. *A Prophetic Trajectory: Ideologies of Place, Time and Belonging in an Angolan Religious Movement*. Oxford: Berghahn.

———. Forthcoming. "O apocalipse angolano: Profecias, imaginários e contestações políticas na Angola pós-guerra."

Blanes, Ruy, and Abel Paxe. 2015. "Atheist Political Cultures in Independent Angola." *Social Analysis 59 (2)*.

Coleman, Simon. 2000. *The Globalisation of Charismatic Christianity: Spreading the Gospel of Prosperity*. Cambridge: Cambridge University Press.

Eickelman, Dale. 1992. "Mass Higher Education and the Religious Imagination in Contemporary Arab Societies." *American Ethnologist* 19 (4): 643–55.

Faria, Paulo. 2013. *The Post-War Angola: Public Sphere, Political Regime and Democracy*. Cambridge: Cambridge Scholars Publishing.

Freeman, Dena, ed. 2012. *Pentecostalism and Development: Churches, NGOs and Social Change in Africa*. New York: Palgrave Macmillan.

Freston, Paul. 2001. *Evangelicals and Politics in Asia, Africa and Latin America*. Cambridge: Cambridge University Press.

———. 2005. "The Universal Church of the Kingdom of God: A Brazilian Church Finds Success in Southern Africa." *Journal of Religion in Africa* 35 (1): 33–65.

Gifford, Paul. 1995. *Christian Churches and the Democratization of Africa*. Leiden: Brill.

———. 1998. *The New Crusaders: Christianity and the New Right in Southern Africa*. London: Pluto.

Giumbelli, Emerson. 2013. "The Problem of Secularism and Religious Regulation: An Anthropological Perspective." *Advances in Research: Religion and Society* 4:93–108.

Griera, Mar. 2013. "New Christian Geographies: Pentecostalism and Ethnic Minorities in Barcelona." In *Sites and Politics of Religious Diversity in Southern Europe*, edited by Ruy Blanes and José Mapril, 225–50. Leiden: Brill.

Hackett, Rosalind I. J. 2004. "Prophets, 'False Prophets,' and the African State: Emergent Issues of Religious Freedom and Conflict." In *New Religious Movements in the Twenty-First Century: Legal, Political and Social Challenges in Global Perspective*, edited by Phillip Lucas and Thomas Robbins, 151–78. New York: Routledge.

———. 2011. "Regulating Religious Freedom in Africa." *Emory International Law Review* 2011:853–79.

Hastings, Adrian. 1992. *The Construction of Nationhood: Ethnicity, Religion and Nationalism*. Cambridge: Cambridge University Press.

———. 1995. "Churches and Democracy: Reviewing a Relationship." In *Christian Churches and the Democratization of Africa*, edited by Paul Gifford, 36–46. Leiden: Brill.

Hobsbawm, Eric. 1992. *Nations and Nationalism since 1780: Programme, Myth, Reality*. Cambridge: Cambridge University Press.

INAR. 2010. *As religiões em Angola: A realidade do período pós-independência (1975–2010)*. Luanda: INAR.

Kirsch, Thomas, and Bertram Turner, eds. 2008. *Permutations of Order: Religion and Law as Contested Sovereignties*. Aldershot: Ashgate.

Mabeko-Tali, Jean Michel. 1995. "La chasse aux Zaïrois à Luanda." *Politique Africaine* 57:71–84.

Mafra, Clara. 2001. *Na posse da palavra: Religião, conversão e liberdade pessoal em dois contextos nacionais*. Lisbon: Imprensa de Ciências Sociais.

———. 2006. "Jesus Cristo senhor e salvador da cidade: Imaginário crente e utopia política." *Dados: Revista de Ciências Sociais* 49 (3): 583–613.

———. 2007. "Casa dos homens, casa de Deus." *Análise Social* 43 (182): 145–61.

Mafra, Clara, Claudia Swatowiski, and Camila Sampaio. 2012. "O projeto pastoral de Edir Macedo: Uma igreja benevolente para indivíduos ambiciosos?" *Revista Brasileira de Ciências Sociais* 27 (78): 81–96.

Mapril, José, and Ruy Blanes. 2013. Introduction to *Sites and Politics of Religious Diversity in Southern Europe*, edited by Ruy Blanes and José Mapril, 1–18. Leiden: Brill.

Neves, Tony. 2012. *Angola justiça e paz nas intervenções da Igreja Católica, 1989–2002*. Luanda: Texto Editores.

Oliveira, Ricardo S. 2007. "Business Success, Angola-Style: Postcolonial Politics and the Rise and Rise of Sonangol." *Journal of Modern African Studies* 45 (4): 595–619.

O'Neill, Kevin L. 2010. *City of God: Christian Citizenship in Postwar Guatemala*. Berkeley: University of California Press.

Pereira, Luena. 2004. "Os bakongo de Angola: Religião, política e parentesco num bairro de Luanda." PhD diss., University of São Paulo.

Ranger, Terence, ed. 2008. *Evangelical Christianity and Democracy in Africa*. Oxford: Oxford University Press.

Sarró, Ramon, and Ruy Blanes. 2009. "Prophetic Diasporas: Moving Religion across the Lusophone Atlantic." *African Diaspora* 2 (1): 52–72.

Schubert, Benedict. 2000. *A guerra e as igrejas: Angola, 1961–1991*. Basel: P. Schlettwein.

Schubert, Jon. 2014. "Working the System: Amnesia, Affect, and the Aesthetics of Power in the 'New Angola.'" PhD diss., University of Edinburgh.

Silva, Teresa C. 2008. "Evangelicals and Democracy in Mozambique." In *Evangelical Christianity and Democracy in Africa*, edited by Terence Ranger, 161–90. Oxford: Oxford University Press.

Silverman, Helaine, ed. 2010. *Contested Cultural Heritage: Religion, Nationalism, Erasure, and Exclusion in a Global World*. New York: Springer.

Smit, Regien. 2012. *More Than Conquerors: Space, Time and Power in Two Lusopohone Pentecostal Migrant Churches in Rotterdam*. Amsterdam: Pallas Publications/Amsterdam University Press.

Tomás, António. 2012. "Refracted Governmentality: Space, Politics and Social Structure in Contemporary Luanda." PhD diss., Columbia University.

Van de Kamp, Linda. 2012. "Love Therapy: A Brazilian Pentecostal (Dis)Connection in Maputo." In *The Social Life of Connectivity in Africa*, edited by Mirjam de Bruijn and Rijk van Dijk, 203–26. New York: Palgrave MacMillan.

Van der Veer, Peter, and Hartmut Lehmann, eds. 1999. *Nation and Religion: Perspectives on Europe and Asia*. Princeton: Princeton University Press.

Viegas, Fátima. 1999. *Angola e as religiões*. Luanda: Edição de Autor.

———. 2007. *Panorama das religiões em Angola: Dados estatísticos, 2007*. Luanda: Instituto Nacional para os Assuntos Religiosos.

———. 2008. *Panorama das religiões em Angola independente (1975–2008)*. Luanda: Ministério da Cultura/Instituto Nacional para os Assuntos Religiosos.

Willert, Trine. 2013. "Religious, National, European or Inter-Cultural Awareness: Religious Education as Cultural Battlefield in Greece." In *Sites and Politics of Religious Diversity in Southern Europe*, edited by Ruy Blanes and José Mapril, 331–58. Leiden: Brill.

11

Politics of Prayer

Christianity and the Decriminalization of Cocaine in Guatemala

KEVIN LEWIS O'NEILL

What are Pentecostal politics? The answer to this question, at least for the purposes of this chapter, does not linger on political biographies. Pentecostal politicians, even Pentecostal presidents, are well-worn objects of study. Not enough scholarship has explored the everyday experiences of believers who perform their politics through their Christian practices. This chapter's intent is thus to shift the analytical focus away from Pentecostal formations of political leadership to Pentecostal formations of citizenship. In doing so, it addresses a particular place (Guatemala), a particular people (Pentecostals), a particular cause (the decriminalization of drugs), and a particular practice (prayer). It is an anthropological approach that begins with a fairly mundane meeting between two political leaders but then fades into a less familiar vision of Pentecostal prayer as political action, ending with the very text that Pentecostals in Guatemala perform to battle the problem of drug trafficking. It is this text, as well as its incantation, that repositions the meaning of Pentecostal politics to include prayer itself. To perform this Pentecostal prayer, this chapter argues, is to participate politically.

A Meeting

On February 21, 2012, at the White House, in its famed Treaty Room, the US secretary of state Hillary Rodham Clinton shook hands with Guatemala's newest foreign minister, Harold Caballeros. The exchange was quick. "It's wonderful to have the new foreign minister of Guatemala here," Clinton announced. "We have a very close and important relationship with Guatemala. We have a comprehensive agenda that we will be discussing, but I wanted to formally welcome him here in his new capacity and to publicly state how much I'm looking forward to working with you." Guatemala's foreign minister proved equally diplomatic. "Thank you very much," he said. "It is such an honor to be here representing my country. And as Madam Secretary has said, we have an intense bilateral relationship and an agenda we'll be talking about. Thank you." They then exited the Treaty Room, making polite small talk (US Department of State 2012).

Harold Caballeros's visit, however, was anything but polite. The immediate focus of this "intense bilateral relationship," as Caballeros described it, was the decriminalization of drug possession in Guatemala. It was an unpopular idea, to be sure. By the time of this meeting, this initiative had already been rejected by the governments of Honduras and El Salvador, and had been received with reservations by Costa Rica (Acercando Naciones 2012). The United States had also rejected it through its embassy in Guatemala. But Harold Caballeros, sent by the president of Guatemala, Otto Perez Molina, insisted that a conversation take place.

The conversation makes sense, for Guatemala, if only because the amount of cocaine passing through Guatemala on its way from the Andean region to the United States has been steadily rising over the last decade. Only 10 percent of this cocaine passed through Guatemala in 2004 (Jordan 2004). But with the continued militarization of Mexico by the US Drug Enforcement Agency and its Department of Homeland Security, Guatemala (with the lowest seizure rates in the region) has become an important point of passage for some 250 metric tons of powder cocaine (United Nations Office on Drugs and Crime 2011, 122). Guatemala's piece of this pie jumped to 24 percent in 2006 and then 44 percent in 2008 (Archibold and Cave 2011). In 2011 nearly 90 percent of the cocaine consumed in the United States touched Guatemalan soil (Miroff and Booth 2011).

With cocaine has come chaos. Drug cartels, for one, pay drug traffickers for their logistical support—not with cash but with cocaine (Grainger 2009). This helps everyone sidestep international money laundering laws. Yet the only way to monetize this powder cocaine in a place like Guatemala is to turn it into crack cocaine and then sell it on the streets. Crack, for the unfamiliar, is the bologna of cocaine.

It is a far cheaper, far more addictive version of powder cocaine that hit North American cities in the mid-1980s (Bourgois 2003). Twenty-five years later, as an unintended consequence of a new war on drugs, crack cocaine ravages Guatemala with a desperate kind of addiction. A relatively small country, whose own genocidal civil war ended in 1996 (CEH 1999), Guatemala now experiences unprecedented levels of urban violence (O'Neill and Thomas 2011). Fewer civilians were killed in the war zone of Iraq in 2009 than were shot, stabbed, or beaten to death in Guatemala. Some seventeen murders occur daily in this small country, with the average criminal trial lasting more than four years and with less than 2 percent of homicides resulting in a conviction (Grann 2011, 42; Wilson 2009). "It's sad to say," one international observer remarked, "but Guatemala is a good place to commit murder because you will almost certainly get away with it" (Painter 2007).

For Guatemala, a conversation about decriminalization is important, if only to shift the country's approach to drugs from a retributive approach (e.g., incarceration) to a restorative approach (e.g., rehabilitation). Decriminalization would also initiate a much larger conversation about the decriminalization of drugs throughout the Americas. The idea would be that less unregulated cocaine could mean less unrestrained chaos.

Harold Caballeros proved to be an unexpected point person for this issue. Admittedly, from a certain perspective, he is a predictable politician. Caballeros was in line with any other politician that Hillary Clinton met that day. Trained as a lawyer at the notoriously rigorous Universidad Francisco Marroquín de Guatemala, Caballeros has a résumé that is impressive by any standard. In addition to a PhD, Caballeros holds a master's degree from the Fletcher School of Law and Diplomacy of Tufts University and has completed postgraduate work at Harvard University's Weatherhead Center for International Affairs. Frequently quoted by the Guatemalan press, Caballeros has also been mentioned in articles published by the *Wall Street Journal* (Riley 2006) and the *Economist* ("Christianity Reborn" 2006). His own campaigns for the presidency in 2007 and 2011 not only developed his political persona but also advanced what many have described as a rather evenhanded (even boring) approach to an unevenly democratizing postwar country.

Yet Harold Caballeros is Pentecostal. A self-professed Christian, an ordained minister, and the founding pastor of a multinational neo-

Pentecostal megachurch in Guatemala, Caballeros has long advocated the practice of spiritual warfare (O'Neill 2010; see Caballeros 2001b). This means that he speaks eloquently and passionately—in sermons, public talks, books, and videos—about how and to what extent demons plague his postwar country. And he does so with great detail, describing with much poetic flair how he wages war against demonic armies and how he fights fallen angels in hand-to-hand combat, hunting down the devils that haunt both his city and his country. In one sermon in 2001, in front of thousands of Pentecostals, Caballeros announced,

> I have been telling you for the last hour that we are at war! And that we are the conquerors! Moreover, we are conquerors in the name of Jesus, who loves us! [*applause*] Aaaah, you must understand this, you must understand. . . . From the day that Jesus saved you, your enemy, the Devil, lost you. [The Devil] was once your father, had tied you up, was never going to free you, wanted you to be eternally lost. (Caballeros 2001a)

Lost and found, sinner and saved, God and the devil—these are Caballeros's political and theological points of reference.

Admittedly, Caballeros is not the first Pentecostal politician in Guatemala. There have been two others. In 1982 a coup d'état resulted in Efraín Ríos Montt, a Protestant military leader, becoming president of the republic (Garrard-Burnett 2010). On the night of the coup he addressed the nation via television, declaring, "I am trusting my Lord and King, that He shall guide me because only He gives and takes away authority" (Garrard-Burnett 1998, 138). Though he is largely recognized as the architect of Guatemala's genocide and has been indicted by international tribunals for crimes against humanity, the Christian dimensions of Ríos Montt's governance are well documented and rooted in a religious conversion that took place in one of Guatemala City's megachurches, Verbo (Stoll 1990, 187–90; Steigenga 1999). President for less than two years, Ríos Montt took a Christian approach to public office that included "codes of conduct" rooted in biblical principles for government workers (*no robo, no miento, no abuso*—I do not rob, I do not lie, I do not cheat), weekly radio addresses to the country that eventually became known among Guatemalans as Ríos Montt's "sermons," and close ties to the United States's growing Moral Majority, which included a guest appearance on the conservative US Christian television show *The 700 Club* (Garrard-Burnett 1998). Amidst a sustained, as well as manufactured, fear of communism, Ríos Montt became Guatemala's Christian soldier. Moral righteousness mixed with extreme violence to define Guatemala's first Protestant president until, in August 1983, he was overthrown in a military coup.

Almost a decade later, in 1991, Guatemala held a relatively fair and open presidential election. The neo-Pentecostal candidate Jorge Serrano ran against Ríos Montt, who, despite his history, remains active in Guatemalan politics to this day. A Pentecostal convert since 1977 and a member of the megachurch Elim, the politically moderate Serrano won with a campaign that emphasized the importance of the family, free market economics, social programs, lawfulness, and respect for God-given human rights (Hallum 2002). While Guatemalans, both Protestant and Roman Catholic, certainly did not vote in droves, the 1991 elections signaled the growing political involvement of neo-Pentecostals: urban, upwardly mobile, nondenominational Christians. Winning the election with 67 percent of the vote, Serrano became the first elected Protestant president in Latin America (Freston 2001, 275). Upwardly mobile voting blocs saw themselves as well as their future in Serrano, until he attempted to dissolve the Congress and suspend the constitution in 1993. In one of the stranger grabs for power in Guatemalan history, Serrano tried to take full control of the country until a combination of protesters, government officials, and international investors stopped his dictatorial efforts. While the full reason for his coup d'état remains unclear, many speculate that the coup was Serrano's own way of avoiding corruption charges, which he continues to skirt to this day by residing in Panama (Steigenga 1999, 162).

Harold Caballeros, as foreign minister, skirted nothing when it came to decriminalization. He insisted that the countries of North America and Central America begin a much-needed conversation about drugs and drug violence. Decriminalization could save lives.

Prayer

Sources closest to Caballeros stressed that he never wanted decriminalization in his political portfolio. His concern was that the entire effort—that is, a former Pentecostal pastor fighting for decriminalization—sounded absurd. And in many ways, it did. But this sentiment obscured the fact that drugs and drug trafficking have always been a part of Caballeros's portfolio. As a pastor, he counseled congregants in the throes of addiction, sermonized on the perils of drug abuse, and initiated and led several prayer campaigns against drug trafficking in Guatemala. It is the latter that this chapter stresses—if only because prayer (from a Pentecostal perspective) can be just as political an activity as a trip to the White House.

To speak of the political power of prayer is not to suggest magic or to make a theological argument. Prayer instead is a kind of cultural work. It is a practice that "works." Robert Orsi says it best when he argues,

> Prayer is not an innocent social or psychological activity. It is always situated in specific and discrepant environments of power, and it derives its meanings, implications, and consequences in relation to these configurations. Indeed praying is one of the most implicating social historical practices because it is in and through prayer that the self comes into intimate and extended contact with the contradictions and constraints of the social world. (1996, 186)

Again, prayer (along with a litany of other Christian practices) "works" because it is a kind of cultural work that produces a sense of self, which believers learn to govern for the sake of Guatemala. Put another way, Pentecostals often work feverishly to combat the problems of postwar Guatemala City, such as drug trafficking, not simply as citizens motivated by their Christianity but also as citizens who consciously work *through* their Christianity. Prayer *is* Pentecostal politics.

This critical perspective helps explain why Pentecostal politics can result in practices and performances that are far afield from what the political scientist would recognize as citizenship participation. In the once overwhelmingly Roman Catholic but now Pentecostal-majority country, Pentecostal politics rarely look like Caballeros's trip to Washington as foreign minister. As is obvious with Caballeros's own political post, Pentecostals in Guatemala do cultivate candidates for elected office, and they also discuss how Christians should vote, but they do so only a fraction of the time. Pentecostals in Guatemala are more likely to pray for Guatemala than pay their taxes; they tend to speak in tongues for the soul of the nation rather than vote in general elections; and active Christian citizens more often than not organize prayer campaigns to fight drugs and drug trafficking rather than organize their communities against the same threat (O'Neill 2010). This is all to say that Caballeros's meeting with Clinton is interesting and valuable, but from an ethnographic perspective it is (at best) an outlier. Pentecostals do a great deal, but they do things that ultimately frustrate Western, secular, and deeply liberal expectations of what it means to participate as a citizen of an emerging democracy—what it means, for example, to battle drugs and drug trafficking.

Campaigns

Take Caballeros's previous prayer campaigns against drug trafficking. These were large-scale efforts organized through his Guatemala City megachurch, El Shaddai. El Shaddai, for the unfamiliar, is a worldwide congregation with twelve thousand members in the capital city alone; the central church holds up to six thousand participants and is shaped like a soccer stadium. The structure is equipped with movie theater–quality seats and top-of-the-line audio and video equipment. More than eighty El Shaddai-incorporated satellite churches dot the Guatemalan countryside, from Chiquimula to Chimaltenango, as well as the Americas, from Bogotá to Boston. Connected via the Internet and radio stations, weekly services use contemporary Christian music to excite large crowds, guiding them through emotional peaks and valleys. Upbeat songs electrify the congregation while sad melodies slow the pace of the service, bringing many to tears. The main church structure also houses a small café, a twenty-four-hour ATM machine, and a bookstore with literally thousands of taped sermons for sale as well as Spanish translations of well-known titles authored by pastors from around the world. As almost a comical gesture to scale, a swimming pool serves as the church's baptismal well.

Historically upper-middle-class, the El Shaddai congregation embodies what critics have come to call the gospel of health and wealth (Coleman 2000; García-Ruiz 2004; Althoff 2005). It is a cultural context that allowed Caballeros to begin (both theologically and politically) with the individual believer. Change the person and you will change the nation. This has long been Caballeros's logic, which has long defined Pentecostal politics. By beginning with the individual, Pentecostalism makes the individual—the self—the very terrain upon which political action takes place (O'Neill 2009).

Pentecostal politics, Caballeros has made clear on many occasions, begins with a decision. It begins with a call for *you* to choose God. During a sermon entitled "Escoge tú" (You choose), Caballeros announced,

> I don't know why the world believes that we can't determine our future, that our future is determined by our past, our circumstances, our situations. The only person who can determine our future is *you*. Do you know who is *you*? Who is *you*? *Me*! In this phrase, *you* means every one of us. And the Bible says here, that amidst life and death, I chose *you*. And between heaven and earth, between blessings and failings, between life and death, I chose *you*.

Caballeros continued, "You choose. *You* are responsible for your future. *You* are responsible for living in blessings or failings. *You* are responsible for life and death. *You* are responsible for living in accordance with the word of God because the decision between life and death is in your hands" (Caballeros 1991). Pentecostal politics hails the individual, charging *you* with the power to change.

Caballeros consistently links *your* decision to choose God not just to the nation but also to each person's attitude:

> Some people point to the situation of the nation, the situation of our currency [the *quetzal*], the situation of your employment, your place of work, your profession. They say that these circumstances mark your future. Your circumstances do not mark your future! Your faith marks your future! Your language marks your future! Your words mark your future!

By faith, language, and words, Caballeros largely means attitude, as he quickly clarified:

> God wants to change your attitude because when you change your attitude, you change your entire life. . . . My attitude determines my future.

I will say it again. My attitude determines my future. Tell me. What can a person with a bad attitude say? Bad things. And what can he obtain? Bad things. And what kind of life can he live? A bad one. . . . Are you listening to me? Brothers and sisters, I am here to help you break the vicious cycle of a bad attitude. (Caballeros 1991)

For Guatemala to change, *you* must change.

Change

Changing Guatemala by changing yourself begins with specific prayers. One is entitled "Against Drug Trafficking." It comes from El Shaddai's principal spiritual warfare project, promoted since the early 1990s, which provides Guatemalan Pentecostals with a body of literature that instructs them on how to wage war in Guatemala. The project's pamphlets, manuals, and archives—yellowing pieces of paper that congregants carry in their back pockets or fold into their Bibles—go to great lengths to equip the believer with the necessary tools to win back Guatemala City from the Devil, to win back the capital as well as the nation from drugs and drug violence. Stowed inside this literature is a series of assumptions. One is the idea that Satan actively attempts to stunt a believer's efforts at prayer. The spiritual war is between Satan and the individual. This paraphernalia warns that Satan will try to make inroads to negatively affect one's own efforts at prayer; Satan will try a number of measures: "Attack our confidence in the Lord, making us feel incapable. . . . Attack our body, thoughts, and nerves. . . . Attack the time that we reserve to pray, making us feel too busy with seemingly other urgent tasks or will interrupt our prayer with things of little importance."

Caballeros had long been a champion of prayer:

The opposition can and must be conquered through prayer and fasting. . . . We have a very active role in obtaining our blessings. If we do not receive the answers to our prayers it is not because God doesn't want to give them to us, but because there is an invisible enemy that wants to place obstacles in front of our receiving, an enemy that it is possible to defeat. (Caballeros 2001b, 8)

But the fight does not come and go. The battle between good and evil, between God and the Devil, is not an infrequent activity.

The logic of these prayer campaigns insists that the successes and failures of each and every person will result in the success or failure of Guatemala as a nation. Participating in the battle for only a short time is nonsense. Every waking minute demands that the believer pray, fast, and speak in tongues. Hesitating for a moment means certain defeat: "Spiritual warfare really constitutes the normal way of life for the believers who have been redeemed by Christ from the slavery of the devil. . . . While we remain on the earth we will have an enemy that is in continual war against us" (Caballeros 2001b, 24). This battle is important for each individual because each individual struggle contributes to the future of Guatemala: "We were suddenly invaded by a sense of urgency. God was putting before us a revelation, giving us a great responsibility" (23). And, as the literature makes clear, El Shaddai congregants, as soldiers for Christ, face an unprecedented battle:

> Now more than any other moment in the history of mankind, God is looking for men and women who are able to place themselves between God and this world, to intercede for Him, for a more just world, for a nation with government officials whose hearts are right with God, for a Church that is always on the offensive, for a strong and united leadership. (Oremos Online 2006)

These prayer projects make it quite clear that interceding in a spiritual war is not a collective activity; intercession is also neither public nor external. Intercession is individual, personal, and internal. The weekly prayer sheets are not used in groups or during church services, but are kept at bedsides and work areas, in one's pocket or knapsack. Fulfilling one's responsibility as a soldier for Christ takes place while praying alone and somewhere quiet. As one informant explained to me, with seemingly never-ending patience and with prayer sheets in hand, spiritual advancement takes effort, painstaking effort, which begins with praying an hour a day. The hour-long spiritual exercise has six phases of active prayer.

Phase 1 asks the Christian soldier to give thanks to God "for the privilege of entering into His presence." In this phase, the prayer guide asks the lonely warrior to recite God's many biblical names, invoking the power that accompanies each name. Phase 2 involves praying for the manifestation of God's kingdom in the present world. The believer at this moment presents his or her petitions to God with only one caveat. The Oremos flier reads, "Remember that we should not pray about a problem without having a solution in mind. The solution to the problem? Yes, examine the Word to encounter what solution God has for this situation. The solution should then be placed in your mind and then confessed." In the third phase, "We pray for a resolution for the needs of our family, church, and nation. This is the intercession." Phase 3 begins the specific prayer-acts made on behalf of Guatemala, turning a devout believer into a citizen-soldier. The prayer manual programmatically provides a prayer, but Gustavo explained that the key here is to have one's own prayer melt into *glossolalia*, or speaking in tongues—to fade from specific words and toward direct communion with the Holy Spirit. Phase 4 asks the Christian soldier to put himself or herself at the service of God and neighbors, focusing on the importance of praying for the needs of others. Phase 5 returns to the explicit language of spiritual warfare: "Dress with the armor of God. Also, pray for God's protection (Solomon 5:12) in our lives, in our family, in our possessions, etc. (John 1:10)." Finally, the sixth phase asks the believer to pray for a specific theme (Oremos Online 2006). One relevant theme for Guatemala is drug trafficking.

Conclusion: A (Spiritual) War on Drugs

The following is part of a prayer that Caballeros once asked his congregants to recite against drug trafficking. While one could easily form a comparison between this prayer, published in 2004, and Caballeros's trip to Washington in February 2012, in some effort to plot out how Pentecostal politics have evolved in a few short years, it is important to note that the El Shaddai church still calls its congregants to wage a spiritual war against drugs and drug trafficking. Again, Harold Caballeros's trip to Washington is (at best) an outlier, while the Pentecostal politics that drive everyday life oftentimes begin and end with prayer. For the student of Pentecostal politics, then, it is best to consider the following prayer as not simply evidence or texture but as the actual medium through which Pentecostals in Guatemala participate in their country's most pressing issues. To read this text out loud or to oneself, to follow the above-mentioned steps, to prepare oneself for spiritual battle, and then to read this prayer—this itself constitutes the stuff of Pentecostal politics:

> Our powerful Savior will defend us. He has chosen us and we pray to Him day and night, asking for help. He will grant Guatemala justice against all odds; He will hear His children and will open his heart and his ears.
>
> Certain paths have led us away from You. The godless do not recognize their limitations and their need for You. This has brought Guatemala to an uncertain reality that we all face as a nation. And You, who respect our will and our desires, no matter how selfish they are, watch with a heavy heart as today we live surrounded by drugs and death. This is not what You desire for Guatemala. Guatemalans and foreigners who lack the Word have created a space for corruption and greed.
>
> Arrogance and disrespect, for both the law and human life, provide plenty of terrain for both organized crime and drug trafficking. The growing presence of drug traffickers also makes honorable citizens feel hopeless. It traps their hearts in a dangerous web of apathy. This is reprehensible because it makes society silently complicit in perpetuating a vicious cycle. It is also reprehensible that the spirits of greed and a thirst for power lead to violence and a destabilized country. In Guatemala men and women are controlled as if by puppeteers. In the name of Jesus, we think this shameful.
>
> Lord, do not allow gangsters to dominate the north, south, east, west, and center of Guatemala. We declare that they will not take over the streets and the roads in isolated towns. They will not construct important stretches of highway; they will not build schools and clinics; they will not rob the hearts of the Guatemalans. They are not the benefactors of the needy. They are not the godfathers of our youth. *No!* Jehovah freed us from our trust in man and in godlessness. . . .
>
> This land is God's land! God has not forgotten and will never blame the innocent. He is a sovereign judge and nothing escapes his presence. We reclaim Guatemala for God and for His glory. We pray that the Holy Spirit breathes a strong wind in Guatemala, and shakes the webs of drug trafficking and organized crime. . . .

Protect the authorities. Do not allow bribes or intimidation to blind people from acting in the Word and in the Law. Allow the authorities to combat drug trafficking and organized crime. We support the authorities, even though it is not in them that we place our trust, but in you, Lord. We ask that the authorities in Guatemala do their work for peace and happiness of Guatemalan citizens. . . . Amen.

REFERENCES

Acercando Naciones. 2012. "Guatemala: Harold Caballeros Visit to Washington Held." http://www.acercandonaciones.com/en/diplomacia/guatemala-harold-caballeros-realizara-visita-a-washington.html. Accessed March 8, 2013.

Althoff, Andrea. 2005. "Religion im Wandel: Einflüsse von Ethnizität auf die Religiöse Ordnung am Beispiel Guatemalas." PhD diss., Department of Philosophy, Martin-Luther-Universität Halle-Wittenberg.

Archibold, Randall C., and Damien Cave. 2011. "Drug Wars Push Deeper into Central America." *New York Times*, March 23.

Bourgois, Philippe. 2003. *In Search of Respect: Selling Crack in El Barrio*. Cambridge: Cambridge University Press.

Caballeros, Harold. 1991. *Escoge tú*. December 18. Audiocassette recording.

———. 2001a. *La batalla entre dos reinos*. October 28. Audiocassette recording.

———. 2001b. *Victorious Warfare: Discovering Your Rightful Place in God's Kingdom*. Nashville, TN: Thomas Nelson.

"Christianity Reborn." 2006. *Economist*, December 19.

Coleman, Simon. 2000. *The Globalisation of Charismatic Christianity: Spreading the Gospel of Prosperity*. Cambridge: Cambridge University Press.

Comisión para el Esclarecimiento Histórico (CEH). 1999. *Memoria del silencio: Guatemala*. Guatemala City: Comisión para el Esclarecimiento Histórico.

Freston, Paul. 2001. *Evangelicals and Politics in Asia, Africa and Latin America*. Cambridge: Cambridge University Press.

García-Ruiz, Jesús. 2004. "Le néopentecôtisme au Guatemala: Entre privatisation, marché et réseaux." *Critique Internationale* 22:81–94.

Garrard-Burnett, Virginia. 1998. *Protestantism in Guatemala: Living in the New Jerusalem*. Austin: University of Texas Press.

———. 2010. *Terror in the Land of the Holy Spirit: Guatemala under General Efraín Ríos Montt, 1982–1983*. Oxford: Oxford University Press.

Grainger, Sarah. 2009. "Guatemala Drug Trade Leaves Trail of Local Addicts." Reuters, September 28.

Grann, David. 2011. "A Murder Foretold." *New Yorker*, April 4.

Hallum, Anne M. 2002. "Looking for Hope in Central America: The Pentecostal Movement." In *Religion and Politics in Comparative Perspective*, edited by Ted Gerard Jelen and Clive Wilcox, 225–42. Cambridge: Cambridge University Press.

Jordan, Mary. 2004. "Pit Stop on the Cocaine Highway." *Washington Post*, October 6.

Miroff, Nick, and William Booth. 2011. "In Southern Mexico, a Neglected Frontier." *Washington Post*, June 21.

O'Neill, Kevin. 2009. "But Our Citizenship Is in Heaven: A Proposal for the Study of Christian Citizenship in the Global South." *Citizenship Studies* 13 (4): 333–47.

———. 2010. *City of God: Christian Citizenship in Postwar Guatemala*. Berkeley: University of California Press.

O'Neill, Kevin, and Kendron Thomas, eds. 2011. *Securing the City: Neoliberalism, Space, and Insecurity in Postwar Guatemala*. Durham: Duke University Press.

Oremos Online. 2006. http://www.oremos.net. Accessed February 15, 2006.

Orsi, Robert. 1996. *Thank You, Saint Jude: Women's Devotion to the Patron Saint of Hopeless Causes*. New Haven: Yale University Press.

Painter, James. 2007. "Crime Dominates Guatemala Campaign." BBC News, May 10. http://news.bbc.co.uk/2/hi/americas/6643935.stm.

Riley, Naomi S. 2006. "Can the Spirit Move You to Join the Middle Class?" *Wall Street Journal*, October 13.

Steigenga, Timothy. 1999. "Guatemala." In *Religious Freedom and Evangelization in Latin America: The Challenge of Religious Pluralism*, edited by Paul Sigmund, 150–74. Maryknoll, NY: Orbis.

Stoll, David, ed. 1990. *Is Latin America Turning Protestant? The Politics of Evangelical Growth*. Berkeley: University of California Press.

United Nations Office on Drugs and Crime. 2011. *World Drug Report*. New York: United Nations.

US Department of State. 2012. "Remarks with Guatemalan Foreign Minister Harold Caballeros before Their Meeting." February 21. http://www.state.gov/secretary/rm/2012/02/184289.htm.

Wilson, Maya. 2009. *Guatemala: Crime Capital of Central America*. Washington, DC: Council on Hemispheric Affairs.

12

Politics of Tradition

Charismatic Globalization, Morality, and Culture in Polynesian Protestantism

YANNICK FER

Jonas "instantly saw the difference." At his first meeting with mission-aries of the charismatic organization Youth With a Mission (YWAM) in 1995 in Tahiti, he remembers being struck by "the freedom in the preaching and the teaching" and above all, by the music and dance. "It's very strict here," he explains. "Everyone—the ministers—thought we couldn't play traditional music for Jesus. When YWAM came, they began to teach that we should use our culture."[1]

This unexpected encounter between the Polynesian "Christian tradi-tion," of which the historical Protestant churches are today the custodi-ans, and the "liberation of self" promoted by international charismatic networks underlines the complex effects of Pentecostal/charismatic glo-balization on local Christian cultures. As John Barker notes, in Oceania "it is very risky to read the complex and transient events of the present into the grand narrative of conversion from tradition to Christianity, as a one-way movement into a uniform global modernity" (2012, 78). The spread of a "charismatic culture" oriented toward personal empower-ment (Coleman 2000, 6) in the Polynesian islands is indeed part of the long history of local Protestantism, which has turned the relationships between culture, body, and morality into a political issue. This history began in Tahiti at the end of the eighteenth century with the arrival of the first missionaries from the London Missionary Society (LMS), in-spired by English evangelical "revivals." This history has contributed to the contemporary shaping of cultural and national identities by associat-ing Christianity and tradition. And it continued in the twentieth century through the confrontation between, on one hand, classical Pentecostal churches advocating a moralization of personal existence as a condition for salvation and, on the other, historical Protestant churches denouncing such religious "individualism" in the name of community cohesion and cultural authenticity.

So the "informalization" of manners (Wouters 2010, 171) and the free expression of cultural "personal" identity fostered by charismatic networks need to be understood within the perspective of a historical incorporation of Christian morality, which has made the discipline of the body a cornerstone of the new system of authority (Eves 1996, 86). "Dancing for God," as YWAM claims, entails both a subversion of the traditional order stemming from Polynesian historical Christianity and a break with the moral conservatism of classical Pentecostalism, which associates conversion (and personal respectability) with a strict control of the Polynesian "pagan nature" smoldering in the corporal expressions of the local culture.

One of the paradoxes of these charismatic movements in Polynesia resides in the way they combine this claim for radical liberation with political activism for the restoration of a "Christian government" that would give precedence to the "salvation of the nation" at the expense of individual freedom.

Christian Tradition and Pentecostal Globalization in Polynesia

Most of the constitutions of independent Polynesian island states today proclaim Christianity as a cornerstone of their national identity, alongside cultural tradition. Thus Samoa presents itself as an "Independent State based on Christian principles and Samoan custom and tradition." Only the French Pacific territories officially differentiate themselves from this political culture that encompasses Christianity and often associates churches with the governance of public affairs. But in French Polynesia too, biblical references still imbue political discourses and, at least since the end of the 1990s, the historical Protestant church[2] has backed the movement for political independence (Malogne-Fer 2007).

The history of these churches—which are still dominant in all Polynesian island nations—has often merged with the history of local states, many churches achieving independence from Western missions during the time of political independence, between 1962 (independence of

Samoa) and 1980. Throughout the nineteenth century, as they translated the Bible into vernacular languages and became a central part of social life, Protestant churches acquired the role of custodian of Polynesian languages and cultures. Moreover, the early involvement of Polynesian "teachers" in the Christianization of Pacific Islands alongside Western missionaries from the LMS or Methodist missions (Forman 1990) has contributed to shaping a common Pacific Christian culture, a "Pacific Christian way" transcending local particularities.

Therefore, when Pentecostal churches were established in Polynesia during the second half of the twentieth century, they were planted in Christian lands and had to find their place within a deep-rooted biblical culture. These churches, coming mostly from a North American background, belong to a classical Pentecostalism stemming from a revivalist tradition oriented toward personal "sanctification" and the restoration of the old-time religion (Blumhofer 1993). They resulted from the missionary ambitions of the first Pentecostal denominations that emerged in the southern United States at the beginning of the century, particularly the Assemblies of God—officially founded in 1914 in Arkansas and present in Fiji since the 1920s (Larson 1997).

These Pentecostal churches have often been indifferent and even hostile to any expressions of local culture in the religious space. Sosene Le'au, a former Samoan leader of YWAM who converted to the Assemblies of God in 1971, in Pago Pago, after having grown up in the main historical Protestant church,[3] describes a church "patterned very much after Western civilization": "We sat on hard wooden pews singing Western-style hymns. In so many ways the church made me feel that my Samoan culture was evil and that I had to give it up" (Le'au 1997, 47–48). On other islands, the Assemblies of God include local songs and musical instruments in their liturgy, but always strongly oppose the Protestant discourse on tradition, in the name of a personal salvation that implies a deliberate break with traditional structures of authority.

But classical Pentecostalism finally stepped into local culture through its reference to the "old-time Christianity," which in Polynesia includes both the missionary era and the mythical time when Polynesian ministers "used to have mana" and could heal the sick. So the rise of these new churches didn't simply rely on the opportunity they offer for individuals to escape from familial and community obligations, or on the attraction of a religious modernity that combined globalization, deterritorialization, and a "holy ignorance" of local cultures (Roy 2009). The "revival" they advocate also addresses itself to a Polynesian Protestant memory that intertwines the legacy of British revivalism with indigenous representations of spiritual power: "I've learnt that in the old days, the Protestant church here lived according to the Holy Spirit, like this church [the AoG] does nowadays," says Nicole, a member of the French Polynesian Assemblies of God.[4]

Thus, in a context of growing religious diversity and the relative decline of historical Protestant churches (Ernst 2006), classical Pentecostalism enables converts to claim a return to the Polynesian Bible (the orthodoxy and the early times of Polynesian Protestantism) as well as a return to oneself (one's own salvation and one's spiritual and practical needs). Pentecostal conversion is also ambivalent in its relationship with the Polynesian norms of self-control inherited from the missionary morality. The experiences of the Holy Spirit, which the converts regard as necessary emotions, indeed put them at odds with a dominant social gaze quick to condemn such emotional outbursts. And yet, the effectiveness of the "changed life" they hope for depends strongly on these emotional experiences, seen as a medium of "transparent and direct" communication with God: becoming able to speak to God and listen to "His voice" is part of an effort of self-reformation that seeks social respectability and *finally* makes them abide, more than others, with the dominant social norms. So these converts differ from mainstream society less through nonconformity than by a kind of hyperconformity, implying a scrupulous respect for the ethical rules of conduct governing the life of "honest citizens." Belonging to a minority church reinforces this quest for respectability, as it constitutes a risk of social disqualification: a double bind expressed by a Pentecostal convert from Huahine (Windward Islands): "You change for the better, and they get upset. I don't know what we have done wrong."[5]

Classical Pentecostalism's discouragement of the expressions—and especially bodily expressions—of Polynesian cultures does not just manifest a deliberate ignorance of local culture inspired by a universalistic and individualist credo (the "new creature in Christ"). Taking up the missionary conviction that a "pagan memory" is fatally smoldering in Polynesian bodies, classical Pentecostalism above all emphasizes how strongly the relationship between body and culture is still a symbolic locus of political authority in contemporary Polynesia. And this is precisely the domain in which the spread of global charismatic Protestantism in Polynesia has its most subversive effects: by fostering a liberation of self that redeems the individual body as a "natural" means of expressing cultural identity, charismatic networks like YWAM contest both the Christian tradition of historical Protestantism and the moral "aculturalism" of classical Pentecostalism.

Charismatic Protestantism, Informality, and Subversion

For the nineteenth-century missionaries in the Pacific, "the reworking of the consciousness of the colonized was bound up with a process of changing the body as a means of changing that consciousness" (Eves 1996, 87). The conviction that "the visible body is emblematic of morality," borrowed from British revivalism and Victorian morality, has given shape in Polynesia to a discipline of the body encompassing self-presentation, interpersonal interactions, and the relationship to cultural memory. On many islands, specifically in Tonga or Samoa (Tcherkézoff 1997, 338ff), this new Christian order features tightly interwoven church hierarchies and social traditional hierarchies, thus subjecting individuals' bodies to the authority of elders—both deacons and heads of families—and to a strong duty of respectability. Jonas remembers the circumstances that led his parents to leave the Marquesas Islands for Tahiti at the beginning of the 1970s, after a ball at which they were seen dancing "too closely":

> My parents had a Protestant youth in the Marquesas. They made a fault over there: there was a ball, and dancers were not allowed to dance too close. That's how it was, in these times. And my parents, they were too close. The ball was organized by the local church, and they were already married. My parents, as well as my uncle who was laughing, were told that they were no more members of the church, excommunicated. That's how they came here, where I was raised.[6]

Besnier notes that in Tonga, during services in mainstream denominations, and in most public contexts, "the fear of ridicule and shame (*mâ*) ensures a dignified and controlled comportment, particularly for adults" (Besnier 2011, 218). This fear, an embodied expression of social control that produces self-discipline, applies in particular to the rules governing cross-sibling avoidance that Besnier describes as the foundation of the Tongan social order (*fakaʻapaʻapa*). By contrast, the two charismatic churches he visited dramatically distanced themselves from this traditional social order, through an emotional effervescence and an informality of manners that even opens "the possibility that one's classificatory cross-siblings witness behavior that foregrounds bodily or sexual matters, or that someone witnesses it in the presence of his or her classificatory cross-sibling" (Besnier 2011, 219). "Feel happy," the leaders of these churches said simply.

The recent growth of these charismatic movements in the Polynesian islands comes with a redefinition of the licit/illicit boundaries, fostered by three main socio-religious evolutions, both local and global. The most evident is a generational break, linked with rapid social change and transnational circulations between the small island states and the strong diasporic communities living in New Zealand, Australia, and the United States since the 1950s (Fer and Malogne-Fer 2014). The belief in an individual salvation echoes the effects of higher levels of education, increasing salaried employment, and migration, which prompt young Polynesians to shift from the simple reproduction of their parents' activity (usually self-subsistence based on agriculture and fishing) and strive to "make their own life." Moreover, as Coleman notes, "the globalizing charismatic habitus incorporates the imagery and practices of youth—physical movement, deployment of contemporary musical forms, technology—and locates them within a context of protest against an established religio-political order" (Coleman 2000, 229). So the charismatic experience can be lived by young Polynesians as a nonconformist liberation that gives them access to a "higher" level of spirituality (according to a logic borrowed from their school experience) and to a cosmopolitan Christian culture.

The specific way this charismatic Protestantism does articulate individualization and globalization, through a deconstruction of the sacred/profane distinction inherited from missionaries, is precisely the second feature that contributes to making it attractive to Polynesian youth. As they promote a less social and more individuated understanding of moral consciousness, charismatic currents contribute—indeed, more deeply than does classic Pentecostalism, which remains attached to common criteria of moral respectability—to shifting the locus of moral judgment from practice to personal character, and from social relationships to the "personal relationship" with God. The question is no longer, "Is it right to do this?" but rather, "Is the person doing this a true Christian?" Bodily movements and cultural expressions (such as dance), which traditionally mark the border between sacred and profane, can then participate in this subversion of traditional order, pursuing the "liberation" of the Polynesian individual.

Finally, a third evolution, at the intersection of Western influence and the internal dynamics of Polynesian societies, enables young charismatics to distance themselves (at least during worship time) from the social duty of self-discipline, and to claim the authenticity of free self-expression. This evolution, a long-term historical process described by Wouters (2010, 171) as an "informalization of manners," is here intrinsically linked with the cultural influences and the reshaping of social order that Christianity brought to the Polynesian islands. The Victorian era, whose values have been ingrained into and nurtured by the traditional Christian morality in Polynesia, was in many respects a climax of the "second nature"—a social order resulting from the domestication of the spontaneous drives of "human nature," which based moral reputation on a personal ability to show self-discipline (Wouters 2010, 161). To the contrary, the rise of charismatic Protestantism appears to be symptomatic of the advent of a "third nature," allowing a greater openness to emotions—even "dangerous" ones—which can now be experienced without shame or fear of losing self-control, as these experiences are felt by individuals who "can take the liberty" of allowing such, because they own (and are seen as owning) an inalienable capacity of self-regulation, based on a set of embodied dispositions (Wouters 2010, 172–73).[7]

Religious globalization once again locates this process within the frame of reciprocal influences and borrowings.[8] At first glance, global charismatic culture seems to deviate from mainstream Western habitus, as its styles of faith and bodily deportment involve "the evocation of bodily possession by powerful, externally derived and divine forces" (Coleman 2000, 139). This is (implicitly or explicitly) inspired by a desire to move closer to the forms of bodily experiences commonly associated with non-Western spiritual realms, such as trance. In the Polynesian context, this liberation of emotions and bodies that expresses "an attempt to recover the 'first nature' without losing the control brought by the 'second nature'" (Wouters 2010, 173) could be simply analyzed as an importation of a Western process of individualization and informalization of manners. But it also entails new opportunities to reconnect with a cultural memory banned by missionary morality, in the name of individual freedom and self-expression.

In the case of Urapmin converts to Protestantism, Robbins has described the persistence of a "double consciousness," a consciousness troubled by the irremediable opposition between the moral duties imposed by local culture and the individualistic values of Christianity, instilling the conviction that one is a "sinner" (2004, 313). In Polynesia, the tension that charismatic Protestantism strives to solve is rather a double bind inherent in traditional Protestantism, as this Protestantism claims its continuity with indigenous cultural heritage while still implicitly identifying part of this culture (especially dances) with a profane Polynesian "nature." Thus the sense of cultural belonging coexists with the patterns of personal salvation inherited from the early missionaries, who saw the body as the very place of a necessary confrontation between culture and Christianity. Charismatic Protestantism then tends to elude this double bind by symbolically acknowledging cultural expression as a means of individual liberation.

Thus the Island Breeze movement, an official "ministry" of the charismatic network Youth With a Mission, advocates the use of Polynesian cultural forms, especially dances, as an authentic expression of Christian faith and a means for evangelization (Fer 2012). Island Breeze began at a school of evangelism led by the Samoan Sosene Le'au in Kona (Big Island, Hawaii) in 1979, with twelve young students, mostly Samoans and Hawaiians. When he remembers this very outset of the movement, the Hawaiian Coleman Kealoha Kaopua clearly situates the beginnings of the liberation and reappropriation of cultural identity in the body: "Because we are Pacific Islanders, we like to move our hands, you know, express ourselves, and we did. And that's when the seeds for Island Breeze started because it was observed that, you know, these expressions were meant for worship."[9]

The liberation of individual bodies fostered by charismatic movements has a very clear political dimension, as it opposes the self-discipline ingrained by the Polynesian Christian tradition and tends to reshape the existing relationships between Polynesian culture and Western domination on one hand, and Polynesian individuals and local traditional structures of authority on the other. But the translation of this charismatic "liberating" credo into the political field, inspired by the global theology of spiritual warfare, has finally much more ambivalent effects, combining the subversion of traditional order through individual liberation with a claim for the restoration of a "Christian government," potentially constraining individual autonomy for the "salvation of the nation."

Charismatic Politics and Christian Order

In many Pacific Islands, the struggle for national independence included the idea of a future government that based its actions on Christian values. So charismatic activists in politics today can legitimately refer to this local history as they endorse the old hope of a "Christian governance" that the postcolonial states seem to have betrayed, notably by letting corruption prosper. This gives to the charismatic engagement in politics the appearance of cultural continuity. But the entry of these new Christian actors into the political field also illustrates a generational break, which needs to be understood within the perspective of global evolutions of charismatic Protestantism on one hand, and transnational circulations between the countries of Polynesian immigration and the islands of origin on the other.

The evangelical missionary youth networks that burgeoned in North America between the end of World War II and the 1960s, and more specifically the charismatic organization Youth With a Mission (YWAM), have strongly contributed to this reshaping of Christian politics in Oceania by facilitating interactions between local Christian cultures and a wider evangelical offensive inspired by firm opposition to Western secularization. These evangelical networks came from a generational shift, against the constraints imposed by classic religious institutions and toward the conquest of a "new world" that seemed now within their reach, thanks to the development of new means of transportation and communication.

In the ideological context of the Cold War, evangelicals first regarded the Pacific as a stepping-stone to Asia, itself a densely populated continent then dominated by communist atheism and non-Christian religions (Cunningham 2001, 150). As they became established in New Zealand, Australia, and Hawaii, they found there the recruits needed for their missionary project: young charismatic New Zealanders took part in the development of new YWAM national bases in the Philippines, Hong Kong, Singapore, India, Indonesia, and Japan. In 1980 Kalafi Moala, a young Tongan man who had come to New Zealand to study at the university, became the first regional Asia-Pacific director. And the China Focus Team, dedicated to missionary work in China, is today based on the YWAM university campus in Kona (Hawaii), which opened in 1978 and now receives mainly South Korean students.

But these missionary networks also contributed to local religiopolitical dynamics within Oceania by locating themselves at the crossroads of two distinct and complementary spaces. The first of these is Christianity from a Western cultural background, weakened by secularization and marked by evangelical "revivals," as in New Zealand. The second is a "Christianity of the South," claiming Christian identity as a distinctive feature of Polynesian culture in a context of increasing transnational movement between the countries of immigration and the islands of origin. Thus at the end of the 1960s, the first steps taken by YWAM in New Zealand coincided with a strong charismatic "revival" that first affected the historical Protestant churches and later contributed to the rise of new Pentecostal/charismatic churches throughout the 1970s and 1980s (Davidson 2004, 171–72). These young "born-again" Christians claimed a greater individual freedom in their quest for a "spiritual but not religious" experience, while advocating a conservative counterrevolution for their country based on a "return" to biblical principles (Evans 1992, 76). They were at the forefront of an evangelical offensive that progressively led a significant part of charismatic evangelicals in most Western societies to take a public stance against the liberalization of dominant moral values, in the name of an aggressive Christianity (Fer 2010). This new generation of Christian activists, from among whom YWAM recruited its first missionaries, has contributed in New Zealand to the development of a new Christian Right, small but influential, organized into association networks defending "family values" and evangelical media until its entry into politics at the end of the 1990s.

"The kingdom of God is in each of us and we carry it with us everywhere we go," the YWAM founder Loren Cunningham writes. "I think for a Christian, the secular world should not exist. Each of us stands in one kingdom or in the other: light or darkness" (Cunningham 1997, 141, 148). The theology of spiritual warfare, elaborated by C. Peter Wagner in the 1980s and actively spread by YWAM, includes the political field and government among the seven main spheres of influence that Christians need to penetrate in order to reform society and ensure the salvation of the nations (Gonzalez 2011). Through the incorporation of a duty of personal commitment—each convert has to "take a stance for God" in the battle against "the principalities of darkness" (Marshall 1992)—and the rejection of the principles of secularization, this charismatic theology establishes a specific articulation between individual experience, national identity, and globalization. It echoes what Liogier describes as an "individuo-globalism" characteristic of contemporary spiritualities, associating individualism with global consciousness (Liogier 2009). It also throws light on a process of "charismatization" through which the evangelical personalization of religious experience may generate new forms of political engagement. In Polynesia, such an encompassing approach to politics matches the traditional notions of relationships between religion and politics. But the complex articulation between individual autonomy and social structures of authority that this charismatic theology promotes also creates many areas of uncertainty and internal contradictions.

On most of the Polynesian islands, evangelical missionary youth networks have established partnerships with the leaders of the historical Protestant churches concerned about competition from Mormonism and the disaffection of youth from church life. However, rather than contributing to an effective reengagement of youth in historical churches, this kind of partnership has more often built new bridges between Protestant youth movements and local Pentecostal/charismatic churches, to the benefit of the latter (Aliimalemanu 1999). This points to the intrinsic ambiguity of the attitude these networks adopt toward traditional church institutions, which they regard as both partners and mission fields. Moreover, in their strategy of political influence, the international leaders of YWAM similarly seek to build alliances with Polynesian heads of state who are close to the same traditional church hierarchies that their missionary activities contribute to undermining. This underlines a sticking point between, on one hand, a national approach that aims to consolidate the position of the local chiefs of "Christian nations" and, on the other hand, an effort to spread the values of autonomy at the individual level, reinforcing the democratic claim. Thus in 2005 Cunningham spoke of Tongan King Tupou IV as "a good friend and a good man,"[10] while Kalafi Moala—the former Asia-Pacific regional director of YWAM and founder in 1988 of the newspaper *Taimi of Tonga*, a banned publication in Tonga—campaigned in his country against monarchy by divine right and for the establishment of parliamentary democracy. This political engagement was inspired in him by his former experience in YWAM, he says, and is a continuation of the "mission" he has received from God ("This is His mission for me"), in the name of the freedom and rights that God has granted to all men: "when a force (whatever that may be) robs humans of their right to choose, such a force must be opposed. And all other human rights that are Biblically based, are God-given: the rights to life, health, happiness, education, etc."[11]

Conclusion

The growth and diversification of Pentecostal/charismatic movements in Polynesia have progressively given shape to a distinct religious field that offers Polynesian "born-again" Christians both a set of common references and a diversity of options fostering the development of personal itineraries. In this field, individual identities are reformulated under the cross-influences of individualization, reappropriation/reshaping of the Polynesian "Christian tradition," and globalization. The transnational circulations between the Polynesian migrant communities and their islands of origin play a major role here, as they introduce an intermediary level where connections are made between religious dynamics specific to secularized societies (in particular the aggressive reaffirmation of a Christian morality) and Polynesian cultural memory and values. Thus the individual agency claimed by young Polynesian Protestants can merge with new forms of religious commitment against secularization, in the frame of a "spiritual warfare" that is both global (Western "dechristianization" versus Christianity of the South) and local (New Zealand dominant culture versus Polynesian Christian culture).

The attempts by the New Zealand Christian Right stemming from the 1970s charismatic revival to convert the moral convictions of Polynesian migrant communities (the "Pacific Peoples," who make up 6.9 percent of the population) into political engagement have been so far unsuccessful, due to the lasting fidelity that these socially disadvantaged groups show to the Labour Party. But in the mainstream Protestantism of New Zealand, ethical issues—especially same-sex unions and the ordination of gays and lesbians—have contributed throughout the 2000s to materialize a "cultural" frontier between liberal Pakehas[12] and Polynesians (Malogne-Fer 2010): the essentialization of theological differences as "cultural differences" nurtures new forms of engagement, inseparably religious and cultural, in affinity with the credo of conservative evangelicalism.

This return of sexual morality to the forefront of the agenda of Protestant churches, even as the informalization instilled by charismatic movements fosters in its own way a liberation of individual bodies, throws light on the contemporary reshaping of Polynesian Christian morality. Discipline of the body remains the focal point for the ongoing elaboration of this morality, which should not be understood merely as the result of a one-way historical incorporation of norms inherited from Western missionaries, but also as a domain of agency and conscious actions "in which actors are culturally constructed as being aware both of the directive force of values and of the choices left open to them in responding to that force" (Robbins 2004, 315).

NOTES

1. Jonas, interview by author, Papeete, Tahiti, May 31, 2001.

2. The Maohi Protestant Church.

3. The Congregational Christian Church of American Samoa.

4. Nicole, interview by author, Papeete, Tahiti, April 9, 2001.

5. Eddy, interview by author, Papeete, Tahiti, June 2, 2001.

6. Jonas, interview by author.

7. The combination of an academic discourse and ecstatic experiences among mainly well-educated upper-class believers at the Vineyard conference described by Bialecki in this volume can be seen as another illustration of this Charismatic ethos.

From their outset, Youth With a Mission and the Vineyard movement have indeed had strong affinities (Fer 2010, 27).

8. On globalization and the shaping of new moralities, especially among youth at the intersection of Western and local influences, see also Krause's chapter in this volume.

9. Coleman Kealoha Kaopua, interview by author, Kona, Big Island, Hawaii, May 3, 2005.

10. Loren Cunningham, interview by author, Kona, Big Island, Hawaii, May 6, 2005.

11. Kalafi Moala, interview by author, e-mail correspondence, December 6, 2006.

12. New Zealanders of European descent.

REFERENCES

Aliimalemanu, Vaega F. 1999. "The Conversion of Members of the Methodist Church in Samoa to the Assemblies of God: Description and Analysis of Contributing Factors." Master's thesis, Pacific Theological College, Suva, Fiji.

Barker, John. 2012. "Secondary Conversion and the Anthropology of Christianity in Melanesia." *Archives de Sciences Sociales des Religions* 157:47–66.

Besnier, Niko. 2011. *On the Edge of the Global: Modern Anxieties in a Pacific Island Nation*. Stanford: Stanford University Press.

Blumhofer, Edith L. 1993. *Restoring the Faith: The Assemblies of God, Pentecostalism and American Culture*. Urbana: University of Illinois Press.

Coleman, Simon. 2000. *The Globalisation of Charismatic Christianity: Spreading the Gospel of Prosperity*. Cambridge: Cambridge University Press.

Cunningham, Loren. 1997. *Tout à gagner: La méthode de Dieu*. Burtigny, Switzerland: Jeunesse en Mission.

———. 2001. *Is That Really You, God? Hearing the Voice of God*. 2nd ed. Seattle, WA: YWAM Publishing.

Davidson, Allan. 2004. *Christianity in Aotearoa: A History of Church and Society in New Zealand*. Wellington: New Zealand Education for Ministry Board.

Ernst, Manfred, ed. 2006. *Globalization and the Reshaping of Christianity in the Pacific Islands*. Suva, Fiji: Pacific Theological College.

Evans, John. 1992. "The New Christian Right in New Zealand." In *"Be Yet Separate": Fundamentalism and the New Zealand Experience*, edited by Bryan Gilling, 69–105. Hamilton, New Zealand: University of Waikato and Colcom Press.

Eves, Richard. 1996. "Colonialism, Corporeality and Character." *History and Anthropology* 10 (1): 85–138.

Fer, Yannick. 2010. *L'offensive évangélique: Voyage au cœur des réseaux militants de Jeunesse en Mission*. Geneva: Labor et Fides.

———. 2012. "Le protestantisme polynésien, de l'Église locale aux réseaux évangéliques." *Archives de Sciences Sociales des Religions* 157:67–87.

Fer, Yannick, and Gwendoline Malogne-Fer. 2014. "Protestantism among the Pacific Peoples in New Zealand: Mobility, Cultural Identifications, and Generational Shifts." In *Movement, Place-Making and Multiple Identifications in Oceania*, edited by Elfriede Hermann, Wolfgang Kempf, and Toon van Meijl, 142–63. New York: Berghahn.

Forman, Charles. 1990. "The Missionary Force of the Pacific Islands Churches." *International Review of Missions* 59: 215–26.

Gonzalez, Philippe. 2011. "De l'évangélisation des cultures à l'hégémonie culturelle: l'Héritage ambigu de la School of World Mission de Fuller Seminary." *Perspectives Missionnaires* 62:57–65.

Larson, Lawrence R. 1997. *The Spirit in Paradise: The History of the Assemblies of God in Fiji and Its Outreaches to Other Island Countries throughout the South Pacific.* St. Louis, MO: Plus Communications.

Le'au, Sosene. 1997. *Called to Honor Him: How Men and Women Are Redeeming Cultures.* Tampa, FL: CultureCom Press.

Liogier, Raphaël. 2009. "L'individuo-globalisme: Nouvelle culture croyante des sociétés industrielles avancées." *Revue Internationale de Politique Comparée* 16 (1): 135–54.

Malogne-Fer, Gwendoline. 2007. *Les femmes dans l'Église protestante ma'ohi: Religion, genre et pouvoir en Polynésie française.* Paris: Karthala.

———. 2010. "L'ordination des gays et lesbiennes dans l'Église méthodiste de Nouvelle-Zélande: Conflits théologiques ou culturels?" In *Protestantisme évangélique et valeurs,* edited by Sébastien Fath, 98–117. Cléon d'Andran, France: Excelsis.

Marshall, Tom. 1992. *Principalities and Powers.* Tonbridge, UK: Sovereign World.

Robbins, Joel. 2004. *Becoming Sinners: Christianity and Moral Torment in a Papua New Guinea Society.* Berkeley: University of California Press.

Roy, Olivier. 2009. *La sainte ignorance: Le temps de la religion sans culture.* Paris: Seuil.

Tcherkézoff, Serge. 1997. "Culture, nation, société: Changements secondaires et bouleversements fondamentaux au Samoa Occidental; Vers un modèle pour l'étude des dynamiques culturelles." In *Le Pacifique Sud aujourd'hui: Identités et transformations culturelles,* edited by Françoise Douaire-Marsaudon and Serge Tcherkézoff, 309–73. Paris: CNRS Ethnologie.

Wouters, Cas. 2010. "Comment les processus de civilisation se sont-ils prolongés? De la 'seconde nature' à la 'troisième nature.'" *Vingtième Siècle* 106:161–75.

Afterword

The Anthropology of Global Pentecostalism and Evangelicalism

JOEL ROBBINS

The editors of this volume of ethnographically rich and tightly argued case studies, focused on various aspects of the lives of Pentecostal and evangelical Christians living in many different parts of the world, remark that the book appears at a time of transition for anthropological studies of Christianity. Dividing the history of this area of study into three phases, they point to a long period, roughly coextensive with the rise of the discipline to its current place in the academy, in which anthropologists only occasionally studied Christianity and tended not to treat it as an object of broad comparative discussion; a period beginning about fifteen years ago, when the development of a comparative field known as the anthropology of Christianity began to become a self-conscious project for some scholars; and a period that is just beginning, during which the anthropology of Christianity, now a large-ish and secure part of the discipline, takes its place as an established subfield marked by well-developed debates and begins to reach out in new directions. Given this historical trajectory, I want to open this afterword by asking what it means for the editors to situate this collection in the space between its second and third phases.

A number of models are available for thinking about the transition from upstart intellectual movement to established subfield. One is the conveniently ready to hand theory of church-sect dynamics that has long been important in the sociology of religion, particularly in the sociology of Christianity (for a classic formulation, see Niebuhr [1929] 1957). In the terms of this model, we would figure the anthropology of Christianity as originally a small sect locked in battle with the scholarly world around it, but now on its way to becoming a reputable, world-accepting church. Another model would draw from Thomas Kuhn's (1996) famous account of the movement between normal and revolutionary science. Normal science, on Kuhn's account, is marked by steady progress toward solving intellectual problems and the possibility of teaching by means of authoritative textbooks that report widely accepted theories, methods, and findings. Revolutionary science appears when anomalies that do not fit normal science views (or, to borrow the now widely used Kuhnian term of art, "paradigms") begin to accumulate. Eventually, as more and more recalcitrant anomalies appear, scholars feel compelled to develop new paradigms to account for them. Periods during which such new paradigms appear are those of revolutionary science. These periods are marked not by steady progress, but rather by creativity, tension, and dispute. Eventually, though, as people begin to settle on one or a few of the new paradigms on offer during the revolutionary period as the one(s) that best account for the anomalies that led to the revolutionary ferment in the first place, a new round of normal science begins. People stop struggling over the very foundations of their work and return to the task of making incremental progress toward well-understood intellectual goals.

Kuhn's model of intellectual change in some ways fits the development of the anthropology of Christianity well, and it highlights aspects of its history that the church-sect account would likely overlook. As the editors note, drawing on some of my own earlier work (which was, as they also discuss, indebted to Mary Douglas's [1966] classic anthropological discussion of anomalies), until roughly the turn of the millennium, Christianity had stood in an anomalous relationship to anthropology. On the one hand, Christianity surely was a culture like any other (or a "part of a culture" or a "religion" like any other—all of these terms have been complicated over the last several decades, but I hope my point is clear enough). As such, it was certainly worthy of anthropological study. Moreover, it was not the primary culture of most anthropologists, at least not when they were acting in their role as academic intellectuals. Therefore, it was also "other" enough to be a reasonable target for a discipline that defined itself as committed to studying cultural difference. But at the same time, even if it was not a foregrounded aspect of anthropological academic culture, Christianity was part of the heritage and cultural surround of the societies from which many anthropologists came, and as such it was also in some respects too familiar an object to be worthy of anthropological study. Douglas has taught us that people tend to avoid or even fear anomalies of this kind—things that are neither quite this nor quite that (like snakes, which live on land but do not walk on legs like other animals that live on land)— and so anthropologists, finding Christianity not quite other to but also not quite the same as their own cultural inheritance, tended to leave it alone.

Like Douglas, Kuhn says that scientists at first ignore or avoid anomalies. They stick to looking at the kinds of things that fit their usual categories and that they therefore find easy to understand. But eventually, he suggests, the anomalies become so plentiful that they need to be addressed. It is at these moments that scientific revolutions begin. Given this, we need to ask why anthropologists in great numbers suddenly at the turn of the millennium overcame their predictable aversion to examining anomalous objects and began regularly to study Christianity. One major cause of this shift has to be the very rapid spread of Christianity in the global south in the wake of the continued growth of the Pentecostal movement and, in particular, the explosion of the charismatic movement in the 1970s and 1980s. Suddenly, anthropologists were finding Christians almost everywhere they went, and these Christians, like the ones readers have encountered in the chapters of this volume, were profoundly involved in their religious lives. Pentecostal, charismatic, and evangelical Christians do not background their religious understandings and commitments, nor do they quietly confine them to hidden, private corners of their lives in ways that would make the religious aspects of their existence easy for anthropologists to ignore. Instead, they allow these understandings to shape many aspects of their lives and thus, in classic Kuhnian fashion, these kinds of Christians represented "anomalies" that were turning up everywhere anthropologists looked and proving impossible to ignore. This meant that anthropologists had to rethink some key disciplinary ideas about what they should and should not study if they wanted their field to remain open to the world as they were finding it. And at the same time, anthropological ideas about the role of the study of otherness in defining the field had been changing since the reflexive turn of the 1980s (see, for example, Clifford 1988), and religion, having reentered the public sphere around the world in the 1970s and 1980s (Casanova 1994), began to gain ground as a topic of interest across the social sciences and the humanities. The time was right, then, for anthropologists finally to feel the need to come to grips with their long neglect of the largest religion in the world, even if it meant leaving some of the comforts of normal science behind (for a more detailed version of the argument of this paragraph, see Robbins 2014).

As the editors note, the revolutionary moment of the anthropology of Christianity is likely nearing its end now. Work in the field looks more and more like normal science—with scholars making steady progress on well-defined topics, rather than fighting pitched battles over the need to take account of new, formerly anomalous objects of study. This shift, however, needs to be seen not as a decline from heights of revolutionary excitement (or as a slide from sect-like fervor to churchly sobriety), but rather, as the editors note, as marking a time when innovations can be more carefully made, debates can be pursued more steadily, and the subfield can begin to reach out to make links with other currently important areas in anthropology. It is with this point in mind that I would like to consider what it means for this book to appear just as the shift from revolutionary to normal science seems to be getting under way in the anthropology of Christianity.

A first thing to note is that the organization of the volume, as reflected in its title, quietly marks a subtle shift in the way the anthropology of Christianity has organized itself to this point. A key category in the anthropology of Christianity has been that of Pentecostal and charismatic Christianity (P/c). This category lumps together those genealogically linked forms of the faith that emphasize the availability of gifts of the Holy Spirit to all believers. These gifts include, among others, speaking in tongues, healing, and prophesying. Historically, P/c Christianity has its roots in evangelicalism, but it is distinct from other strands of the evangelical tradition (e.g., fundamentalism) by virtue of the fact that churches in those strands, on the basis of firmly held theological commitments, deny that contemporary believers can receive Spiritual gifts. One gains a sense of how firmly this difference can set P/c Christians apart from their evangelical cousins when one considers Bebbington's (1989) famous list of key features of evangelicalism, carefully reviewed by the editors in their introduction, alongside Donald Dayton's (1987,

19–23) equally influential list of the four key features of Pentecostal theology. Like other evangelicals, P/c Christians subscribe to conversionism, Biblicism, activism, and crucicentrism, but when it comes to their theology, their focus is on the fact that Jesus offers salvation, Jesus heals, Jesus baptizes with the Holy Spirit, and Jesus is coming again. In the P/c list, the emphasis on Spiritual gifts stands out strongly, and it does so in P/c everyday life as well. For this reason, other evangelicals, particularly fundamentalists, often find Pentecostals beyond the pale, and Pentecostals likewise do not see themselves accurately reflected in the mirror of these other evangelical streams (Robbins 2004). Indeed, some scholars even suggest that P/c Christians are so distinct from other kinds of Christians, including other evangelicals, that they deserve to be defined as a fourth stream of Christianity, alongside Catholicism, Orthodoxy, and Protestantism (Jacobsen 2011). In this emerging classification, other evangelicals are securely within the Protestant fold, while P/c churches are treated as fully distinct from the broader stream from which they first emerged.

These historical and classificatory considerations matter for our understanding both of the history of the anthropology of Christianity and of some of the unique qualities of this volume. P/c churches, rather than evangelical churches more generally, are the ones that have been both growing very rapidly and spreading globally very extensively in recent decades. For this reason, and because the emphasis on Spiritual gifts gives them a somewhat "exotic" quality that renders them a good fit for common anthropological conceptions of religion (see Douglas 2001), a majority of early works in the anthropology of Christianity have focused on them. This is, for the most part, true of this volume as well. Only Omri Elisha's chapter focuses solely on evangelicals who are not Pentecostal. Jean DeBernardi's chapter also focuses in large part on the Brethren, generally classed as fundamentalists (although, as if to help make our point about the differences, she does mention that some Brethren women in Penang and Singapore left for charismatic churches because the latter allowed them to preach, presumably because those churches count Spiritual inspiration, rather than gender, as the overriding qualification for taking up the preacher's role). The rest of the chapters focus primarily on members of P/c churches (even when they sometimes refer to them as evangelical), and the characteristic importance of Spiritual gifts for these kinds of Christians is in almost all cases on display. But it is also true that the volume's introduction discusses evangelicalism in some detail and very helpfully considers some of the key historical relations between evangelicalism and P/c Christianity. Together, then, the introduction and the two chapters on evangelicals make this volume unusual for the way it includes both P/c and evangelical cases, rather than focusing on P/c Christianity alone.

It is a real advance on the editors' part to bring scholars studying evangelicals and those studying P/c churches together in one volume. The anthropological study of non-P/c evangelicals has grown rapidly of late, and initiating a comparative conversation that encompasses these kinds of Christianity and P/c churches is an important current task for the anthropology of Christianity (for an important full-length recent study of an evangelical group, see Webster 2013; for an ethnographic comparison of cases across the P/c and evangelical divide, see Robbins, Schieffelin, and Vilaça 2014). The chapters collected here are not for the most part explicitly comparative in this sense, though all of them take up theoretical issues, like those of language, embodiment, affect, media-tion, political relations, and so forth, that bring with them the poten-tial for staging comparison across Christian traditions. Moreover, taken as a set, they do put some comparative resonances in play within the volume itself. Thus, for example, it is clear that the Manichean moral understanding of the world as dominated by a struggle between good and evil, and the language of Spiritual warfare many believers use to develop their own plans of action in relation to this struggle, cross the P/c and evangelical divide (for a very fine early ethnographic account of this moral vision in a fundamentalist context, see Ammerman 1987). This moral understanding is at the center of Kristine Krause's chapter, but it is much in evidence in many other chapters as well. Read together, these chapters show that while views about the Spiritual gifts may differ between evangelical and P/c groups, views about the moral condition of the world appear to be much less varied. As one reads through the vol-ume, one cannot help but recognize the tremendous potential for com-parative work on how these moral views shape the lives of a wide range of Christian groups around the world.

A second point worth making about the way this volume brings to-gether cases that have until now often been kept somewhat separate is that by doing so the contributors here remind us that categories like evangelical, Pentecostal, and charismatic are folk categories as much as, and before, they are scholarly ones. As categories Christians themselves deploy, they are subject to all kinds of negotiations in use. This can lead these categories to appear, as the editors note in their introduction, to be quite open and polythetic. But as anthropologists we can do even more than make this important point, for we can also study how people come to define and use these categories in the varied situations in which they live. In a piece that appeared before the anthropology of Christianity developed, and for this reason perhaps has been somewhat neglected, Kent Maynard (1993) argued that where he worked in Ecuador, terms like "evangelical" and "charismatic" are segmentary and relative, just like corporate group terms such as "lineage," "clan," and "tribe" are relative, at least in classic anthropological models of social structure. One further task this volume thus raises for the anthropology of Christianity is that of beginning to track carefully how Christians situate themselves in relation to other Christians. We need, in other words, anthropological studies of Christian self-definition, interdenominational dispute, and grassroots ecumenism (a term I borrow from Richard Werbner, personal communication; see also Robbins 2013; for a related point, see Garriott and O'Neill 2008). By crossing boundaries on an academic level, this volume opens up precisely these kinds of issues concerning boundaries and their negotiation, and it suggests that we can explore them ethnographically to good effect.

I have dwelled on the novelty of this volume as a collection that analyzes both evangelical and P/c Christianity because I think its innovative qualities in this regard might not be obvious to all readers. But there is also much else that is important in these chapters, either by virtue of the ways they push well-established topics in new directions, or for the ways they broach new topics that deserve further development. In the former category, one can point to the way Jon Bialecki raises new questions for well-developed discussions of Christian language ideologies by cross-pollinating them with ideas about affect. Martin Lindhardt nicely contributes to a long-running anthropology of Christianity interest in materiality, and Kelly H. Chong presents an important case in which the widely remarked P/c tendency to transform (but not erase) pre-conversion patriarchal relations shows up in very full form in the

Korean churches she studies, but does so to completely conservative local effect.

Of the new directions limned in some of these chapters, I would like to add two more to the list offered in the introduction. First, I would group Martijn Oosterbaan's and Mathijs Pelkmans's contributions as ones that interrogate with unusual care the shifting dynamics of charisma and conviction in P/c life. In both chapters, we move beyond static models of how P/c believers can see the Spirit in play in the world, to follow the work of discernment they constantly carry out in order to gauge the true nature of the powerful events and forces they encounter. Second, I would note a relatively novel attention some of the contributors pay to issues of what we might call Christian social organization. While Omri Elisha's contribution is explicitly focused on a currently rapidly developing debate within the anthropology of Christianity over the extent to which Christianity promotes individualism, he also presents fascinating material on the evangelical understanding of social relations, and gives us some sense of the role of small support and study groups in organizing Christian life. At a very different scale, but taking up related issues, Thomas Csordas lays out the complex, transnational social linkages that constitute the global world of charismatic Catholic communities, while Yannick Fer's account of the global para-church organization Youth With a Mission offers comparable material on the sinews that bind together various spots on the global charismatic world map. Somewhere between the small group and the global ecumene, Ruy Blanes and Kevin O'Neill offer us insight into the articulations that hold between Christian churches as social groups and the nations in which they live. Working at a number of these scales, Kristine Krause (like Elisha) reminds us of how much work P/e moral thinking does in providing the terms by which believers define these social groupings and understand the relations between them. The study of Christian social organization is something of a frontier for the anthropology of Christianity, and we still need much more work on the internal organization of churches themselves (Robbins 2014). But the chapters here make a good start on opening this area up for further investigation.

As the editors note in their introduction, one of the key strengths of this volume is the consistently high quality of the ethnographic accounts offered by its contributors. One can learn a great deal about what P/e

Christianity looks like in various parts of the world from the chapters collected here. One can also get an initial exposure to many of the key debates that have marked the first decade and a half of work in the anthropology of Christianity. I have singled out only a few of these debates for discussion here, and I have mostly let the ethnographies speak for themselves. But I hope I have been able to help situate this fine volume in relation to the anthropology of Christianity more generally, and to point to some of the many avenues for further exploration that it opens up.

REFERENCES

Ammerman, Nancy Tatom. 1987. *Bible Believers: Fundamentalists in the Modern World.* New Brunswick: Rutgers University Press.

Bebbington, David. 1989. *Evangelicalism in Modern Britain: A History from the 1730s to the 1980s.* London: Unwin Hyman.

Casanova, José. 1994. *Public Religions in the Modern World.* Chicago: University of Chicago Press.

Clifford, James. 1988. *The Predicament of Culture: Twentieth-Century Ethnography, Literature, and Art.* Cambridge: Harvard University Press.

Dayton, Donald W. 1987. *Theological Roots of Pentecostalism.* Peabody, MA: Hendrickson.

Douglas, Bronwen. 2001. "From Invisible Christians to Gothic Theatre: The Romance of the Millennial in Melanesian Anthropology." *Current Anthropology* 42 (1): 615–50.

Douglas, Mary. 1966. *Purity and Danger: An Analysis of the Concepts of Pollution and Taboo.* London: Routledge and Kegan Paul.

Garriott, William, and Kevin Lewis O'Neill. 2008. "What Is a Christian? Toward a Dialogic Approach in the Anthropology of Christianity." *Anthropological Theory* 8 (4): 381–98.

Jacobsen, Douglas. 2011. *The World's Christians: Who They Are, Where They Are, and How They Got There.* Oxford: Wiley-Blackwell.

Kuhn, Thomas S. 1996. *The Structure of Scientific Revolutions.* Chicago: University of Chicago Press.

Maynard, Kent. 1993. "Protestant Theories and Anthropological Knowledge: Convergent Models in the Ecuadorian Sierra." *Cultural Anthropology* 8 (2): 246–67.

Niebuhr, H. Richard. (1929) 1957. *The Social Sources of Denominationalism.* New York: Meridian.

Robbins, Joel. 2004. "The Globalization of Pentecostal and Charismatic Christianity." *Annual Review of Anthropology* 33:117–43.

———. 2013. "Afterword: Let's Keep It Awkward; Anthropology, Theology, and Otherness." *Australian Journal of Anthropology* 24 (3): 329–37.

———. 2014 . "The Anthropology of Christianity: Unity, Diversity, New Directions (An Introduction)." *Current Anthropology* 55 *(Supplement 10): S157–S171.*

Robbins, Joel, Bambi B. Schieffelin, and Aparecida Vilaça. 2014. "Evangelical Conversion and the Transformation of the Self in Amazonia and Melanesia: Christianity and the Revival of Anthropological Comparison." *Comparative Studies in Society and History* 56 (3): 559–90.

Webster, Joseph. 2013. *The Anthropology of Protestantism: Faith and Crisis among Scottish Fishermen.* New York: Palgrave.

ABOUT THE CONTRIBUTORS

JON BIALECKI is Lecturer in Anthropology at the University of Edinburgh. His work has been published in several edited volumes and in academic journals such as the *South Atlantic Quarterly*, *Current Anthropology*, *American Ethnologist*, *Anthropological Theory*, and the *Journal of the Royal Anthropological Institute*; he was also a coeditor of a special issue of *Anthropological Quarterly* that focused on Christian language ideology.

RUY LLERA BLANES is Postdoctoral Researcher in the Department of Social Anthropology at the University of Bergen and Associate Researcher at the Institute of the Social Sciences at the University of Lisbon. He is the author of *A Prophetic Trajectory* and coeditor of *The Social Life of Spirits*.

KELLY H. CHONG is Associate Professor of Sociology at the University of Kansas. She is the author of *Deliverance and Submission: Evangelical Women and the Negotiation of Patriarchy in South Korea.*

SIMON COLEMAN is Chancellor Jackman Professor at the Department for the Study of Religion, University of Toronto. Previously, he was Professor and Chair at the Department of Anthropology, University of Sussex. He has been editor of the *Journal of the Royal Anthropological Institute*, and is currently coeditor of *Religion and Society: Advances in Research*.

THOMAS J. CSORDAS is Professor and Chair of Anthropology and Director of the Global Health Program at the University of California, San Diego. He is the author of *The Sacred Self; Embodiment and Experience; Language, Charisma, and Creativity; Ritual Life in the Catholic Charismatic Renewal; Body/Meaning/Healing;* and *Transcendental Transcendence.*

JEAN DEBERNARDI is Professor of Anthropology at the University of Alberta. Major publications include *Rites of Belonging: Memory, Modernity, and Identity in a Malaysian Chinese Community* and *The Way That Lives in the Heart: Chinese Popular Religion and Spirit Mediums in Penang, Malaysia.*

OMRI ELISHA is Assistant Professor of Anthropology at Queens College, City University of New York. He is the author of *Moral Ambition: Mobilization and Social Outreach in Evangelical Megachurches.*

YANNICK FER is Researcher at the French National Centre for Scientific Research and the author most recently of *L'offensive évangélique: Voyage au cœur des réseaux militants de Jeunesse en Mission.*

ROSALIND I. J. HACKETT is Professor and Head of Religious Studies, the University of Tennessee, and an Adjunct Professor in Anthropology. She has received fellowships from Harvard University, the Rockefeller Foundation, and the Pew Foundation. She has published extensively on religion in Africa, notably in the areas of new religious movements, art, gender, media, and conflict.

KRISTINE KRAUSE is Assistant Professor of Anthropology at the University of Amsterdam. She is the coeditor of *African Diaspora: A Journal of Transnational Africa in a Global World* and *Travelling Spirits: Migrants, Markets, and Moralities.*

MARTIN LINDHARDT is Associate Professor of Cultural Sociology at the University of Southern Denmark and the author of *Power in Powerlessness: A Study of Pentecostal Life Worlds in Urban Chile.*

KEVIN LEWIS O'NEILL is Associate Professor at the University of Toronto Department for the Study of Religion and its Centre for Diaspora and Transnational Studies. He is the author of *City of God* and *Secure the Soul.*

MARTIJN OOSTERBAAN is Associate Professor at the Department of Cultural Anthropology at Utrecht University. He has published on Pentecostalism and media in Brazil and Europe.

MATHIJS PELKMANS is Associate Professor of Anthropology at the London School of Economics. He is the author of *Defending the Border: Identity, Religion, and Modernity in the Republic of Georgia* and editor of *Conversion after Socialism* and *Ethnographies of Doubt.*

JOEL ROBBINS is Sigrid Rausing Professor of Social Anthropology at Trinity College in Cambridge University. He is the author of *Becoming Sinners: Christianity and Moral Torment in a Papua New Guinea Society.*

INDEX

aisthesis

219 prayer is cultural work